# The Poems of Tukārāma

*Translated and Re-arranged with Notes and Introduction by*

J. Nelson Fraser

and

K.B. Marathe



MOTILAL BANARSIDASS PUBLISHERS
PRIVATE LIMITED • DELHI

*Reprint: Delhi, 1981, 1983, 1991, 2000, 2007*
*First Edition: 1909*



ISBN: 978-81-208-0808-9 (Cloth)
ISBN: 978-81-208-0851-5 (Paper)

MOTILAL BANARSIDASS

41 U.A. Bungalow Road, Jawahar Nagar, Delhi 110 007
8 Mahalaxmi Chamber, 22 Bhulabhai Desai Road, Mumbai 400 026
203 Royapettah High Road, Mylapore, Chennai 600 004
236, 9th Main III Block, Jayanagar, Bangalore 560 011
Sanas Plaza, 1302 Baji Rao Road, Pune 411 002
8 Camac Street, Kolkata 700 017
Ashok Rajpath, Patna 800 004
Chowk, Varanasi 221 001

*Printed in India*

BY JAINENDRA PRAKASH JAIN AT SHRI JAINENDRA PRESS,
A-45 NARAINA, PHASE-I, NEW DELHI 110 028
AND PUBLISHED BY NARENDRA PRAKASH JAIN FOR
MOTILAL BANARSIDASS PUBLISHERS PRIVATE LIMITED,
BUNGALOW ROAD, DELHI 110 007

# PREFACE

The translation here offered to the public aims at presenting Tukārāma's poetry in readable English; and accordingly it has not been made on strictly "scientific" principles. Literal translation has often been replaced by accurate paraphrase; and religious expressions peculiar to the Hindu system have been rendered by the nearest equivalents. It is believed this will not mislead a scholar, while others, who might take a passing interest in Tukā's spiritual experiences, will not be repelled from this version by unnatural English.

No attempt has been made to settle the text of Tukā. We have simply followed the edition of S. P. Pandit, published at the Indu Prakash Press in 1869, occasionally preferring an alternative reading in the foot-notes.

The life of Tukā is an abstract of that printed in the same edition. Should I be able to do so, I hope to collect some day all accessible information regarding him, and to publish it along with a study of his poetry. In the meantime I may say, for myself and my collaborator, that we hope critical readers will pardon occasional mistakes in our translation and will treat with consideration cases where they will find we have chosen a rendering which they would have rejected. The many difficulties and obscurities of Tukā's old Marathi leave ample room for error and difference of opinion.

J. NELSON FRASER.

# CONTENTS

# The Life of Tukārāma

THE poet Tukā was by caste a Śūdra, and by occupation a vani or retail dealer in corn. He was born in the little village of Dehu, sixteen miles north-west of Poona, probably in the year 1608 A.D. His father's name was Bolhoji; and from his thirteenth year Tukā had to undertake the management of the family business. In this he was successful for some time, but a famine brought distress and bankruptcy, and several of his relatives died.

Upon this he turned seriously to religion. His family had always been distinguished for piety; and he, naturally, devoted himself to the family god, Viṭṭhobā of Pāṇḍharpura. He continued, however, to reside in Dehu, and a hill, named Bhandara, is pointed out as a frequent scene of his meditations.

He soon became a well known teacher, and crowds of people were attracted to his Kathas and Bhajanas.* Some jealousy and enmity were aroused by this success, which was not welcome to his Brāhmaṇa contemporaries. Tukā was personally assaulted by one of them, Mumbaji Gosavi, and another, Rameshvara Bhaṭṭa, induced the headman of Dehu to expel him from the village. Tukā met these antagonists with submission, and soon obeyed an order of Rameshvara's to throw his poems into the river Indrayāni. They were recovered, however, whether by a miracle or by the simple process of

---

* A Bhajana is a hymn in praise of the Deity; a Katha is a sermon on a sacred text or theme, interrupted by frequent hymns, which, like those of the Bhajana, are often composed *ex tempore*.

taking them out again; and Rameshvara Bhaṭṭa relented. An abhanga is preserved in which Tukā bestows his forgiveness on his foe.

Other troubles assailed him, of a domestic kind, for his wife was incensed at the poverty which her husband's religious life entailed. Some abhangas are preserved in which her conduct is related and deplored.

Finally, however, Tukā's character and influence were established. Sivāji himself sent him a flattering invitation to visit Raigad. Tukā declined this honour, with his usual modesty, but he wrote seven abhangas in which he thanked the king, and offered him some advice on public affairs.

The circumstances of his death are unknown. The popular account states that he ascended into Heaven in the car of Vishṇu; a note on the Dehu manuscript of his poems says that "Tukoba started on pilgrimage"—and was, apparently, seen no more.

His memory is well preserved in the Deccan. Brāmhaṇa and Śūdra alike are familiar with his poems; and there are Varkaris, or regular pilgrims between Dehu, Alandi, and Pāṇḍharpura, who know thousands of them by heart. Unfortunately they do not always know their meaning, for Tukā's Marathi, now archaic, is often difficult and obscure. It is much to be regretted that no one has produced a good Marathi commentary on his works.

Their form is simple enough; an irregular rhymed metre, which in course of time makes itself felt if not understood by the English ear. They deal little with outward circumstances and much with the inward life of the spirit. Every word of the writer is set down with great force and naiveté; and no suspicion of affectation offends us while we read him. We easily comprehend him for what he is, an unlearned man struggling with the mysteries of faith, by such light as he can find. This light is sometimes reflected from the great Sanskrit classics; it is sometimes borrowed from the traditions of the Kṛishṇa worship and the Bhakti school of Bengal. It is always concentrated, however, on the image of Viṭṭhobā at Pāṇḍharpura, in which Tukā finds a power actually present to help and save him. It has been conjectured that this was only his early attitude; that this faith in the power of images gradually left him. But there is no foundation for this view that I know of; and we must not support it by any "internal evidence" from the abhangas; we do not know in what order they were composed.

Whatever view we take of Tukā's creed, he was undoubtedly in many ways a man able to discern spiritual things; and no one who is interested in these things can fail to learn from him. He appeals to no miracles and no direct vision of any saint or deity; he proclaims the need of man for God's grace, the power of God to bestow it, and the peace and happiness which it brings. He never forgets the duties of morality; if his code (like all moral codes) is limited, it is clearly conceived and enforced. We may sometimes wish he had faced the world with more resolution, but we shall never find him wanting in honesty.

He has no philosophic system to propound; and he does not open up any paths of mystical intuition. He is a plain man of the people, who has set out, under all the limitations of his age and class, to find a faith sufficient for himself and his countrymen.

Viṭṭhobā is probably a relic of Buddhist times; and Tukā's creed is in some ways a far off reflection of Buddhism. No one, however, knew this less than he.

He has many analogues in literature. King David is one of them—a figure not unlike that of Tukā's own prince, Sivāji, and a composer of hymns not unlike Tukā's abhangas. John Bunyan is another—not so much of a poet, but a seeker after truth, who emerged from a similar station in life.

I refrain, however, from further criticism at present. This translation is only meant to provide the materials for it, should circumstances allow it to proceed.

It remains to add that the arrangement of the poems is simply adopted for convenience, similar poems being brought together under suitable headings. But of course the significance of the headings must not be pressed too far.

The present volume contains abhangas 1—1,500 in the Indu Prakash edition, which are one-third of the whole. Some abhangas by Tukā's brother, and all the Hindi abhangas, are omitted.

# I

# Autobiography

## I.—Thoughts about the World

### 1

LET God loose me not from his hand; I have come with devout faith to seek his protection. Consider me thy own; I perform for thee a neem-fruit ceremony with my own soul. Sitting amid the saints, I have learned to know the consort of Lakshmī; I had nothing to call my own; thus my thoughts were fixed on thee. Hindrances arise to keep us from thy worship; they raise before us the temptations of the world. Men love what is base and call it sweet; as we look upon them we discern their clownish natures. Men are ever dying and have died, innumerable; it is good for us to gaze upon them; therefore I come to entreat thy mercy; grant me to be patient and steadfast. Let men censure me, at their ease; I will not answer them. You, O Nārāyaṇa, are our first father; your feet are solid gain. If I will not seek my own advantage, if I am content to depend on my merit, then I am a worthless sinner; the saints will laugh at me, says Tukā.

### 2

THE country people cover their dead and go on sowing without loss of time; so must you seek your own gain, since a body of flesh is bestowed on you. The grain drawn forth by the hand sprouts sooner than what is left in the bag; thus is it with the welfare of man. We have no authority over time; the wise must solve this riddle. Tukā says, The wise man takes counsel with himself in this mortal world.

3

DID not the sages of old know this? They kept the world at a distance. They on whom the eight mystic powers descended would not come into contact with the popular mind. They ate roots and leaves to nourish the humours of the body; they dwelt in the forest; they sat still with fixed eyes, they wore the seal of silence. Tukā says, Thus, O infinite One, do thou with my spirit; keep the people far from me.

4

HE who knows the affection of the devout heart, he is God's darling. I desire myself no other, be he wise or learned. Who so fixes his thoughts on God's name and form, his servant am I. Tukā says, He knows in their purity the nine forms of worship.

5

O GOD, I am consumed by the fever of the world, in the service of my household. Thus I have forgotten thy feet; come speedily to me, O mother Pāṇḍuranga; I am oppressed with the burdens of many lives, I know not the secret of escape. I am beset by thieves on all sides, no one hears my cry for pity. I am sorely troubled, sorely bestead! I have long been utterly weary. Tukā says, Run now speedily to me; this is thy glorious name in the world, O Lord of the helpless.

## 6

THIS is not my own country or garb; by chance I have wandered here. What can I claim as mine? Where have I found a resting place? Though I call my feet and my hands my own, how bereft I am of them! I am a friendless stranger blind and lame. O Lord, regard and relieve me; I have neither brother nor child, I commit myself to the saints. I tremble as I follow the path before me, whereon many have travelled and none returned. I cannot see what happens though my ears perceive a sound. I sit at the cross roads, holding thee fast in my thoughts. I cry out for mercy like one that has lost his way. My belly is never filled; my feet are never at rest. I am weary with wandering through the eight million villages. I cling to this inhabited spot; what can I trust to? Who will bring me an unexpected alms? Oft have I heard its praises sung in such a strain that now I cry, O meritorious Lord, be my friend! I am very hungry, but thou givest freely. Any merits I had, I resign. Wealth, family, son, mother, all these ties I have cast off. O God, I have renounced desire, for so it was decreed I should do. Tukā says, You are now my all-powerful protector.

## 7

AS an actor plays a part, as a heron assumes a contemplative attitude to catch fish, so a hypocrite wears a garland and marks his forehead, but he keeps his secret guile from the sight of the world. As an angler offers a morsel to the fish but keeps them ignorant of the guile within; as a butcher kindly protects his beasts, while he carries a knife to cut their throats; Tukā says, Even so I am a simple man in the world, but you are merciful, O Pāṇḍuranga.

8

I HAVE renounced the world, sprinkling my head against it; now I shall let no trouble touch me. Why should I pollute my hands, to wash them again? Thus hindrances beset us in the way we have to walk. God has ordained everything and assigned everything to its own place. Tukā says, When we forget to think of ourselves, we cease to speak of "ours" or "another's."

9

I CANNOT bear to hear of restraint; my spirit is weary. I cannot bear any one's company; I find it pleasant to sit by myself. I weary of the life of sensuous desire. Tukā says, The snares of desire and illusion, that keep us from God, increase our pain.

10

IT is vain to tell the secret to the world; we must leave men to their own wanderings. In vain do they pretend to run after us; they return empty and dejected. Though we teach them, they will not learn and lay the matter to heart. Tukā says, Unless they have true experience they will still be wretched.

11

DO not praise me, O ye saints; your words will make me proud. That burden of pride will keep me from your feet and will not suffer me to cross the sea of the world. Tukā says, A high spirit will pursue me and I shall be severed from the feet of Viṭṭhobā.

12

WE must listen to nothing that will bring us sorrow and separation from your feet. I tremble when I see destruction so near men; I make them ashamed, but they will not listen. What can I do, O God? I have no strength to beat them and drive them before me to the path. Tukā says, O Pāṇḍuranga, do not set such mad men in my sight.

---

## II.—Humility, Sin and Misery

13

I AM a cripple, O God, in hands and feet; I am seated on a self-willed mount; if I spur him, he will not see fences, hedges, stumps of trees or holes. I have none to lean on, either father or mother. O generous people, bestow a gift on me, I am going to Pāṇḍharpura; convey me there, O friend of the feeble! I have wandered on my crutches from door to door till I am quite worn out; I find none to relieve me or save me from the pains of mortal life. Let Hari show me that power which the saints extol; he who dwells at Pāṇḍharpura gives limbs to the cripple. For the sake of my belly I have become dependent on the world. My cries of "mother and father" procure me nothing; there is no lack of contempt for me. Some say, "Move on!" they feel no pity; the dogs attack me. Many fierce desires possess me. I know not what faults I have committed in time gone by; I know nothing of my merits or demerits, I recollect nothing of them. I have lost all my wits, like a moth that flutters round a lamp. Give me in some measure the gift of life, O ye that are holy and deep in experience. I have travelled far, I have suffered harrowing pain; this was the purpose that brought me here. Hard it is to find you, but I have met you; I have greeted your feet. I, Tukā, fold my hands and make my bow to the saints.

## 14

I HAVE no faith myself; I merely utter a song to adorn the world; but do thou, O Saviour of the sinful, make true my words! I call myself thy servant, but in my spirit dwell passion, and worldly hope. Tukā says, I assume the outer garb but within me I have nothing at all like it.

## 15

I AM desolate and guilty, void of good actions, slow in understanding; I have never sent thee any word of mine, O sea of mercy, my father and mother. I have never sung or listened to thy praises. Through shame I have turned from my own true welfare. When the saints are assembled, I delight not in thy story. I have often slandered others. I have neither done nor procured good deeds. I harassed others without compassion. I have dwelt in unlawful traffic; I took on me the burden of a family. I have neglected to visit holy places. I have devoted hand and foot to the service of my body. I have offered thy saints neither service nor gift; I have neither worshipped nor looked upon thy image. I have fallen into evil company, unjust and impious acts; I have forgotten to seek my true welfare; my conduct I would wish to forget and speak no more. I have destroyed myself, I have been an enemy to all my neighbours. But thou art a sea of mercy; O carry me over to the end, says Tukā.

## 16

I CANNOT give up food, or dwell in the forest, so I cry to thee, O Nārāyaṇa, for pity! I have no authority to con the Vedas! Tukā says, Man's life is short, a hard riddle.

## 17

THIS pompous ornament becomes me not, it is false upon me. I am but dust upon your feet, a sandal on the saints' feet. I cannot recognize your primal form, I offer you faith, so far I can see you; I cannot see the perishable world merge into the imperishable ; in my mind there dwells no distinction of spiritual and non-spiritual and so forth. I am nothing at all, says Tukā, I will fall at your feet, O listen to these words!

## 18

MY life has been passed in seeking every pleasure; I have not pursued for one moment liberation. I have vexed myself with wandering in every region; my life has been shrouded in illusion. There is none who knows my true welfare, none to help me but myself. Even the saints know not the true source of bliss, the beginning or the end of it. How can I tell the torments of the womb, though I have endured them? O Nārāyaṇa, I was conscious of the flesh and its secretions; when I tried to think of thee, when I drew near to death, I knew thee not, though thou wast near to me. Dust returns to dust; the store of the past clings to the soul. Now I entreat thee, grant that I may serve thee. Tukā beseeches thee, O Keśava, show him the path through life.

---

## III.—Prayers

### 19

WHOMEVER I meet on this road I enquire of him, "Will God be merciful to me? Will he keep me from shame?" I have forgotten all other interests; in this alone I occupy myself. Tukā says, I am full of anxious wonder—who will meet me and tell me?

### 20

O PROTECTOR of thy worshippers, O kind to the humble spirit, O Viṭṭhala, that art our only mother! How comes it thou hast forgotten me? There is something wanting in my lot; what shall I do? Tukā says, Burn up the history of my past, make it perfect and meet me.

### 21

WHY do you wait for a sacred or auspicious day? My spirit is growing weary. Send me speedily, O Pāṇḍuranga, a tender morsel; do not keep me waiting. Consider not that I am faulty and full of transgression; be not angry against me: why do you make us weep, your ignorant children,—your elder and wise no less? Why do you stand with your hand upon your hips, to crush your little darlings? Tukā says, Now I will tie a knot in my mantle and I will not forget to stay with you.

## 22

WHY do you not speak, O God? Why do you make me wretched? With my life in my throat I wait for an answer; it seems you have ceased to care for me. To-day you have muffled yourself in a mantle to avoid the pollution of my presence. I am ashamed to call myself God's; you will not ask after me, though it costs you nothing, says Tukā.

## 23

WHY do you not pity me, though you are seated in my heart? O Nārāyaṇa, cruel and merciless, I have cried on thee unheard till all my voice is lost. Why has my spirit found no repose? The stirrings of sense never pause. Tukā says, O why are you angry? We know not, O Pāṇduranga, whether our guilt be over or not.

## 24

OF yore I used to gaze on all that lay before or behind me; then I lost my sight, a film passed over my eyes. They were shrouded in darkness ever thicker and thicker; I trembled, O God,—where was the fruit of my birth? Give me now the gift of sight, O Pāṇduranga, my father and mother! I have come to thee for protection, seeking to avert my sin. Do thou anoint my eyes and make the path easy for me. I will follow the path of the saints, the path that leads back to life no more. My spirit is afflicted, I can remember no good thought. I relied on mankind, but I lost that support; I can turn neither to this place or that, utter darkness has fallen upon me. My companions have all turned away from me; no one supports me. As long as man is active, others call him their friend; great and small honour him to secure their own comforts. But when the senses have decayed, they say, "This old bugbear is come! how changed a man he is, though his person is the same!" I am entangled in this worldly life; how blind I have become! Ever dwelling on "I" and "mine" and strengthening the bonds of illusive desire I do not see my true interest; I have killed myself. Death pursues me; desire and passion accompany me; as I walk along, my good and bad qualities trip me up. Now I have left that path; I have become another man; I look toward your dwelling-place with abundant hope, Tukā says, O great physician, dweller in Pāṇḍhari!

## 25

WHEN I was at ease, I took a rope and tied it round my neck myself: now what am I to do? I am fast bound; I cannot stir forwards or backwards. I finished all my means; I ran into debt; I left my field unweeded; I starved my wife and children. I plundered many people's houses; I could not save myself whatever I did. Tukā says, We must give up desire; we must cast it away altogether.

## 26

O GOD, be merciful to me and show me the truth; how pitiful thou art! Such is thy glorious name in the world. With a mere glance dost thou chase away the power of Time. Tukā says, O God, do thou protect me!

## 27

AS the Ganges fails not to quench the desire of the thirsty, so do thou, O sea of mercy, fulfil my desires! Thou art chief of the generous; it is little that I ask. Tukā says, Look upon me with a merciful countenance be my help!

## 28

I LIVE in the world so far as I am required to, but let my faith dwell at your feet. O generous master, what can I do? You have bound me fast; I am trudging along with the load that is set upon me. The body performs its appointed duty; O mind of mine, let not the secret lapse from you. The forces of the world drag me from place to place, but let me never be slothful in contemplation. Let the senses perform their own part; do thou give their fond passion a resting place at your feet. Tukā says, Do not, I entreat thee, hand me over to destruction.

## 29

I CANNOT sing or speak with clear utterance; but I have brought body, speech and mind to seek thy protection. O accept me, reject me not, O Hari! O Saviour of the sinful, vindicate thy name! I know nothing of faith or devotion; I call myself thy servant; if you abandon me, who will be disgraced? Tukā's brother says, I have embraced thy feet; now whom else have we but thee?

## IV.—How he Awoke

### 30

I DREAMED that I was impressed in a gang; but when the dream ended, it all turned out to be false. I cried for mercy in vain; that very cry was the source of my trouble. King, noble and peasant—the whole picture was unreal, but my sufferings were real, till I awoke; my bodily experiences witness it, for it was pain that made me open my eyes. Tukā says, The saints brought me to my senses at last; otherwise the lock-up was ready waiting for me.

### 31

I WAS caught in the net of the illusory world, but this Viṭṭhala took mercy on me. He rescued me and set me apart and showed me the form that I view with fond and curious love. I see others leaping and dancing and displaying fond interest in the world; they have found their pleasure in treating the false as though it were true. Others too I see weeping and sobbing and breaking their heads for grief; in weeping for their friends they bring on their own deaths. Tukā says, I marvel at my own words.

### 32

I LEFT the world by my own resolution, for I was bound up in it heart and soul. When butter and buttermilk are once separated, you cannot find either present in the other. One process of churning brings both into existence, but their natures are distinct. Tukā says, When the pearls have been discovered, the pearl-shells are left alone.

33

IN my own life I have experienced both good and evil fortune. I have witnessed both; I have found and shall find both displeasing. I have lived in the forest, but even here pain overtook me. Tukā says, I will take God with me and make him my guide.

34

'TIS well I was created a Kunbi, otherwise I should have perished of pride; thou hast done well, O Lord God. Tukā leaps to his feet and dances. If I had had any knowledge, I should have been in danger, I should have missed the service of holy men, I should have fallen into fruitless ignorance; I should have been puffed up with conceit, I should have followed the path of destruction. Tukā says, Where human greatness is, there follows hell, the punishment of pride.

35

WHEN a child is learning to form the letters, pebbles are placed to guide him; but when he grows familiar with their shape, what need is there of these? The false fears I had in the past were due to my ignorance. Tukā says, Now I know the truth, I have no fear of bugbears.

36

AS far as renunciation goes, without set purpose, I accomplished it in my mind, O Viṭthala! Experience of life soon brought distaste for life; unavowedly I became an ascetic, in my own mind. My body felt weary through the burden of debt; I was weary of the world. Tukā says, Now disgust and weariness have quitted me; I have put off the guilt of misconduct.

37

IT is well I have got rid of this straggling crowd, they have gone each to her mother-house. It cost me grievous pain to take care of them; now I am ashamed of those greedy desires. When they strayed, I had to suffer myself; I had to pay away my wages in fines. I would not remain still for a moment, I suffered misery till to-day. Their tricks were innumerable; they broke their tethers; I have neither time nor will to tell the tale. Tukā has given over charge of these cattle to God.

---

## V.—His own Disqualifications

38

I DO not know a single trick to take away men's senses; I sing your praises, I celebrate your excellent deeds! I cannot display a knowledge of herbs, or marvels of sleight of hand. I have no following of pupils; I do not pretend that I am not a beggar. I am not the head of a school, I am no lord of lands. I preside over no formal worship, I have not opened a shop of that kind. I have not propitiated Vetala; I cannot declare secrets. I am not a reader of Purāṇas; one whose actions resemble not his speech. I do not understand dialectics; I am no miserable scholar, I do not carry burning fires, crying *Udo! O anandi!* I do not count a rosary, gathering an idle crowd about me. I do not know the secrets of the

Atharva-veda; the charms that arrest and deceive, and remove enemies. I am not like these men, says Tukā; I am no mad fellow dwelling in hell.

## 39

SOME one may say of me, "You are a poet," but my speech is not my own. It is not my own contrivance that is at work; the pervader of the world sets me speaking. Weak as I am, what power have I to disarm? What I say is what Govinda prompts. I am appointed to sit and measure out, but I am nothing, the authority of master is all. Tukā says, I am a faithful henchman, I bear the seal of my master's name.

## 40

OUTWARDLY I receive honour from the world, but within I do not deserve it. Therefore, O Lord of Pāṇḍhari, I feel uneasy; I feel ashamed when I confess it. The saints look on all mankind as images of Bramhā; they do not perceive my faults. Tukā says, I know myself very well; I am just what I was.

## 41

I AM a man of low degree—why should I be proud? It is you that people honour in me, O Nārāyaṇa. What pleasure or pain can I find in that? Honour and dishonour spring from the qualities of men. I am like a rag that men set on their heads to honour it, because it once held a golden coin. Tukā says, People honour me, but I am not what they honour; what reason is there to delight in so feeble a creature?

## 42

I QUOTE the words left behind by the saints; what can a clown like me know himself? I cannot utter the name of Viṭṭhala aright—how could I draw the true moral from it? Like a child I linger over it with stammering lips; chide me for it, if you will. Do you forget what I am by birth? I cannot dwell on this thought. Tukā says, It is God who makes me speak; he alone knows the secret meaning of what I say.

## 43

DOES the cock keep the author of day true to his time? Why, O God, do you place on my head such a burden as to bid me be a saint? Will masters starve, if servants refuse to cook food? Tukā says, The infinite one knows how to bring all things to pass.

## 44

I BELONG to no village, I stay alone in my own place. I have no fixed round of wandering and all my words pass unheeded. I count nothing my own or another's; verily I belong to no one; I need neither live nor die; I remain continually as I am. Tukā says, I have neither name nor shape; I stand apart from actions good and evil.

## 45

I SPEAK though I am silent; I am dead yet alive; I am in the world yet out of it. I have renounced all, yet I have my fill of pleasure; I am alone yet not alone; I have severed all ties. Tukā says, I am not what I seem, if you ask what I am, ask Pāṇḍuranga.

## VI.—His Motives

### 46

SPEECH is not local, it does not choose to travel in one direction and not in another. Even so my accents travel throughout the universe. The arrow that once was lodged in the quiver must go wherever it is shot. Now what needs Tukā do here? He merely wears the seal of his lord.

### 47

WE may look on the world as divine, but I blame this disposition of men; I feel a compassion that seeks to help them, for they will fall into the hands of death. I have no friend nor any enmity towards strangers. I speak this by way of prelude, says Tukā, to lay bare the heart of the matter.

### 48

I HAVE come to smooth paths, to distinguish truth from falsehood. While I utter my voice, Viṭṭhala is my witness; therefore no doubt dwells in my mind, through the power of my lord alone. Tukā says, In future I shall speak no idle words.

### 49

TO preserve faith is the end of my efforts. I declare the righteous precepts of the Vedas; I do as the saints have done before me. Unless a steady spirit possesses you, you are a miscreant to leave your worldly duties. Tukā says, Such a one is a vile wretch; the worship of Hari turns to guilt in him.

50

I TUKĀ am smaller than an atom, yet vast as the sky. I have relinquished the body, for the world is error manifest. I have relinquished the triad of knowledge; I have lit a lamp within the vessel of my body. Tukā says, Enough of me is left to serve mankind.

51

I WILL consult my own soul; why should I care for the views of men? All men know their own interest; if you use force to them, they feel aggrieved. Whether they listen to my preaching or not, I shall go home and sleep soundly. What influence have I? I can point out the way when I have seen it. Tukā says, I will point out the mercy of God; he who wishes can enjoy the fruit of it.

52

I PROCLAIM these resources to benefit mankind; I have no delight in any other task. I am filled with compassion for the world, for I cannot bear to see it drowning. Tukā says, I shall see their sufferings, which they will comprehend when the time comes to endure them.

---

## VII.—The Nature of his Mission

53

THOUGH a man be a transgressor, yet if he utters the name, I am his servant, body, speech and mind. Though a man has no faith, yet if he sing of Hari's attributes; though he offend in action, yet if he utter the name of Hari, I am his. Whatever lineage be his, pure or vile, yet if he calls himself Hari's, Tukā says, blessed is he.

54

I HAVE shown as with a lamp what lies behind, midway and before; you must now make an effort for yourself. In my function as a servant I have shown you my master's treasure, in which there is nothing that is not perfect. By due measures I have stilled all longing desires; through God's authority such authority has come to dwell in me. Tukā says, I sit here and send my messages abroad over the heads of you all.

55

I HAVE laid up a stock of goods and opened a fine shop; whatever you want, whenever you want it, here it is ready to hand. I have honestly distinguished articles good, bad and indifferent. Tukā sits in his shop and displays wares corresponding to the price offered.

56

THIS is our delight, to show the world what is right, to make those ashamed who have strayed from the path. How can a man be injured by delivering his message? What harm can the anger of the world do me? What can the exertions of ignorance effect, so sharp are the arrows of Kṛishṇa's name? Tukā says, This is a shop where genuine goods are sold; no false wares will pass current here.

57

THE eyes are brightened by the unction of Kṛishṇa's name, so that one distinguishes the various tribes of men. I interfered with them by serving as a measure of communicated wisdom; and I loved the task because I filled the measure with Nārāyaṇa. Those who work faithfully in the household of the fortunate become fortunate through the act of service. Tukā says, He who earns his bread honestly finds his own place amid the surroundings that rightly belong to him.

---

## VIII.—Appeals

### 58

I BOW down before all, and entreat you, laying my head at your feet; ho! people all, speakers and listeners all, examine this well and tie it up in your bundles. I have dispensed a rich store, my master's property. I am only the porter who carries it. Tukā says, Its value is known in the four regions; it has passed the test, and is found to be genuine.

### 59

BY day and night I will employ myself with the praises of Govinda. All my desires are in God; I have offered my body to him; I stay not a moment, but apply all my senses to him. Tukā says, I sing his praises; I rouse the people.

### 60

I HAVE girt up my loins, and wrestled stoutly against Time and Death; I have made a footpath across the river of the world. Come, great and small, men and women, people of low degree; remember that none need feel anxious fear. Busy and idle, devout and austere, come together; drums resound to invite the liberated and those who seek liberation. He has sent me into this world with a seal of general authority; I bear his name with me, says Tukā.

## 61

SINCE I have spoken to profit you, pardon me if I am poor in speech. You should not be angry with one who shows you the path, a straggler will be ruined, his soul will perish. The neem is applied to crush the disease within; you spread it outwardly, it penetrates within. Tukā says, The beholder sees the advantage of it; the blind fall into the well.

## 62

I AM merely a blind man on the path that leads to the unbodied self; I have renounced the life of many impulses for the life that is at rest in him; in him I see the world no more. "I" and "mine" are lost in the very spot where they arose. All that was visible now has grown invisible. I have swept clean the place of the world and fallen sweetly asleep On the summit of the triple hill there is a free gift bestowed; I have cast away the dish and the wallet, deeds good and bad and desires. I have escaped from the tumult of the world, the attachment of the three qualities; I am well assured I shall have to beg no more. My seventeenth quality is turned round, had it fulfilled all my desires, with uplifted face I have uttered the words "I am He." By fond affection turned towards him I have aroused the unbodied source; he has bestowed on me Absolute Truth and Knowledge of the Absolute Self. He has absorbed my name into his own form, he has set aside all distinction between us. These words are satisfying and full of ample relief; he has made them current for men to come; in their train follows a line that has attained the mystic heights; they have passed beyond the world. This is the only secret, to believe in him; the spirit of self is an oppression; it does not suffer us to reach our home. Therefore cast off the ties of the world, embrace the monist faith. Tukā says, This is the resource which the saints devised of old.

## 63

A SHOPKEEPER may spread out various goods, but each one chooses according to his own desires. Each one makes his proper purchase in the end, though people like to see many things to satisfy their curiosity. A warrior understands the movements of the enemy; others look on them as something to talk about. Tukā says, My speech plays on themes of its own; worldly wisdom I have sacrificed to the untainted One.

## 64

THAT the All-powerful dwells in all being, this first law I know well. I have been shooting forth arrows; he who is struck by one knows its power. First we must make our instruction blameless, and then we may impart it. Tukā says, If you miss the path and stray into the jungle, you will meet with thorns.

## IX.—His Sense of Authority and Assurance

### 65

I AM no obstinate preacher, filled with my own opinions; I teach under the authority of the truth. You must test my doctrine by experience; mature knowledge will show if it is true or false. This utterance belongs not to one spot; if any will receive it, he will find it fill the universe. Tukā entreats the wise not to distress themselves by conflicting opinions.

### 66

I SPEAK words mingled with Nārāyaṇa, in his own presence. I need not grope about, I go forward sowing faith. The treasure I have belongs to that generous master; where am "I" to be found here? Here Tukā has raised a sudden shout.

### 67

I HAVE shown men a path according to the authority I received. To each has been shown a path according to his capacity; he will learn to know it as he follows it. You need not burn the boat when you have reached the shore; many will depend on it hereafter. Tukā says, If the physician is ill, he will never heal mankind.

### 68

THIS is not my own speech, it all comes from Viṭṭhala. Cease all anxious pining, and cling to what will bring you profit. The spirit of self is a false guide; I have given it up in spite of men's remonstrances. Every one will recognize what is best for himself, says Tukā; I am only a measure to portion it out.

## 69

WE dwellers in Vaikuṇṭha have come for this purpose, to prove by our faith the words of the Rishis. We will sweep clean the paths of the saints, for weeds have choked up the world. We will take the leavings of the saints' meals. The ancient forms have lost their meaning, for idle skill in words has ruined them. Men's minds are greedy of pleasure; the way of salvation has vanished; we will beat a drum in the name of devotion. We will appal Time and Death. Tukā says, Raise a joyful shout of acclamation.

## 70

THE measure says, "I measure all," yet its master fills it and lays it aside empty. O God, let pride have no power to arise in me! This seal is current through the country, without it who would receive a wretch like me? Tukā says, The majesty belongs to him who holds all the strings in his hand.

## 71

WHAT power had gone forth to proclaim my name from land to land? The wind was bidden to bear the measure of it; so mighty is my father: whose power was it that gave the power of words to my speech? Tukā says, Confidence in him has removed all fear from me.

## X.—A Prayer for a Pupil

### 72

O LORD of the world, show me this kindness, give me a pupil who will continue my rules; beckon forward such a one, who is fully expert in the knowledge of Bramha, whose banner is known in the three worlds. Tukā cries aloud at the door of his Viṭṭhobā.

### 73

GIVE me, O God, a pupil versed in knowledge of Bramha, who is a glorious image of faith and loving devotion. In his mind let such a skill be deeply planted, that victory over passion may have its station in him. If I find such a one in the flesh, I will wave round him the neem-tree leaves to shield him from harm!

---

## XI.—Consolation and Happiness in God

### 74

I CANNOT sing; there is no music in my voice; I will cast my burden on thee, O Pāṇḍuranga. I know nothing of tune, time or accent or metre; I place my spirit at thy feet, O Pāṇḍuranga. Tukā says, I care nothing for the world; I care for thee alone, O Nārāyaṇa.

### 75

I AM a man of low degree, feeble in brain, miserable in aspect; other defects of mine too he knows; yet Viṭṭhala has accepted me, knowing what my purpose is. Whatever I do, I seek my own true interest, so experience has taught me. Infinite bliss and joy are bestowed on my soul; he who is joy in the highest has taken my burden. Tukā says, He is proud of his name, so he puts forth his strength to save his suppliant.

### 76

WHY should I pursue glory or pride or popular honour? Show me thy feet, O God! Let not thy servant turn aside to vanity. Grandeur will be a burden on my soul; it will lead me away from thy feet. What do mankind know about the faith of the heart? They honour each other according to outward appearances. Tukā says, I find adversity sweet, if it leads me to thy feet.

### 77

I WAS worn out by desires, O mother; they oppressed me without pity: I took refuge in thee and all was well. I went to thee, now again I entreat thee. Tukā says, Through thy influence, O Kānhobā, the oppression has ceased.

### 78

IF I stay apart from you for a moment, I come crying to you. I love to be with you; we are no new friends; we are one by nature. The high and mighty call me away from you; I will have none of them. Tukā says, You dearly love the faithful, O embrace me heartily!

### 79

THE essence of the Śāstras, the image of the Vedas, he dwells with me as the friend of my soul. I desire, therefore, none but him, I have all in his name alone. He who is both qualified and unqualified, even he comes to sport with me, says Tukā.

## 80

THE good guide and master has shown favour to me; yet not through any service that I did him. He met me on the road as I was going to the Indrayāni; know that he laid his hand on my head. He asked me for a little butter to eat; I fell into a dream and forgot him—somehow a difficulty arose, so he grew impatient and went away. Rāghava Chaitanya, Keśava Chaitanya—he told me these names to indicate his teachers; he told me his own name was Bābaji, and gave me as a mantra Rāma Kṛishṇa Hari. It was Thursday the tenth of Magha; finding it auspicious he received me into the order, says Tukā.

## 81

KNOWING my faith, my lord and master taught me the way; he taught me a spell well pleasing and simple, that severed all the bonds of the world. There are saints still moving on, there are others that have crossed the sea of the world; wise and foolish alike, he has provided them with vessels well pleasing to them—gourds, rafts and floats. Tukā says, Pāṇḍuranga has shown me a vessel, for he is a sea of mercy.

## 82

I HAVE cast down my burden; I am free from anxious care; the saints have entrusted me to Viṭṭhobā. He put out his hand and caressed my head; he bade me lay aside care. His hand is on his hip, fair are his even feet on the brick; he stands upright on the bank of the Bhima. My mortal toil is over; I have embraced thy feet, O Keśava! Tukā says, Now, O infinite one, do thy will! any shame of mine belongs to the saints.

## 83

KNOW that this is my resolve, I have become indifferent to the world. I shall embrace none but thee; I have cast away fear, shame and doubt. O infinite one! there is an old bond between thee and me; a close bond formed by the saints. I have laid down my personal self at thy feet; it exists no more; any shame of mine belongs to you. Tukā says, The saints have escorted me to you. Now I will not leave your feet, O Viṭṭhala!

## 84

EVERY moment I am watchful and observe myself. I have put a check on myself, not to be parted from thy feet. I consider before I speak; I keep myself pure. Tukā says, Once I was afraid; now I am wakeful.

## 85

THIS is the diversion of the goddess within me; why do you not recognize it? Who is at work here, if I do not heed pain or joy? I myself am here no more, the words are all you can recognize. I am converted into her; surely my faith cannot be concealed. Now ask me your own questions, of things dear or things indifferent to you. With this goddess firmly fixed in my mind I shall know what you mean or what you are asking about. Tukā says, You must not keep still when such a season of gain is offered you; where shall you go to find such an opportunity?

## 86

SHOULD evil spirits seize you, they will vanish in time; when this god has entered you, he will never depart. Now speedily so deal with me that I shall never have to bear any other burden. Take me and place me on the bank of the Chandrabhāga; there is nothing left of my own soul within me now. Tukā says, I have understood the tidings, my own voice has vanished away.

## 87

VIṬṬHOBĀ alone is generous to the blind and lame; he has created the world and he knows all. Without an effort he organizes and destroys our store of merit and demerit; who but thou can save us from the pain and cares of the world? Let thy kingdom prevail, O merciful Lord! Easily thou knowest the heart though we speak not. Pundalika rolled before thee on the pebbly shore; blessed is Pāṇḍhari, on the bank of the Nira and Bhīma; I see nothing else, my eyes have begun to see the unseen; the source of love has descended there and brought a shower of imperishable knowledge. Moreover Upamānya, a little child, who could not see nor walk in the ways of the world, he threw himself down and called with loud cries on Hari's name; therefore Hari came to him with hasty steps. The child Śuka, that was born blind, lay in the shed, wearied out by the pain of many a re-birth; he remembered thee in due time. "I fear no more the pain of the past," he said to Gopāla. Thereupon he came and by his skilful power he saved him from shame. To the blind man who sees not the world he shows himself; he is free from pain and grief, he relinquishes the greed of wealth. He knows no distinction of "Self" and "Other"; he recognizes neither brother nor friends. Tukā has reached the same stage; therefore be pleased, O Nārāyaṇa!

## 88

MY spirit is dull; I cannot learn to know the truth, but I meditate in my heart on thy lotus feet. What do I know about the differences of the scriptures? I spend the time in meditation. I know nothing, but I call myself his servant, he will be proud of me. I have departed from the comforts and beaten paths of the world; at one stroke I have thrust the world from me. It clung to me before, but I have severed it now; in solitude I have preserved my mind. Tukā says, O husband of Rakhumai, protect thy worshipper who calls on thee.

## 89

O GOD, for thy sake I am dead, while yet I live; how free from all desires my spirit reposes! It never falls into error. My feet and hands stir not; how my sight has been turned towards God, seeing I see not the perishable or imperishable world! O Viṭṭhobā, give us a gift worthy of your name! Your glory has been proclaimed; your fame has spread to regions afar; you alone bestow joy, liberation, and attainment; we have abandoned all and cried to thee, therefore thou hast set us free from grief and fear and shame and affliction; O God, come now before us and grant us thy merciful favour. The sea of mortal life is the source of misery; the scandalous voice of mankind is like a scorpion concealed in a bed. The organs of sense are like arrows piercing us; I feel a heat like flame passing over me. I have endured it all;

what shall I do? These evil wretches are hard to bear. Your name in the three worlds is like a tree full of leaves and branches; I have climbed up the trunk, trusting to the support of faith. I arouse men and women; may your rule prevail throughout all worlds! Through merit men attain to happiness; these are mere cries of ours. I cannot remember what is mine or others,—what shall I do? I have lost the thoughts that lead like a smooth way to happiness; I have set on your head as a burden my cares of getting and keeping. Stretch out to thy suppliant Tukā thy hand that calms all fear!

## 90

I HAVE dispersed the crowd; my mind is at rest; Tukā has come hither to avoid the uproar. Let him rest on a cot and sleep, himself and Rakhumai together. I have come hither with cymbals and vina to worship the feet of my lord. Tukā says, Now with respect let Pāṇḍuranga listen to my stammering accents

## 91

WE must tell thee what we want; we must ask of thee the secret desire of our hearts. O Viṭṭhala, humble in spirit, loving and merciful, mother of ours, you will deal gently with our fancies. We have laid at thy feet our devoted faith. You are all in one to us. I will let no breath of any other being touch me; I will visit no other house but thine, all power rests with thee; I know thou wilt give me what I ask; therefore Tukā ceases from this time to entreat thee.

## 92

NOW thou shalt do as seems fit to thee; if thou wilt, save me, or slay me if thou wilt; keep me near thee or far from thee; bring me back into the world or not. I have sought thee, all ignorant, I know nothing of faith and devotion. I am void of all understanding, needy and worse than needy. I cannot steady my mind, I cannot rule my wayward senses; I have exhausted every effort; peace and rest are far from me. I have offered thee perfect faith, I have laid my life at thy feet; do now as thou wilt, I can only look to thee; O God, I trust in thee, I cling firmly to thy robe. Tukā says, It is for you to deal with my efforts.

## 93

NOW I shall attain perfect happiness. I have left every strange region, I see nothing but my mother's house. Viṭṭhala and Rakhumai are near me, my sister, brother, father and mother; he is the head of all my family. I need recognize no stranger. I have stretched out my authority throughout the world. I have shaken off subjection to others; all is my own now; I have dismissed shame and anxious care. I indulge my wishes to stay at home, in my mother's house where I have my way. I do as he bids me; I am not afraid of making mistakes. I long endured to dwell with my mother-in-law; I was troubled by many desires; now I forget worldly interests. My father and mother caress me with fond affection; they answer me gently and bid me tell them my childish desires. Tukā will speak freely henceforth, in his stammering accents.

## 94

VERY sweet is the food we get with him; therefore I have preferred the pursuit of Kṛishṇa to life itself. The delight of his company grows from moment to moment. Henceforth, says Tukā, I shall teach mankind to be as fond of him as I am.

## 95

YOU have given shares to all; look upon me! Along with my companions I formed great hopes. Why are you silent? Give me my own share! I have given up all my own provisions; now I will not be left out. O infinite one, I am hungry; you who know everything, why don't you know that? I am tired out with tending the cows of self-will and extravagance. Tukā cries out for mercy, Hari casts a morsel to him; Tukā takes it up and rejoices and divides it among his friends.

## 96

THE little cowherds meet together and begin to make a plan, "Come, let us go and steal butter, to-day; let us take with us the Lord of the Moon. Comrades, there is one who has kept us waiting all this time." Govinda leads the way, the cowherds follow; he moves about in his essential nature, he goes to and fro unknown to any. He sees a lonely house with nine kinds of butter in it. He enters himself, he supplies them with lines of butter-pots. He does not let them speak; he says, "Be quiet; when I give the sign, eat the milk." After full contentment, Tukā serves God.

97

HIS companions begin to cry, "Kānhobā, you never let us get the better of you. We won't play any more; we have found out what you are like. We cannot bear the weight; you ride on our shoulders so long together." Tukā grows angry against the devotee's life, but God will not let him retire.

---

## XII.—Admonitions to Himself

98

OH speech of mine, henceforth remember God. You mischievous creature, have done with quarrelsome idle speaking! You left off repeating "Viṭṭhala! Viṭṭhala!" but now, says Tukā, you are sworn to serve the Lord, be assured.

99

I GO on deferring to wife and children, and humbling myself before objects of sense. Run now and deliver me, O Nārāyaṇa, I cannot govern my desires! Stand thou between me and shame of the multitude; for I see that this dispels your worship. Tukā says, Wherever you find us entangled, O God, you must protect us.

100

I HAVE constrained myself to wear an outward appearance; but I have not renounced my inward nature. So my experience constantly tells me; the fruit is known to any mind. I have not even dreamed what it is to be awake; I go about forgetful of all. My mind has not emerged from worldly life; it is still engaged in its old occupations. Tukā says, Like an actor I have changed my outward garb, but inwardly I am still what I was.

---

## XIII.—Some Incidents in his Life

### 101

BY caste I was a Śūdra, I became a trader; this God from the first had been worshipped by my family. I ought not to talk of this, but since you have asked the question, I respect your speech, O saints! When my father and mother had finished their course, I was grievously harassed by the world. A famine used up my money, and took away my good name; one wife of mine died crying for food. I grew ashamed and was tormented by this grief; I saw that I was losing by my business. The temple of God which we had was in ruins; I resolved to do what occurred to me. I began by preaching and singing on the eleventh day; but at first my mind was not in practice. So I learned by heart some speeches of the saints, being full of resource and faith in them. When others sang first, I took up the refrain, purifying my mind by faith. I counted holy the water wherein the feet of the saints had been washed; I suffered no shame to enter my mind. I served others when the chance was given me, wearying out my own body. I paid no heed to friends who loved me, I was heartily sick of the world. I bade my own mind testify to the true and the false, I paid no heed to the voice of the crowd. I honoured the instruction my teacher gave me in a dream, I believed firmly in God's name. After this the impulse of poetry came upon me; I embraced in my spirit the feet of Viṭṭhobā. A blow fell upon me: I was forbidden to write; thus for awhile my spirit was grieved. My pages were sunk in the river; I sat down like a creditor; Nārāyaṇa comforted me. If I told all the story, the tale would be long; it would grow too late, so enough of it now. You see now my present purpose, my future course God knows. God never neglects his worshipper; I have learned that he is merciful. Tukā says, This is all my capital, I utter the verses which Pāṇḍuranga bids me utter.

### 102

IF one begs for titles with tears, what sort of ornament are they? If God gives anything himself, it is sweet; its flavour and its delight continue. Sow your field, and you will reap corn for sale, corn for beggars, corn for seed and corn for charity. Tukā says, Without long endurance how can a diamond be formed?

### 103

NĀMADEVA came with Pāṇḍuranga, and roused me in a dream. "I appoint you a task, write poetry, do not talk of vain affairs." Nāmadeva counted his own verses, Viṭṭhala kept the tally; he told me the total he arrived at, a hundred crores. "What is left undone, you must finish, O Tukā."

### 104

IF thou wilt give me a place, I will stay with thee for ever, sitting at thy feet in the row of saints. I have given up a place that delighted me, so now be not heedless of me! Give me the lowest place, for my office is lowest; trusting to that I shall find peace. Tukā has visited Nāma's feet in a dream; this favour he has stored up in his heart.

## 105

"WHERE I am concerned he has renounced the world; what enjoyment of his own has he given up? For him all pleasures come walking to the house; but *I* cannot escape disgrace. Whom shall I marry to keep things going? How much family trouble must I suffer? What shall I give the children to eat? They will devour me for very hunger; it would be a good riddance if they died. He has swept the house clean and emptied it; there is not a cow left to give us dung for the floors." Tukā says, Miserable and thoughtless wretch; she loads her own head and grumbles at the burden.

## 106

"PERHAPS the brute was my enemy before we were born, and has gained his end now by marrying me. How long must I bear this unceasing misery? How often must I beg my food from others? Curses on this Viṭṭhala! What has he done for me and my family?" Tukā says, These are my wife's vagaries; she laughs one moment and cries the next.

## 107

"I HAD a bag of grain sent me; he would not let the children eat it. He fills up baskets for other people. He is a gluttonous thief!" She grew quite wild and seized his hand like a wolf. Tukā says, It is idle to talk of a harlot's stored-up merit.

## 108

"NOW, my son, what will you eat? My husband is grown a devotee of the temple. He wears garlands on his head, he does not care to be a shopkeeper as he was. He has made arrangements to feed himself. He has no interest in us. He goes about with cymbals and open mouth, he sings before God in the temple. What are we to do now? He is gone off to the jungle." Tukā says, Show some patience now, if you never did before.

## 109

"GOOD; he is gone; now we have got all we want! Now I shall have plenty to eat; bread and soup and all. Wretch as I am, how could I go on quarrelling with him for ever?" Tukā says, When I showed that I despised her words, she began to like me.

## 110

"HE cannot follow his trade; he gets bread thrust into his mouth; he gets up and strikes his cymbals and makes no end of a noise. He is a dead man; he has pounded up shame and swallowed it. He forgets all about his family; they are ruined; his women folk are frightened to death, they hate their own existence." Tukā says, All right, wife, I will leave you alone; I give you a written promise.

## 111

"WHY do people come to our house? Have they not their own business to attend to?" "Through God the whole world has become a part of me; what does it cost you to give a gentle answer? For love's sake people come to see me who could not be appeased by respectful entreaties." Tukā says, This vile woman can find no pleasure in a jewel; she runs after people like a mad dog.

## 112

MY wife died; she was set free; God released her from the world of illusion. O Viṭṭhobā, you and I will enjoy the kingdom; we need no other. 'Tis well that my boy died, God released him from the world. My mother died looking upon me. Tukā says, I have lost anxiety.

## 113

IT is well, O God, that I became bankrupt, and was crushed by the famine; this is how I repented and turned to thee, so that the world became odious to me. It is well that my wife was a scold, that I was dishonoured, and lost my good name, my wealth and my cattle; it is well that I did not fear people's opinion, but sought thy protection, O God; it is well that I built up thy temple, and neglected my wife and children. Tukā says, It is well that I fasted on the eleventh day, for so I kept myself awake.

## 114

HE found the deer-skin under his arm a nui sance; it made a crackling noise, so he threw it away. Listen, O listen to my complaint; the shameless man has no shame. There is a cry from everyone, "Rāma, Rāma"; no one practises his religious duties. Men fall at the feet of the saints, and yet the saints conspire to oppress them. Ṭukā says, They have both brought shame on themselves; they have satisfied themselves by wickedness; in bringing discredit on their own garb they have ruined themselves.

115

WHY, O God, why is this shame brought upon me? I ought not to have forgotten the primal secret that he and I are one. What was to be has come to pass; now remorse is idle. Tukā says, I have had enough now of the company of the wicked.

116

I HAVE reached God, I have reached him; my store of merit was excellent, for it has brought this to pass; now what shall I say? The road was covered with thorns; I went to remove them. Though I did the act, says Tukā, I was saved from showing malevolence.

117

THOU hast done well, O Viṭṭhobā, that seeing within me a spirit of forgiveness, thou didst cause me to be pierced with thorns. Reproaches, abuse and injustice were bestowed on me with grievous ridicule. Tukā says, Thou didst not leave me subject to anger.

### 118

I WILL not, I will not, I will not leave the feet of Viṭṭhobā! Though I be crushed to death unmercifully; though armed men cut me into a hundred pieces, yet I fear not. Tukā says, Before I acted, I resolved to be firm and vigilant.

### 119

WHAT shall I eat?—where shall I go?—under whose protection shall I live in the village? The Patil and all the people are angry with me—no one will give me an alms. He has lost all his senses, they say; they have set me down among the mad men. Good people have put the idea into his head, and ruined me—helpless that I am. Tukā says, His company is not good; let me go now to seek Viṭṭhala.

### 120

MY body is burning, like a forest on fire, run! O Keśava! It is kindled with all the hair on it; I cannot stop the fire, I am burned up like a *holi*. My heart is about to burst—why dost thou look on? Bring water and run quickly; no one else can help me. Tukā says, Thou art my mother, who else will help me in the last hour?

### 121

O NĀRĀYAṆA, do not send me the fellowship of women, nor even that of dolls, clay or wooden. This woman has taken from me the remembrance of God and his worship; my mind was tempted and I could not forbear talking to her. At the sight of her face death entered in through my senses. Beauty is the true root of sorrow. Tukā says, If fire should become a saint, it has the power to burn one who touches it.

## 122

I LOOK on other women like Rakhumai, for so I have been resolved from the first. Begone, O mother, cease your efforts; we servants of Vishṇu are not what you think. I cannot bear your sinful inclinations, desist from this evil speech. Tukā says, If you need a paramour, are there not many men about?

## 123

I CANNOT bear to see this turmoil; I am distressed by the sufferings of others. O God, it seems you have left us; we ought not to have witnessed this calamity. What brings an invading army to the dwellings of Hari's servants? We desire not to see them in the land we inhabit. Tukā says, I am ashamed of your service; O God! my life has grown wretched.

## 124

WHY should I hold that the story of Hari brings salvation to all mankind? Lo, here is destruction begun; O Viṭṭhala, an invading army is upon us. Sin never arises without sin; here is clear evidence to prove it. Tukā says, Where your servants dwell, how can we say now that you dwell too?

## 125

I AM not afraid of my own death now; I cannot bear to see the people suffering. Our holy order is perishing; O generous one, how is it you perceive it not? Our worship is broken off; this indeed is death; we cannot bear an instant without it. Tukā says, O generous one, I ask thee for a place where no wind of violence can touch me.

## 126

HEAR my words, O saints! I am a sinner beyond all men—why do you love me with such tenderness? My heart testifies within me, of a surety I am not saved; men look upon me with honour, because I follow a track that others have laid down. I was sorely troubled by my worldly business, I became a cattle driver, a twister of oxen's tails. Even so, I could not maintain myself, so I took to my present course. The little money I had was soon finished; not that I renounced it, I gave it to Brāmhaṇas and beggars. I cut myself off from wife, sons and daughters, and became of course a low, stupid wretch. I dared not show my face to the world; I crept into holes or retired to the jungle; thus I entered on a solitary life. I was vexed by the cravings of the belly; and I thought that God had no mercy. If any one offered me a dinner, I readily said "Yes." My fathers served this God before me, this is why I worship him. Tukā says, Come, some of you, offer him faith and take him in exchange for it.

## II

# Descriptions and Invocations

### 127

FAIR is the sight of his even feet on the brick there; O Hari, let my restless mind repose. I desire no other illusory joy; send me, O God, no striving for such. The realms of Brahma and the rest are extreme misery; you permit the thoughts of men to be drawn thither. Tukā says, We have learned the secret of faith in him; works of all kinds are ruinous.

### 128

FAIR is the vision where he stands on the brick, with his hand upon his hip. On his neck is a Tulsi wreath, his robe is of silk; I delight for ever in that form. The pendant fish sparkle in his ears; the jewel Kaustumbha shines at his throat. Tukā says, Herein is all my pleasure, I will contemplate his holy face with joy.

### 129

LET my eyes be fixed for ever on thy image, dear husband of Rakhumai; sweet is thy form, sweet is thy name, I will give thee my love for ever. O mother Viṭṭho, give me this excellent gift, dwell in my heart and pervade it. Tukā says, I need nothing else; there is complete joy in thy feet.

### 130

HE is noble and full of grace, the very image of Madana; in him the rays of the sun are eclipsed; he wears on his forehead the spot of musk, his body is anointed with sandal, about his neck hangs the garland of tulsi. He wears the crown and earrings; fair is his holy face, moulded out of happiness; about his waist is thrown a robe of golden silk; such, O women, is he of the dark cloud and dark face. Come, all of you, accompany him. Tukā says, I can be patient no longer.

### 131

WITH thy hand upon thy hip and thy garland of tulsi, show us thy form, O Hari! standing with thy two feet on the brick, show us thy form, O Hari! with thy gorgeous robe of silk about thy loins, show us thy form speedily. As thou appearest on Garuḍ's plinth, so men recall thee. I am wasting away to a skeleton; come, O Lord of Pāṇḍhari, to meet me. Tukā says, Fulfil my hopes; be not heedless of my desires.

### 132

BORNE on Garuḍa, wearing his silken robe, I shall see him, the dark one, the lovely one, the god of the purple cloud, who wears on his neck the fair garland of tulsi. The crown on his head shines like millions of suns, the pure jewel Kaustumbha sparkles at his throat. His holy face is moulded out of happiness; on his left stands his spouse, Rakhumadevi; Udbhava and Akrūra stand on either side of him; Sanaka and the rest sing his praises. Tukā says, There is none like him, my friend Pāṇḍuranga.

### 133

WITH his tulsi garland round his neck the lord of the world stands on the brick; gazing on Pundalika the lord of Pāṇḍhari stands by the Bhīma. Joy and liberation are his handmaids, prosperity and perfection cling to his door. The holy disc moves round him; death trembles and flees from it. The mother of the world stands on his left. Bhimaki his consort stands beauteous by. As lightning flashes from a cloud, so the greatest guilt is crushed by the sight of him. He is the sea of joy, bliss supreme, the delight of the cowherds and the damsels. Govinda blows his flute in joy, entrancing birds and beasts. Handsome is his face, the four-armed god, the rider of Garuḍa, who entrances the mind. Tukā says, My lord comes speedily in return for devotion.

## 134

A JEWEL fades under the shadow of poverty; adversity eclipses the best of the things. Beauty and prosperity are not found apart from Pāṇḍuranga, generous master, sea of mercy. If you set materials for a feast before one who knows not how to cook, these conveniences are all wasted on him. Tukā says, If you put a jewel on a goat's neck, it looks a mean thing for that very reason.

## 135

LET me contemplate him, who bestowed this life upon me, Nārāyaṇa, the life of the world; I will sing his attributes. Him who stands by the Bhīma hand on hip, whose even feet are lovely to see, him I will clasp within me. He who slew the demons, who guards his worshippers, who diverts himself with perfect skill—at his feet I lay my head. He who wore the wreath of wild flowers sporting among the cowherds, who took Bali down to the pit, who stayed there with him, he is my Lord, he to whom this image belongs. Who unites in himself every power, who wears the wreath of basil on his neck, before him ever and anon I fall. He whose name destroys all guilt, whose servant is Lakshmī, to him belongs this surpassing lustre, him Tukā worships with full devotion.

136

VITTHALA is our life, the source of all the Vedas and Sāstras ; Viṭṭhala is perfect attainment, the repose of rapt contemplation. Viṭṭhala is our ancestral God, treasure, family and spirit ; our merit, our highest goal; we love the throne of Viṭṭhala. Viṭṭhala is diffused throughout our race. He fills the seven regions of hell ; he pervades the three worlds, and the souls of the sages. Viṭṭhala is the darling of our hearts. Our gracious and tender master, the embodiment of our love; it is he who puts the world in motion. Viṭṭhala is our father, mother, uncle, brother, sister ; apart from him we care not for our family. Tukā says, Now we have none but him.

137

FORSAKING Vaikunṭha he stands upright on the brick. The lord of the world has come ; he has come to meet his worshipper Pundalika! On the further bank of the Chandrabhāga he stands with his hands upon his hips. Tukā says, The sky resounds with shouts of acclaim.

138

THE throne whereon he sits is studded with jewels ; on either side is a besom of peacock's feathers; Rakhumai and Rādha stand near him. All mystic powers attend as handmaids upon him. Tukā takes off his shoes and stands by as a minstrel to sing of his praise.

### 139

LIKE a diamond set in gold, like a mine of rubies, so glorious is Nārāyaṇa to the sight. His face is a jewel moulded out of joy. Therein is the lustre of a million moons, full moons of the fullmoon day. Tukā says, Our eyes cannot turn away. They are fully satisfied to behold him.

### 140

UPRIGHT on the bank of Bhimā he stands towards the south looking upon us. Evildoers tremble and run away, when those that are bold in his name cry aloud. He endures all with a patient smile; from his speech proceeds a nectar of perfect joy. The sages tasted in their souls this sweetness, when the cravings of their bodily life were stilled. He has taken a firm hold on the minds of men, for he is generous enough to give them their hearts' desire. Excellent is thy name, O mother Viṭṭhā, to which all perfections resort. He stands upon the brick, unclothed, grasping the joint of his waist, to reward devotion. Show us the path across the sea of the world, O Viṭṭhā, mother of those that have attained or seek perfection. Make haste, first enter the path, then you will reach infinite bliss. Tukâ says, Everything has come to Pāṇḍhari; the universe is maintained by the light that proceeds from it.

### 141

O VITTHALA, that standest on the Bhīma's bank, thou hast wearied thyself for thy worshippers, with many a care and many a visit to the earth. Thou art gentle to us, but destructive to the demons. Thou wast reclined amid the sea of milk, when the earth was infested with demons; therefore thou didst appear in the cowherd's house; Pundalika stayed thee at Pāṇḍhari. Tukā says, Thou canst be gained by faith.

### 142

LIKE a mother's feelings, when she hears the auspicious news that a son is born, such be even my feelings when I sing or hear sung the attributes of Hari. The deer is fascinated by the sound of music; he forgets his own existence. Tukā says, The offspring of the tortoise gazes on its mother for nurture.

### 143

THE cooking is done; Rakhumai waits for you; the water is heated in the pot; she has ground beneath her feet the powder for your bath. O Pāṇḍuranga, the feast delays for you; the Gopis have brought the pot and are waiting to pour water for your face and hand. All the damsels stand expectant to serve you; Udbhava and Akrūra have come to give you an invitation. A couch of fragrant flowers is spread; jewelled lamps are set on the trays with khus-khus grass and betel leaves, prepared for your delight. Tukā entreats you, Look hither, O Lord of Pāṇḍhari; he says, Be vigilant every one of you.

## 144

WE count as the murder of a Brāhmaṇa the praise of any other than thee, O Pāṇḍuranga! We slaves of Vishṇu fix our faith on thee alone; we call none God besides thee. My tongue shall be cut into a hundred pieces if I turn back from this assertion. Tukā says, If I attach myself to any other, I shall be guilty of all sins.

## 145

O HUSBAND of Lakshmī, listen to my words! I pray to thee in my wretchedness. With folded hands I wait while thy song is sung; draw near to me thyself. Listen to my cry; I ask for nothing more. Tukā's brother says, O God grant this little petition.

## 146

YOU are wearied with granting the wishes of your servants; you make it your pride to accept us. O Lord of the abject, O visible image of joy, right well do these titles become you! Many have asked thee to bless them; many hast thou blessed and satisfied. Tukā says, O loving father, who can fathom your playful kindness?

## 147

I WILL extol Keśava, Mukunda, Murāri, Rāma, Krishṇa, mighty names that annihilate all guilt. O Life at once and Death of the world, who art at once the Dwarf and the Universe of manifold glory; O container of good and evil, slayer of Madhu; thou who severest mortal ties, who bearest the disc and the mace, strong hero that didst overthrow the demons! O warrior that wearest the jewelled crown, O generous master that givest the world to men, O image of Madana, entrancing the spirit, in whom the cowherds and the damsels delighted. O Kānhā, master of dramatic skill, endowed with every perfection, possessed of every attribute, beyond all attributes, who beholdest and knowest all things; thou who hast created the sun and other lights, yet dost allow no sense of pride to approach thee, how can I serve this God? What little can I offer him? Without faith he cannot be comprehended. Tukā suffers not his soul to quit his feet.

## 148

O VIṬṬHALA, thou art the prince of the generous, the life of the world. Thou art a heap of generosity, all perfection dwells with thee. Thy name is passing sweet, thou dost fulfil our fond desires. Thy holy face is very good; I have begun to fix my thoughts on thee. O utter the sweet name of Viṭṭhala; we have heartily desired him. Tukā cries lamentably on thee; do thou run speedily to him!

## 149

O VASUDEVA, lord of the humble, lotus-eyed glorious eternity! O thou who givest happiness to thy worshippers, there is nothing void of thee! O infinite one, master of the world, most noble form, image of Vāmana! Creator of Brahmā, Lord of Vaikunṭha, inaccessible to the Vedas and Śāstras. O all-pervading one, whose arm is everywhere, unfathomable! Eye of the world, God of the world, ancient father of Brahmā! O Pāṇḍuranga, servant of thy worshippers, thou that dost crush their fears, O best of beings! Infinite one, that dost fill the minds of all, that dwellest apart from association and solitude! O Lord of the senses, thy noble form is unknown to thy simple worshippers; assume thy embodied shape, and set them to adore thee, says Tukā.

## 150

O THOU that dwellest in the sea of milk, and dost repose on the serpent! O thou that dost take a form for thy diversion and didst delight the Gopis! O thou that visibly appearing art thy worshippers' ornament, a sea of attributes whose true form is unknown! O thou who hast assumed unnumbered shapes, whose true shape is limitless! O abode of pity! O Lord God, who dost protect the deities, dispel the mortal fears of thy worshippers! O thou that dost pervade all and liest beyond all, Lord of Vaikuntha, saviour of Gajendra! O thou who givest happiness to thy simple worshippers, there is nothing void of thee. O thou who dost put our minds in motion, a mass of knowledge, thyself champion of thy worshippers, slayer of the demons! O Nārāyaṇa, proud of thy servants, O Pāṇḍuranga, life of the world! Parent of Brahmā and the rest; author of all deeds, thyself doing none; pervading every atom and particle; saviour of the sinful! these are Tukā's words.

## 151

IF I praise any other than thee, let my tongue rot away. If I care for any other, let my head be crushed. If I find pleasure in others, surely it is sinful that very instant. If the ears drink no nectar of God's glory, what use are they? Tukā says, If I forget thee for one moment, what purpose can life serve?

## III

# Pandhari

### 152

COME to Pāṇḍhari! You need not toil after emancipation! The gods come to salute his feet with natural joy and exultation. The dust raised by their dancing feet keeps company with us as we go. Tukā says, There are heads raised on pillars to point the way; there is the spotless throng of the Vaishṇavas.

### 153

WHEN you have seen Pāṇḍhari, you will praise no more the glory of Vaikuṇṭha. There liberation wanders from door to door, needy in aspect like a servant. There is the tulsi-plinth, the courtyard washed, bright hues and garlands, ceremonies ever new from house to house. His name is repeated, his story is told and his praises are sung; as they pound the rice, they recite verses of Pāṇḍuranga. There is perfect happiness unbroken; in a word, Bramhā dwells there. Tukā says, What toilsome efforts cannot attain, there you see visible before you, standing on the brick.

### 154

BE a pilgrim and gaze on Pāṇḍhari; why need you practise other means of salvation? You will gather the fruit in perfection from this. No pride survives here; every craving is satisfied. Tukā says, Dark-blue Viṭṭho dwells before my eyes.

## 155

THE original source of all sacred spots, the fruit of all vows, Bramha himself embodied is Pāṇḍhari; we have seen it with our own eyes; our longing fasting eyes are satisfied. Life of all life, companion in happiness, he stands upright hand on hip. Father of the world, sea of mercy, he destroys the wicked and loves the humble. This is the form unqualified, adored of gods and contemplated by sages. Tukā says, I did not meet it in the Vedas; I found it as I sing of it in songs.

## 156

YOU cannot find sorrow at Pāṇḍhari, though you wanted it for medicine; the joy of love is ever present there. Pundalika has established a market there, he has brought thither all Vaikunṭha. In all dealings there, no loss overtakes one; people make a profit that satisfies them. There is enough for all the country side; it is stored in great heaps; for ten miles round the land is fattened. Tukā says, The saints are well contented; they dwell for ever in Pāṇḍhari.

## 157

BOTH gods above and places of pilgrimage come continually to visit this pure abode by the Chandrabhāga. This is no story I have heard; I describe what I have seen, for its unequalled splendour passes description. No guilt enters the ten miles of its circuit; the worst of sins burn themselves up by a natural fire; men and women are purged from lust; they become divine; the joy of Bramha dwells in every house.

Tukā says, Though you have no trace of merit, go to Pāṇḍhari and receive merit infinite.

### 158

SUCH is the glory of Pāṇḍhari that if we seek aught to equal it, we find no such place, for there God meets us at once. All other holy places take time to yield their fruit. Tukā says, This is a mart of bliss, a heaven upon earth.

### 159

THERE is a city on the bank of the Bhīma, whose name is Pāṇḍharpura; the Patil there has four arms, and sixteen thousand wives. Let us go dancing to play at that town; he will give us joy and rest. Our predecessors have grown bold, they will describe for us their goal of joy. He is mighty above the mighty, ruler over kings; the age of evil cannot enter his dominion. The Patil Pundalika has established a farm, he has escaped from the sorrow of the world; the saints and sages have opened shops there, you can buy what you will. You can buy liberation there for nothing, for nobody wants it! Both markets are thickly crowded; there is an endless stream of pilgrims; they say, "We care not for Vaikuṇṭha, for we have seen Pāṇḍhari; I hoped for it long, now by toil I have won it." Tukā says, O saints, it is through your merits that I have reached his feet.

### 160

COME, let us go and see for ourselves the festival of Kārtika; Vaikuṇṭha has come near to Pāṇḍhari. There is a harvest of invocations; the heavens cannot contain our love; every house in

Pāṇḍhari overflows. They go steadily on, bearing images of Garuḍa; with resolute hearts they clash the cymbals, raise the note of song and beat the drum. Tribes of happy men are gathered there; how they stagger for joy! With stout hearts they move forward, outstripping each other. The nectar of his name is poured out in floods; their senses are all choked up. The army of the Vaishṇavas draws near; the forces of Time and Death tremble. Brahmā and the rest are filled with desire, when they see the joys of the pebbly shore. "Blessed, blessed are mortal men," they cry, "how fortunate they are." One must pass through death to liberation at Benāres; Gayā does but pay off the debt which we owe our fathers; but at Pāṇḍhari there is nothing left in abeyance before the feet of Viṭṭhala. Tukā says, Why should we be anxious now? He who gives all gifts in perfect measure, he will never disappoint us.

## 161

THE guilt which cannot be purged by searching the Śāstras is altogether put away by the sight of Pāṇḍhari. Blessed, blessed is the bank of the Bhīma, the lake of Chandrabhāga. The warrior form of Viṭṭhala is at Padmatīrtha; the place of his sport is at Venunāda. Here is the mother of all sacred spots; Vaikunṭha on earth, unchangeable. His name is proclaimed with shouts; the demons of destruction tremble. There is no spot to compare with this; none that can be weighed against it. Fortunate is the lot of those who behold Pāṇḍhari; since you are born into the world, come, look but once upon it! What is left of your sins, when you have seen the god and his worshippers? Such is the city of Vishṇu that all grow divine in it, both men and women. The wheel of Vishṇu goes round the town; Time and Death cannot enter it. To describe that joy I have no means nor spirit; they who visit Pāṇḍhari have reached Vaikunṭha. Tukā says, He who believes not these words of mine, he is vile here and hereafter; he loves not Pāṇḍhari!

## 162

THE goods we want have come in abundantly; we need wander to and fro no more. He stands upright on the brick; the market of Pāṇḍhari is his inheritance. The streets are crowded; the world breaks into blossom. Tukā says, Bring a true measure, dear friends!

## 163

IN the square of Pāṇḍhari a game has been started; all the Vaishṇavas have gathered together. With cymbals and sticks they make a sound in concert; they have taken the child of Devakī for their leader. Come, my brothers, let us behold this marvel; why are you engrossed in wordly desires? Blessed are those who have joined him; there is no pleasure like this in the three worlds! Their conversation is full of joy and delight; they show to one another their fond affection. They are earnestly bent on the Six, the Eighteen, and the Four; they dance and circle in a pure measure. As cymbals of devotion they wear jewels and sandal-wood; their energy is glorious, and skilfully they wind their clothes about them; they proclaim his name with loud cries. Hari, Hara, Brahmā and the thirty-three crores of gods meet in the holy Bhīma. They all stand marvelling. Amraoti is abandoned; they cry, "Glorious is Vaikunṭha, but it cannot compare with Pāṇḍhari." Tukā's servant says, Be not slothful; I call on men and women.

### 164

WE are obstinate little children entreating you for the happiness of your love; our desires we have centered on your feet, and we have spurned the knowledge of Brahma. When I am invited to Pāṇḍhari, I set my eyes on that road. Tukā says, There I shall see all notable spots together in one.

### 165

HE who visits Pāṇḍhari forgets his father and mother; he becomes Pāṇḍuranga and nothing else; he continues to embrace him. He needs neither wealth nor house, he quits the sensuous life. Tukā says, This spot annihilates impurity at once.

### 166

PUNDALIKA'S inām is full; the roads are crowded; every article is brought there; the omens are good for all kinds of profit. All difficulties overgoing these are swept away; all balances of debts due and payable. Tukā says, Whatever gain you make there, it belongs all to yourself.

### 167

MY treasure consists in worshipping at Pāṇḍhari, I know nothing else but that, O Lord of Pāṇḍhari! I am Viṭṭhala's own slave stamped with his own name. Tukā says, Now I cannot turn back at all.

### 168

TO reach Vaikuṇṭha you need not mortify your body nor take away your life; Pundalika has provided a means thereto, a means of putting off the burden of the world. Tukā says, He has provided an easy path; Pāṇḍhari is Vaikuṇṭha upon earth.

### 169

IF a man has visited a million holy places, but has not seen Pāṇḍhari, accursed is his birth, for he has not seen the even feet. He may have gone through forms of sacrifice and union innumerable, but he has not seen the even feet. Tukā says, In Viṭṭhala's feet, lo! unnumbered holy places meet.

### 170

WE are born and go on our way; we eat the curds and rice of the world. Not so in Vaikuṇṭha, there you get no mouthful of the world! We go on feeding each other, we rejoice in the whirl of existence. Tukā says, Excellent are the level sands of Pāṇḍharpura; what is humble is best!

## IV

# Dehu

### 171

BLEST is the village of Dehu, holy is that spot of earth, for there lives Pāṇḍuranga, our God. Blest are the husbandmen there, happy are they, who cry upon his name. With his hand upon his hip the father of the world stands there; by his left is Rakhumadevi, our mother; at the door stands Garuḍa with his hands joined together. On the north is a peepul tree, on the south stands the Ling of Śankar; beautiful is the bank of the holy stream Indrayani. There is the wood of Lakshmīnārāyaṇa Ballal, where the Lord of perfection dwells. Without is Bhairava, who smooths the way, with Hanumanta near at hand. There do I, Tukā, preach and sing, with the feet of Viṭṭhobā in my heart.

# V

# The Nature of God

## I.—In Himself

### 172

WE hear it said that Janārdana lives in mankind; how is it we fail to perceive this? Who is it that passes through birth, age and death, through pain and disease? Guilt and merit, conduct pure and impure, who is it that has taken these on himself and why? We die and pass away; but not so thou; how shall we assure ourselves of this? Tukā says, Do thou unfold this mystery and show me the truth.

### 173

OF what material is the " I " made; how difficult it is to look into its nature. We cannot forget the idea, though it is nothing but ourself. When darkness overpowers light, the ground under our feet is changed. Tukā says, If you take God with you, he will show you where you are.

### 174

ALL our possessions belong to Kṛishṇa; not knowing this, the mind imagines otherwise; therefore evil spirits assault it; the five elements come besieging it. We conceal our possessions from their true owner, and bring punishment on ourselves. Tukā says, Time throttles us in its grasp, yet we go on crying " I," " I."

175

THEE, without attributes, let me contemplate as one with attributes; all on a sudden I feel the sense of difference between us. Henceforth there will be no conception of union between us; it is well as it is, let us keep our respective positions. In trying to approach thee I have wasted words. Tukā says, A feeling of indifference pervades my frame as it does thine, O infinite one!

176

RAISE no question whether Hara and Hari be different; one resides in the other, as sweetness resides in sugar. If one cares to distinguish them, it is but a *vilanti* that marks the difference. Tukā says, The right side and the left form one body.

## II.—His Relation to the World

177

BRAHMA and Māyā exist together, as the shadow follows the body. If you try to cut it off, you fail; if you try to destroy it, it has an existence of its own; if you cover it up beneath you, it is there, out of sight. When it is inseparable, why should we persist in calling it separate? We lead ourselves into a confusion of mind. Tukā says, The taller you grow, the taller it is; the shorter, the shorter; it varies with yourself.

178

IF God intervenes, then the action passes over to him, I am a silent witness; knowing this, all vexation about purity and impurity passes away. The toy notion of individual and supreme spirit was created for a diversion of the fancy. Where then are the worlds? They are an illusion that passes away. Of a truth the world is of one substance with Vishṇu; under this notion all our ideas fall into their place. The variety of castes and creeds is a diversion of his; the whole texture is woven of one; then how can there be a distinction of like and unlike things? Such is the conclusion reached by Nārāyaṇa in the person of his Vedic author. This essence of gracious favour Tukā has obtained; his dwelling is close to his feet and not far from them

## 179

THE mind serves as a crucible wherein all pleasures are thrown together. One serves to make another deeper, but each returns at last to its native form. When a drop of rain falls into the sea, how can it be distinguished? Tukā says, The new drops cannot be recognized even by God.

## 180

HOW could we contrive a ferry across the mirage of the world, to cross to the farther side of it? When children play at shop with coins of broken potsherds, what real loss or gain is made in that business? When girls play at a wedding, does any real relation between them follow? Whatever joy or grief we experience in a dream, when we wake we find it was a false impression. It is false that all are born or dead, or bound or free or suffering, says Tukā.

### 181

WHY should I trouble about actions good or bad? I have found the true secret. You are like your name; you have not revealed yourself at all. You have parted with nothing; you are still stored up. Tukā says, What will my burden be to you?

### 182

KNOW this, the devout have no store of merit; they have reached the state where all is God, immanent and transcendent. Purity, ignorance, passion and pain can never touch the devotees of Hari. In all their members it is nothing but God that eats or speaks or acts. Tukā says, There is no such distinction as "God" and "His worshippers."

### 183

BY this means our independence of spirit is cast forth; whether we take or refuse pleasure, it is Pāṇḍuranga dwelling in us who takes or refuses. The semblance of a cause being destroyed, we cease to count loss or gain, much or little. Tukā says,- Let us return to our tasks, but cease to identify ourselves with them.

## III.—Union with God Necessary

### 184

ENOUGH; I need urge no more reasons. The diversity of gods is an offspring of our own thoughts; there is no truth in it; God is one. Among duties of worship, as they are reckoned, who can distinguish between good and bad? who knows what should be done and what should not? Let us leave them all alone and put from us a chance of suffering. Tukā says, Sing the praises of this God; sing them, O my soul, with satisfaction.

## 185

I WENT to ask for provisions for the way; I felt bewildered in your world of illusion. Apart from you it yields nothing to any one; in expressing my own soul I lost it. It was in vain I visited your home of illusion; enough, I say, enough of it now! Tukā says, For this very reason, O Gopāla, stay apart from us!

## 186

WHAT should I do with any other God but the Lord of Pāṇḍhari? When a river has joined the ocean, all other names of it vanish. When the sun rises, all other lights are lost. Tukā says, I know none but the Lord of Pāṇḍhari.

## 187

MOREOVER, we are greatly strengthened; we shall hold you by your pledges. What is past and gone is past and gone; by finding the vital principle all objects are secured. To break off all bonds produced by movements of the world, we ought to be pure in the presence of the pure one. Tukā says, Such is your nature that through you knowledge of the true self comes to us easily and unbidden.

## 188

WHY do I care where the Ganges meets the ocean? My desire is to allay my thirst.

I store up in my heart for ever the lovely form of Viṭṭhala. It is the butter that men want: who cares to store up butter-milk? The mother gives the child a morsel conveniently to its mouth: the child need not be anxious. Let us sing and dance and perform rites of joy; alas! that I have not a fuller faith! Tukā says, I am altogether one with God; why need I desire the future world?

## 189

O KEŚIRĀJA, thus I will worship thee; putting aside all sense of difference, I will reverence thy feet. I will shun no direction; I will go straight to any point. Tukā says, I will not be one-sided in matters of praise or blame.

## 190

HENCEFORTH I shall reverence all spirits. I shall conceive thee to be present every moment, O Nārāyaṇa. While I hold the Vedas authoritative, I shall except those passages that teach difference. Tukā says, Then I shall want no other companions.

## 191

YOU cannot separate the sun from its rays; even so through faith our God inheres in ourselves. How can you separate sweetness from sugar? Tukā says, Where a sound arises, it melts into the vault of the sky.

## 192

IT was you who created me: how could I be different from you? Consider now yourself if I am not just like you, neither more nor less. In the place where you set me I have continued, obedient to you. Tukā says, Now I declare plainly, I am free from actions, like yourself.

193

WHATEVER I do, O God, I offer thee as a service. O Nārāyaṇa, spirit supreme, there is no distinction between me and thee. We know none but thee; our own mind testifies this to itself. Tukā says, O Lord of the world, is not this the truth?

194

O GOD, I see why you answer not. You are ashamed to be called one who speaks; yet I will not seek to catch you in a dilemma. Why should I fear to call you dumb? Take me beyond all limits to yourself, giving me this for a response; if you will not receive me, I shall be perplexed indeed. But remember this,—between giver and receiver this is the rule of piety: the gift must be such as the other can receive; if either be careless of the other, both sides are guilty. Therefore I hope and long to hear your voice; to this end I patiently strive departing not from my resolve, I will not go till I have had an answer from you; know that this is my fixed intention. You may say yes or no, as you will, says Tukā.

195

THOUGH the idea of a second is dispelled, yet Hari remains undiminished: we need not search for his seat outside ourselves. If you desire to know so much, know it by the mind within the mind; know it as the expert hunter knows the signs where game may be found. First, is the body a reality? Are the correlatives of the body facts? It is a mere scarecrow: it is something that the thief takes for a sentinel. Tukā wakens you and cries, Do not be idly frightened! Open the inner eye, you will find you are in himself.

196

I HAVE learned your secret by my own faith; now I shall keep my form concealed within me, like a tortoise. I shall meet you eye to eye; I shall not allow any separation to part us. Tukā says, O God, to contemplate you is to serve you.

197

WILL men turn up their noses at the smell of sandalwood? Will they object to gold—can such a thing happen? Sugar is sweet to all alike, young and old. Tukā says, If my mind were pure, why should people censure me?

198

YOU are yourselves immortal—see whether this be true or false! Do not speak of "This body of mine," and then you will believe what I say. What are you afraid of? Every thing is yours. Tukā says, In very truth you are better than the gods.

199

THE world is all God—true, but the chief thing needed is good advice. First, destroy yourself, then you will pass this test. You have gained the treasure of divine knowledge, when you can speak confidently on this point. Tukā says, This is the fifth stage of emancipation, when you see the effect absorbed into the cause.

## 200

MANY have died who were dear to me; how is it, O Hari, you have survived them? Come, tell me now, O Viṭṭhala, how is it you have lived so long? My father died with his eyes fixed on you, my grandfather and great-grandfather. Childhood, youth and the staff of age have chased me hotly; but you have lasted so long, because you had none to withstand you. Tukā says, Thus I conclude that all men, myself too, have to be placed in you as a deposit.

## 201

BLESSED is the time that is passed in contemplation; among the auspicious it is most highly auspicious. The servants of Hari need not cross the sea of the world; they know not what dwelling in the womb is. Deserts and peopled places alike are filled to overflowing by this ocean of mercy, Pāṇḍuranga. Tukā says, God and his worshippers are bound up together, they appear separate but they are really one.

## 202

IF he is the true substance of the Vedas, why do the Vedas say of him "Not this not this"? It is clear the Vedas are distinct from him. When thou hast revealed thy own secret nature, how can it be said, O infinite one, thou knowest it not? Since thou dost enjoy the sacrifice, why dost thou not help to complete it? If aught is missing, thou art angered. Thou dost dwell within us mortal creatures; then why, O Hari, hast thou set forth a difference between us and thee? Since thy form can be seen by austerity and pilgrimage, why does pride step in to keep us apart? Tukā entreats thee to pardon him, he stands and cries at thy door.

## IV.—Distinction from God Necessary

### 203

AS sweetness pervades sugar, so God pervades my frame; now I will worship him as best I may; God is within and without the soul at once. A ripple is not different from the water it belongs to; gold is still gold, though it be known as an ornament. Tukā says, So are we in him.

### 204

HOW can a child's longing fail to be gratified? We who are God's babes trust not to knowledge of Brahma or union with the supreme soul. We will master by experience those words which have been published. Tukā says, This shall be the effort I make in my simplicity, when the last end comes I will show this fond desire.

### 205

FAITH was designed to spread the glory of God; otherwise whence in the nature of things arises a second to speak of? To display his glory the test of worship was designed. Tukā says, The worshipper of God is an ornament to mankind.

### 206

WITHOUT a worshipper, how can God assume a form or accept service? The one makes the other beautiful, as a gold setting shows off a jewel. Who but God can make the worshipper free from desires? Tukā says, They feel to each other like mother and child.

## 207

WHAT does the lotus flower know of its own perfumes? The bee enjoys it all. Thus thou knowest not thy own name, but we know the happiness of love that proceeds from it. The mother cow eats grass, but the calf enjoys the sweet milk; he enjoys who produces not. Tukā says, The pearl lies in the shell, but the shell cannot see or enjoy it.

## 208

LIBERATION belongs to you, O God; keep to yourself that hard acquisition. What I prefer is worship; I will not renounce that delight. According to your powers, take care of that generous master. Tukā says, It is enough if you meet me once in the last end.

## 209

TO repeat your name is to string pearls together; this pleasure in your embodied form is ever new. I have ceased to desire the unembodied God; your worshippers do not seek liberation. With you it is still left possible to give and to receive. What avails the spot where a dish stood, when it is taken away? Tukā says, Give me the gift of freedom from fear; say, O thou that pervadest the world, I have given it thee!

## 210

I AM not starved for want of food, but it is Janārdana who deserves my reverence. I have looked on God as one who sees everything, in bright and dark days alike. God is like a father with his child, who feels and gives pleasure at once. Good acts and bad acts vanish. Tukā says, God's glory alone is left.

211

CURSED be that knowledge which makes me one with thee; I love to have precepts from thee and prohibitions. I am thy servant; thou art my lord; let there be still between us such difference of high and low; let this wonderful truth be established, destroy it not. Water cannot taste itself, nor trees taste their own fruit: the worshipper must be separate, thus alone pleasure arises from distinction. The diamond looks beautiful in its setting; gold, when it is fashioned into an ornament; if there were no difference, how could you contrast the one with the other? After heat one enjoys shade; at the sight of her child the milk comes into the mother's breast—what delight there is when they meet each other! Tukā says, This is a great thing gained and so I view it; I am thoroughly resolved to desire liberation no more.

212

THIS is why I have left my house and gone to the forest; my love will be spoiled by the evil eye; I shall lose my love of him. I will not listen to this doctrine of unity. Tukā says, This doctrine that God and I are one is false, I shall not let it interfere with me.

213

HAD I not been a sinner, how could there have been a Saviour? So my name is the source, and hence, O sea of mercy, comes thy purifying power. Iron is the glory of the Parisa, else had it been but an ordinary stone. Tukā says, Through the petitioner's faith comes the honour of the tree of wishes.

---

## V.—The All-Pervading Character of God and His Relation to the Created World.

### 214

WHAT manner of faith shall we offer; what single thing is fit to present you? You fill all and lie beyond all; you are present in our bodily form, whether we speak, eat, taste, or smell. How shall we control our organs, and sort out merit and guilt? What ceremonies or deeds shall we perform? Where is the scene where you are not present? What do I gain by closing my eyes? What spell or charm shall I utter? Where shall we place our faith? Where is the spot in which you are not? Whither shall we turn? Where shall we set our feet? There is no spot known to us that is void of thee; how can I search for such a place? Tukā says, Nothing but thy name shall be to us worship, liturgy, rosary, incense, lamp, fruits, betel-nut, flowers and water!

### 215

THOU art to me mother, father, brother and bosom friend; treasure, family and darling of the soul. Now I need no other grounds of assurance. I have placed on thy head all my burden of gaining and keeping. Thou art the sum of action, deeds of piety, thou art deity and family, in thee deeds of austerity, place of holy resort, religious vows, teacher—in thee everything is comprised. Thus says Tukā's brother, O God, who doest and makest man to do, in thee is fulness of faith, devotion, worship and attendance on God!

## 216

THIS Hari dwells in every spirit, pervading it as fire pervades wood. Light is reflected in every vessel, yet it does not perish when they perish. If you pound grass, you find no milk in it, yet when the cattle eat grass it turns to milk; he alone knows the secret of this who pervades all things and yet remains without them. The fruit appears at the end of the plantain tree; yet if you search within the stem, what do you find there? Cursed be the impatient man, his life is wasted; he gets no fruit or flowers; his labour is wasted. The reflecting medium occasions the name; but the reflection is nothing more; the essence remains behind in the dense body. Since the medium is impure, how can you see the essence within? Do not go on increasing sin and merit. Employ the true secret, have done with pretences; thus I Tukā entreat you; need I fall at your feet? If your desires are set on children, wife and money, consider, what will be left you at the end?

## 217

THY feet are everything to me; let me trust in thee alone. I see thy feet everywhere; the three worlds are pervaded by Viṭṭhala. Discussions of thy nature are a maze of error; let me refuse to enter into them. Tukā says, There is no particle without thee, yet I see thou art greater than space itself.

## 218

RĀMA is royal power and subject and protector of the people; in him all are comprised. There is no speech of him that is not auspicious; he is an infinite mine, a heap of good things. He has destroyed the idea of master, and every sort of service: whom else need we desire? Tukā says, The whole earth is buzzing with God's name; there is nothing left for us but to sing of him.

## 219

NĀRĀYAṆA gives and himself enjoys the gift; now what is left to say? Few words remain to speak. Whatever object our eyes behold is our own form dancing before us. Tukā says, Every sound is Govinda.

## 220

SPEECH cannot describe it, though you should utter all the words to our satisfaction. God's body is as it were a mirror, where each may see his own form. Infinite is the ripe crop that faith alone produces. Tukā is embarrassed by the heap of corn and sits dividing it out.

## 221

YOU have created amusing games to soothe your eyes with watching them; apart from that end, we all know what the world is—a wooden tiger and a wooden cow! There is unity at the bottom, but he has set an amusement afoot; he has made one light into many. Tukā says, There is no real form in the mirror, the reflection serves as an amusement.

## 222

WHEN you have the evidence of your mind, why do you need public opinion? You have your own advantage within yourself. The true faith you should hold is your own reflection that God pervades all, within and without you. With pure faith on your side, you need not abandon the world; the truth will come to light anywhere. The man who has tasted inward sweetness values it; he cares no more for outward show. Tukā says, Pure faith brings this about; God will belong to those who possess it.

## 223

TIME devours all this visible world; all things are ever passing from birth to destruction. As the sprout lies hidden in the seed, so is the infinite one the last resort of all things. Tukā says, Sound is resolved into the sky; thus men fail to perceive this great secret.

## 224

IN this reflection there is pleasure ever new, it should be discussed among the saints. If we remember the form of a thing, it becomes one with ourself; it does not stay apart a single moment. If you mean to worship him, then conceive him as the universe; in vain it is to limit him to one spot. Tukā says, Such is my perception of him; I lay my head in submission at his feet.

## 225

WE love this worthless world only while we fail to see him who pervades it. Nārāyaṇa is the father of the world, Nārāyaṇa pervades it, when we take him for our standard, all else becomes false. We need lamps no more when the sun arises; their light disappears in the lustre of the day. Tukā says, The store of our past makes the world cling to us; the undoubted secret of salvation is with Nārāyaṇa.

## 226

WE have hurled a stone upon the sensuous life; we have put death to death. You pervade the world: how can I be separate from you? Now why need I struggle to teach you? How can I expel anything from myself? How can I admit any thing to me? We may enter on dry discussions, but you remain beyond them; we are only thrusting imaginary torments on ourselves. You have all kinds of workmen dwelling in your house; you distribute wages according to their labour done. Tukā says, We know nothing of loss or gain; let him who is master preserve the house.

## 227

WITHIN and without is Hari; Hari has imprisoned me in my heart. Hari has set a stone upon desire; he has robbed me of worldly wealth. Hari has given me his soul in exchange for mine; he has caused a breach between me and mankind. Tukā says, Hari is not apart from us he surrounds us on every side.

## VI.—Universality of God's Grace

### 228

BECAUSE a girl is enjoyed for two years by Gandharva and Agni, do men or animals cast her off? A cow feeds on filth with her own mouth, yet she is pure; so is a stream when it has mingled with the Ganges. A peepul tree grows from a crow's excrement; if you consider the birth of the Pāṇḍavas, it was guilty. Śakuntalā, Suta, Karṇa, Śṛingi and Vyāsa—their names destroy sin. Consider Gaṇikā, Ajamela, Kubja, Vidura—consider too who was Pingalā, Valhā, Viśvāmitra, Vaśishṭa, Nārada—was the origin of these men pure? Yet men and women whose actions would not save them were saved by their repentance and by remembering Hari. Tukā says, Lord Hari does not remember a man's origin; he who considers that goes to hell.

### 229

I HAVE renounced all vehicles of sense; I shall not allow any trouble to come near me hereafter. Why should we have to clean our hands? Why should we put obstacles in a practised path? What has God not created for you? Every thing is in its proper place. Tukā says, When our pride disappears, with it goes the relation of I and you.

### 230

YOU cannot make cakes without pounding wheat; if you are idle, you will spoil them. Do not be angry if I tell you the secret! The thread-bound pole dances when the conjuror beats the ground with his rod. Tukā says, The secret is in the rod; it puts its skill in every thing.

231

WHY primal form is beyond mind or speech; so devotion has been invented to measure thee withal. With the measure of devotion I count out the infinite one, for verily there is no other way to do it. By sacrifice and austerity and union through the body, by recourse to contemplation, thou canst be found. Tukā says, Accept, O Keśava, as we offer it, the service we lay before thee in simple faith.

232

WHAT limit of his have we found by search, by considering further him who fills the world? Atoms and masses alike are divisible for ever; if the Śrutis say he is not, they too are exhausted before they define him. To a grub within a fruit there is a sky proportioned to his size; but how many such fruits there are on a tree! The infinite one showed Arjuna within his belly new creations and the world of Kṛishṇa. Tukā says, Cling to the robe of the saints; if you try to fathom him, how can you live long enough?

233

THE Yogis gaze on the reflection of your splendour; we see the original before our eyes. He stands upright with both hands on his hips; from his body glances a purple lustre. He pervades the world, yet dwells far from it; within all things he is hidden unmodified by all. He has neither shape, nor outline, nor name; we must approach him in our spirits. There is neither end nor limit to him, nor room for distinction of caste; he has neither family, nor caste, head, hands or feet. The joy of faith enlightens the ignorant, through their own fond desire, says Tukā.

## 234

IF I would praise thee, lo! the Vedas cannot do it; what are my efforts worth in comparison with that? But I find it very sweet to speak of thee; my tongue longs to taste the draught. Where is the intellect that can describe thy form? In every hair of thy body unnumbered worlds arise and pass away. Tukā says, True as thou art, and thou alone, there is no speech than can truly describe thee.

## 235

HOW can I see or meditate on thee! Show me the secret,—beggar that I am. Tell me how I can worship or serve thee, what faith, O God, will bring thee to me. How can I praise thee or conceive thee, or know whose or what thou art? How can I sing thee or meditate on thee! Show me what are thy thoughts, and thy ideas. Tukā says, As thou hast made thy servant, so, O God, teach me this by experience.

## 236

I HAVE no abilities to praise thee; the Śrutis stand still and dumb before thee; the four modes of speech stand dumb and helpless,—such is thy form, O Hari! That form is such that our eyes may not behold it, for the sight of it deceives Brahmā and the rest. Brahmā and the rest are embarrassed by Karma; hence they must wander from birth to birth. Tukā says, Thy attributes, thy name and form, are unmeasurable: how can we describe them?

## VII.—God's Power

### 237

THE high yogis sit contemplative in closed rooms; he comes up behind to protect them; he satisfies their hunger and thirst; he cools them when they are hot; they have learned to disregard the sensations of the body. What society delights them save that of Hari alone? What earthly pleasure or joy affects their souls? They would not choose for an instant the pride of kings. Tukā says, Poison becomes nectar through the gracious favour of Nārāyaṇa.

### 238

HERE is a little secret of your love, O Lord of the world; I remember the tale and will tell it to you. A deer and two fawns were grazing blithely in the wood, when suddenly there came a hunter with two dogs. He spread his nets on one side, he stationed his dogs on the other, he fired the grass on one side and waited himself on the other. The deer were beset on all sides; they began to remember your name. "O Rāmkṛishṇa, God of Gods, come at once! who will save us in this strait, but thou, O father, Lord of the world?" You heard their words and your pitiful heart was troubled; you ordered the rain to quench the fire speedily. You roused up a hare and the dogs pursued it; the deer joyfully bounded off, crying "Govinda has saved us!" Thus art thou full of mercy, beloved of thy worshippers; they delight heartily in thy praise, O spouse of Rakhumai, says Tukā.

## 239

IF I speak of goodness, he satisfies every desire; if of sweetness, how sweet is his name! If of mercy, behold, he is altogether righteous; of humility, he will not vex his servants. In generosity he is ready to give his spouse away; he triumphs over Time and Death. Regarding wisdom, he is a heap of noble qualities; but all to those who know him alone. He is as old as time; his way of diversion cannot be fathomed. Among the cowherds, he was a rude cowherd, a subtle cheat among the weak women. We may call him a simpleton, for he is submissive to faith; greedy, for he loves the morsels left by others; ugly, for he fell in love with Kubja; timorous, for he dreads sin. As to games he alone can play them; in dancing he alone knows a dancer. He hides within our spirit, yet, though we grasp thee, O God, thou art not apprehended. If we call thee high, behold thou art highest of all; or low, then thou art lowest. Tukā says, I have spoken the truth; I have paid no false worship.

## 240

WHAT lack we at the feet of Viṭhobā? No single thing. To distribute the mind among all the objects around us is to make it a beggar from door to door. Who is mighty save my Viṭhobā? Tell me any that is glorious save him.

Tukā says, There is liberation in Viṭhobā's village! let us carry off this treasure that costs us nothing!

### 241

IF Nārāyaṇa is weak, why do the Purāṇas resound with his praise? No drum is beaten save in the name of a glorious prince; else why do not men praise some other? Therefore declare that he lives for ever; it is his noble nature to make the lives of men happy. The excellence that is in him is incomparable, therefore his holy form has penetrated our hearts. No one is great who does not obey Hari; no prince should rise up against him. Tukā says, The truly great will serve him; with him there is no deceit or envy.

### 242

TELL me of any one else like Pāṇḍuranga; it is he who bestows salvation upon this Iron Age. There is some weakness in every other; look in your own heart for the place where he may be formed. Sin committed elsewhere vanishes in holy spots; sin committed there is like a line graven upon adamant; but the sin committed at Pāṇḍuranga's abode is absorbed in him and continues not in the sinner. This secret was told by Śiva to his wife. Tukā says, This deity comprises in himself all holy places.

### 243

IF God is your friend, then all the world is kindly to you. Experience shows us this, yet men are troubled without cause. If God protects a man, fire cannot harm him. Tukā says, Hari protected Prahlāda.

## 244

HE who pleases the saints is the death of Death, even as the child of a rich man is rich. If you listen to him, you will hear of none but the One; he protects you from weariness of fond desire. He has means to set you free from any guilt you have incurred; look not upon any other source of destruction. Tukā says, The shade of the wishing-tree is the chief thing: what compassion is not to be found there?

## 245

KRISHṆA is my mother and father, sister, brother, aunt and uncle. Kṛishṇa is my teacher and boat of salvation. He bears me over the river of the world. Krishṇa is my own mind, my family, and my bosom friend. Tukā says, Holy Kṛishṇa is my place of repose; I am resolved I will not be parted from him.

## 246

O GOD, give us some hope of support! There is no lack of aught with thee: what does it cost thee to grant us repose? My mind is frenzied with desire to serve thee. Tukā says, O Nārāyana, thou dost own thy worshippers' control.

## 247

LISTEN, people, how you may recognize your own interests! You must bring to mind the prince of Pāṇḍhari; if you utter the name of Nārāyaṇa, how can you be fettered? From this shore you may pass over the sea of the world. He will bring the age of Kali into subjection; the mirage of the world he will chase away. Prosperity and mystic powers will all be bond-slaves of his. This is the essence of all the scriptures, the secret purpose of the Vedās; if you look, you will see it is the purport of the Purāṇas. All are empowered to approach him, Brāhmaṇas, Kshatriyas, Vaiśyas, Śūdras and low-caste men; children, harlots and all others. Tukā says, By experience I have found this much out; other creatures may perchance enjoy this pleasure by good fortune, through their faith.

## 248

WHAT or whom shall we ask for but thee, O thou who fillest the globe and the universe? Who else knows how to fulfil our heart's desires? What of other princes and kings? There is none other in the three worlds that grants liberation, none that saves us but thou. When we think upon thy name and form, sin and fever run away in fear, desire is destroyed. Hari, this name of thine is truly called such in the Purāṇas, for it drives away death and re-incarnation from those they have seized. Why should I waste my speech? It is fruitless for me to praise any other than thee. O thou that destroyest the world, the great serpent is wearied with describing thee. Let my spirit repose in confidence at thy feet; it is vain to ask for aught else. Thy title, "Lord of the humble," is justified in the eyes of men; thou hast saved many a humble, many a guilty, many a sinful man. Tukā dwells at thy feet; preserve him, O God! I ask that I may serve thee.

## 249

WE feed upon this essence; we distribute it to others; come take it, do not ramble in the waste! He whose even feet are set upon the brick, he alone is a hero in generosity. All your desires will be satisfied, if your mind dwells steadily at his feet. Tukā says, He has sent me with the message, that this path is easy and pleasant.

## 250

WHAT puzzle can we find in the sea of the world, if he shows us the path and goes before us? Pāṇḍuranga is a good ship; he suffers not our feet or our bodies to be wet. Many holy men have gone over already, and reached the further shore. Tukā says, Now is the chance, come, let us run speedily after him.

## 251

THROUGH the virtue of the magnet iron stands upright and changes its nature. Such is the effect with us; thou dost play about us within and without. The flame devours a thread, but an amulet will preserve it. Tukā says, The sandal tree raises its wood to the highest honour.

## 252

WITH his wheel and mace in hand, he ever protects his worshipper at his feet and destroys the wicked. The unknown one has assumed a form, the excellent one has shown himself to us. Tukā says, Viṭṭhala fulfils the desires of every man.

## 253

BEFORE now thou hast saved many suppliants, therefore they call thee lord of the helpless. Thou didst not weigh guilt or race or lineage; thou didst save Azamela and the Bhil woman. Thou didst set the child Dhuru in a firm place; thou didst offer the sea of milk to Upamanya. When the beast Gajendra was injured by the denizen of the waters, thou didst rescue him from the sea of the world. Thou didst save Prahlāda in fire and flood, turning poison into nectar by thy name. When heavy burdens fell on the Pāṇḍavas, thou wast their champion. Tukā says, Thou wast the Lord of these helpless people I have heard the tale, I am come to thee.

## 254

OH brother, the Ganges is no common water, the banyan and peepul are not mere trees, tulsi and rudrāksha rosaries are not necklaces, they are manifestations of God. The sea is not a stream, you must not call the linga a stone. The saints are not like worldly men; you must not call the ascetic's staff a cane, nor holy food by the name of wheat; Rāma-Rāma you must not call words of common conversation. The sun and the moon are not mere stars; Meru is not a hill. The serpent of Śiva and Vāsuka are not poisonous snakes. Garuḍa is not a bird. The bull of Śiva is not a head of cattle. The wishing-tree is not a mere tree, nor the wishing-cow a cow. The tortoise of the world is more than a tank tortoise. Varaha is not a wild boar. Brahma is more than the soul of man. Lakshmī is not a mere woman. A holy sprinkling horn is not a bone; the silk robe of a goddess is not a piece of cloth. The magic stone Parīksha is not a stone; it is a manifestation of the goddess. Gold is not a common metal, nor salt a kind of sand; the ascetic's deer-skin and tiger-skin are not hides. Pearls are not flints, nor diamonds pebbles; the soul is not a guest to be dismissed when you desire. Dvāraka is not a mere village, nor Kṛishṇa's image a mere figure. The Gomatī is not a mere place of pilgrimage; the very sight of them brings liberation; Kṛishṇa is not a mere pleasure-seeker, nor Śiva an ascetic. Tukā says, He has obtained in Pāṇḍuranga alone all the bliss that these things can give.

## 255

MEN of strength have fought their way swiftly to the goal; but we are weak, we will cry to you for mercy. They have made a stepping stone of that mighty enemy. Tukā says, They are true heroes, steadfast saints, a very sea.

## 256

THE vile and stubborn demons tremble, for the bank of the Bhima rejoices in the town of Pāṇḍhari. Now shout aloud the thousand names at once! Viṭhai enters her worshippers' bodies and drives out any demon that has lodged there. Sīta was seized by a demon and taken to live in the aśoka forest; yet a mother came to her in the form of a goblin with loose hair. Mahisāsura made Prahlāda mad, suddenly Viṭhai came to the scene, gnashing her teeth. When seven children of Vasudeva had been devoured, she came at the appointed time for Vāsudeva's sake. When the poor Pāṇḍavas were forced to wander in the forest like madmen, she ran and saved them, protecting them in the flesh. Wherever men fix their thoughts on her name, thither she runs herself: she considers not the low degree of any men where she sees faith. O ancient goddess of our line, O mother, says Tukā, Why should we fear now spirits of evil or servants of Yama?

257

YOU saints need feel no anxiety; nor wonder how you can turn a crystal into a diamond. You must test a thing by the rules of its own place and time, and allow it whatever its worth may be If you punish one, you will frighten many; this reproach will be in many mouths. Tukā says, My words are not foolish, no madman's ravings.

258

WHATEVER good you do a child, his mother is aware of it. The child is dearer to the mother than her own life; if you take the child away for a kindly purpose, still the separation is poison to her. Tukā says, It follows the same law as that which refreshes the eyes when the feet are anointed.

---

## VIII.—The Power of God's Name

259

SUCH is Viṭṭhala's name that it heals the disease of the world, the sum of action stored from the past. If you utter it, you annihilate rebirth. Guilt cannot dwell along with it, the three-fold fever passes away. Tukā says, The illusion of life becomes your servant and falls at your feet.

260

VIṬṬHOBĀ'S name is ever true and good and welcome, it severs all ties, its praise is heard in both worlds. He who has faith among his possessions profits by it very speedily; simple as he is, says Tukā, he knows how to conquer Time and Death.

261

BE assured that this perishable body will be destroyed: why then do you not utter his name? Countless millions have been saved by his name; it has given them a place in Vaikuṇṭha. There is nothing in the three worlds of such virtue as his name: why do you not recall it? Tukā says, His name is more glorious than the Vedas; Gopāla has bestowed it on us freely.

262

HIS name is the essence of all essences; the servants of Yama come to beseech it. Let your speech glorify the best and the highest of beings. He who wore on his head the moon, he saved himself by repeating this name; even so Valhakoli saved himself. Tukā says, Why should I describe it? The feet of Viṭṭhobā are full of salvation.

263

TEACHERS themselves do not understand the secret of the Vedas: what authority do others possess? The name of Viṭṭhobā is easily mastered;

with one impulse it bears you over the sea of the world. The wise know well that charms are impracticable, likewise acts and seasons prescribed; other men are all foolish. Tukā says, We have lost sight of the commandments and prohibitions; this path has been annihilated.

## 264

THOUGH you have made friends of the mighty, they cannot help you in the last hour. Rather utter the name of Rāma; make this provision, the best of all, or Yama will gnash his teeth and rend you. Amass, if you will, crores of wealth; it will not release you from the grasp of death. No train of followers or host innumerable will save you; only till death appears you may waste your might. Tukā says, Good sir, cut short the revolutions of birth and death!

## 265

YOU are set free from all obligations, if you recite the name of Viṭṭhala continually; when you utter the name no sin can stay near you. Uttering his name it takes not one instant to burn up millions of the five great sins. You have sinned in time passed; sin, if you will, in time to come; we shall stand security for you. Commit what sins you can commit; what other names of sin need I mention? Tukā says, Time and Death cannot enter here; our sins are consumed in flames.

## 266

CONSIDER him as a Brāhmaṇa beyond all doubt, vile though his birth may be, who utters correctly the name of Rāma Kṛishṇa and remembers his purple form. Peace, love and compassion are ornaments upon him, his patience is still unbroken. Tukā says, The six enemies have altogether left him; he is Brahmā himself.

## 267

THE pleasure which his name gives—know that it is God himself. I do not say this in ignorance, for I have the approval of the saints. That he who utters the name needs any other means of attainment—do not say so. Tukā says, Through his word that man attains happiness whose father and mother are both of them pure.

## 268

I HAD fallen into the eddy of the world; I had been oppressed by care; I had missed the path and urgently I had raised a loud cry. I had been caught and imprisoned by the senses. Tukā says, All is well now, for I uttered the name of Viṭṭhala.

## 269

THERE is nothing else that I trust to, I have made it my business to utter "Viṭṭhoba." I have girt up my loins, and issued a challenge; I shall not allow Time or Death to stir against me. With faltering speech, as best as you can, cry out, Hari! Hari! Tukā says, We have discovered the true seed of all the Purāṇas.

## 270

DESIRING the bait, a fish swallows the hook; his throat is laid open and he dies: as he writhes in the hour of death, he remembers the merciful one; in his last moments he utters thy name. Tukā says, His happiness passes all bounds.

## 271

WHAT is not accomplished by the contemplation of Viṭṭhala alone? In him all means of attainment are summed up; he carries us over the sea of the world. That name bestows the fruit of many austerities. Tukā says, Those three syllables are a form easy to repeat.

## 272

THOUGH the name is close to his lips, a man utters it not day or night; the name of Viṭṭhala destroys desires and annihilates the world. Why do you not secure this dwelling-place, this pleasant neighbour for your heart? Tukā says, Why do you not lay up this excellent store?

## 273

THOSE who live in the world cannot be servants of a teacher, they cannot renounce passion, for they tremble through fear of lust. Such is not thy name, O Lord of Pāṇḍhari, that requires no toil from anyone; it is perfect sweetness and we need not wash our face before we taste it. We shall not hanker after wealth, we need not fear the world. A single life is not enough to fulfil our destiny, and good deeds multiply their consequences; the name of Viṭṭhobā alone destroys the sorrow of the world. You may give up doing and undoing, or looking into sacred texts. Tukā says, All is concluded by the name of Viṭṭhala.

## 274

EVERY fruit that appears on a tree is sure to ripen, if it falls not from its stem; this name will enable you to attain the end, if you abstain from vice. It is a well-trodden path and will take you to the goal, if no obstacle interferes. Tukā says, If adversity arises, it will bring destruction of your gain.

## 275

THOUGH you have no sweet speech, though God has given you no music in your voice, yet Viṭṭhala suffers no loss for lack of that; utter the name of Rāma Kṛishṇa as best as you can. Ask God to give you that sweetness of worship, the face that brings love and confidence. Tukā says, I bid my spirit be resolute from day to day.

## 276

THIS miraculous power of mine is developed to its height in music; this is your own gift. O God, grant me to serve you continually! Therein is a flood of love, that neither ebbs nor flows. As you utter his name, says Tukā, you perceive a deep mine of nectar.

## 277

REDUCE your speech to silence, keep it away from all objects of sense. Every effort is weariness that is not spent upon his name. Our own plans draw the mind after them; merit and guilt are alike in this. Tukā says, Let my spirit find a resting-place in Nārāyaṇa.

## 278

THE Purāṇas tell his story in song; where his praises are sung he stands waiting himself. In the throat of Dattātreya the spell of his name prevailed; he repeated only the praise that delighted him. This name is an essence of supreme power; amid the ritual acts of the Brāhmans this name stands first. Nārada wandered amid the three worlds with a vīna in his hand and this name on his lips. Parīkshita was condemned to die within three days, but he escaped by uttering this name. The fame of the fisherman spread far and wide; he composed the life of Rāma ere Rāma was born. The Vedas call you embodied and unembodied. Tukā says, Your name is the same in both aspects.

## 279

THE utterance of his name brings no liberation; such is the teaching of some. Wicked indeed are their words; we should turn a deaf ear to them. Those who kept his name within their minds have attained to him. Foolish men have died groping in darkness, chattering nonsense as they died. They who censure the nine rites of worship, they are born to be reproved, they are like swine that have entered the world. Why should I repeat this time after time? The vile do not remember it. Merely because he recited this name, a child was hidden in the sea of milk. For his own name's sake he chased the demon Śankha; he tore his entrails open and took out the four scriptures. It is well known in the world that through his name Gaṇikā was saved. Others too were rescued, guilty and sinful wretches. This at least has been loudly proclaimed, that his mind was in Prahlāda's mind. He saves men in danger from fire and water; poison has no power over them. Why should I display, says Tukā, by such examples the glory of his name? Those who denounce it go down to hell.

## 280

GOD serves his servants, he cannot suffer them to want anything, he throws away the dish prepared for himself and runs to help them. Such is the sea of mercy that stands on the brick; complete in generosity he displays himself in return for devotion. On his breast appears the sacred footprint, the ornament that his worshippers have set there. He feels it no hardship; he gladly suffers himself to be spurned. Satyabhāmā makes a gift of him; he cares not to conceal it. He sets his servant's feet on his head and goes about his task. He keeps Bali's gate; he drives Arjuna's chariot. He serves his servants like a true dependent. From due respect he will not speak to Pundalika, he stands decorously behind him. Tukā says, Why do you not worship so kind a mother?

## 281

IF a child calls his father uncle, why should he be rebuked? If our faith be pure, however imperfect it be, Viṭṭhala fulfils our longings. If you call sugar stone, does it not still taste sweet? Tukā says, The words may be irregular, but no word will be fruitless.

# IX.—God's Generosity and Condescension

## 282

HE calls himself his worshippers' debtor; he is ever grateful to them. By singing his praises we have induced the formless to assume a form. So the Lord of Pāṇḍhari fulfils to each his desire; he has presented himself to his devotees to pay off his debt of gratitude. Nārāyaṇa was born for the Rishi Amba's sake; such is his love of devotion that he serves his servant. In obeying their commands he hesitates not; he became a door-keeper in the house of Bali. He is deeply grateful for devotion; he finds no resort away from them. He who is Lord of the world trains the steeds in Arjuna's chariot. Such is his grateful love of devotion that he follows his worshipper's heels; at Pundalika's door he stands with even feet on the brick; he never stirs, but stands still with his hand upon his hip. He is subject to faith and devotion; truly is he called Lord of the humble. Tukā therefore lies and embraces his feet without moving.

## 283

WHO is such a heap of generosity as you? You give your servant a place with yourself. You consider not whether he is pure or abject, or what his lineage is; you purify him by dwelling in his body. In his house you will eat even bitter food, but you will not relish dainties from impious people. You will not leave your servants' houses though you are beaten there—you, who will not visit the Yogi's minds. Tukā says, True are your titles to honour, so the four Vedas declare.

## 284

HIS servants feel no uncertainty of salvation; Pāṇḍuranga is a haughty champion; with him is mercy and the gift of life. He can save you from death by flood or fire. Tukā says, For our sake his heart is stirred to mercy.

## 285

IN my fear, I have forgotten my fatigue; so I call on the Lord of the world with piteous cries My father is a mighty man, a jewel in a crest; my words shall cause him to arise. When my prayer falls on his ears, he will not be slothful; he gives strength to his suppliant, he relieves him from anxious fear; he sets him down at a banquet and gives him to eat freely. He bears him on his shoulder, he takes him home, he visits him oft and oft. Tukā says, Let my lord regard my stammering speech.

## 286

HOW merciful he is! in those who are helpless he feels his chief delight. He bears their burden on his head; he undertakes the care of acquiring and keeping for them. He suffers them not to stray from the path, he takes them by the hand and leads them. Tukā says, This is the reward if you follow him with absolute devotion.

## 287

THE stories of Hari are mother's milk that never cloys; people take kindly to them, the saints delight in them. Nectar stays ashamed in the rear of this sweet juice, because of the deep joy that Brahmā gives. The guilty and sinful become as men that sanctify assemblies; they become four-armed like God himself. All delights blossom in that spot where the crowd of Vishṇu's worshippers is gathered. Void of form, like an actor he has put on form; through love to men he dances and sings in the person of the saints. Tukā says, He has sifted the true means of attainment; he stands forth easy to attain by songs of praise.

### 288

O PROTECTOR of the fallen, your praises shall fill the world, if you take up the cause of your suppliants. We have learnt in our own dealings how true is the praise the Purāṇas give thee. You cannot bear to see your servants weak, therefore you stand upright before us, with disc and mace and weapons innumerable in your hands; where you see aught needed you run to supply it. Tukā says, It was our faith that brought about your full incarnation.

### 289

GOD dearly loves the man who has given up the world, he comes running after him and bears himself his joys and sorrows. The grace of Viṭṭhala does all for him, he has only to repeat the name. Tukā says, Simple and tender is Viṭṭhala's kind heart.

### 290

SEE what manner of God he is—mad after devotion and simple-hearted! He comes the moment he is called for—so ravenous of service he is! He growls in the dry wood unashamed. Tukā says, He assumed the form half male and half female.

## 291

THE consort of the Gopis is merciful to his worshippers; unsummoned he stands at their door; unbidden for them he toils. Wherever he sees pure faith, he sets the dust of his feet on men's foreheads. Tuka's brother says, Why will you not worship so kind a master?

## 292

WHY have you left such a leader? and why do you look so wretched? Your heart is full of passions; you have nothing in your hand but dust. Pāṇḍuranga is a proud and generous master; he needs but a tulsi leaf and water, he hungers after meditative devotion; you need not ask what office he will give you, nor send a pleader to plead your cause with him. He himself presides over his service and chastisement in his service. Tukā says, You will find no impediment if you go to meet him; go silently and embrace his feet.

## 293

THOUGH our Lord is so great, yet faith can make him dwell in a casket. He assumes the form that his worshipper has imposed on him; he fulfils his desires as he conceives them. Though he who gives us the world is so great, yet he asks us for a leaf of tulsi and water. He has assumed name and shape; he has made himself easy to reach, says Tukā.

## 294

VIṬṬHALA dwells by the Bhīma in Pāṇḍhari; he keeps Pundalika by his side, he is generous in compassion. Viṭṭhala is tender, if you remember him; he is highest in the height. He supports all the worlds, he finds his diversion in assuming forms. He stands upright, but he feels no weariness; there is no other saviour than he. A wealthy man keeps but one kind of food in his house, he succours the afflicted every instant. His servants bring them tasty food with all respect, he never stands aloof from them. With the exalted he is exalted, with the lowly he is lowly. You cannot seize him by an effort of strength. If you close your eyes, he comes before the mind, he dwells in the heart, and notes the opportunity to give you your desire. When the mother is ready to nurse, she has every breast full and none empty; we children go on sucking when the milk is ready: thus soul mingles with soul, says Tukā.

## 295

A RICH man need make no distinction of castes; he has materials at home to feed every one who comes. When he is honoured, he shows abundant honour; where any one calls for food, he serves him abundantly. Surely he does not distinguish friends and relations; prince and peasant are alike to him. Where he sees faith, he comes and busies himself; he leaves the dull of spirit to themselves. He forgets not the beggar; by soft persuasion he puts an end to his doubts. Tukā says, He gives enough to eat and leave uneaten; he leaves on their faces signs that they have felt satisfaction.

## 296

NOW beneath this strong compulsion the lord of Pāṇḍhari stands ready and waiting for us.

Now let us receive into our hearts him whose limit cannot be discerned. We have forgotten our bodily form and have ensnared him by repeating his name. He considers not race, family or name, when he purposes to save his saints. It is good that we have found the secret; we need wander no more in search of it. He is immortal, full of help, a generous master; the four-armed God respects his saints. He makes himself great and small as he pleases; his form is fair and lovely; he is full of love to the devout, he shows his respect to the saints by employing their aid: we have found this secret, therefore we have come to supplicate the saints. Tukā says, I will cleave to the lord of Pāṇḍhari with perfect devotion.

## 297

THE cattle are cared for because they yield us curds and butter. This is the secret that we faithful people know, hence we have embraced the name of Rāma. Steel, flint and cotton serve to produce fire; else who would carry them about? Tukā says, Spades and iron-bars are only kept till we find this treasure.

## 298

THE wishing-tree despises not those who apply to it; but you are better than all wishing-trees, for you require no application. O listen! if you bestow a gift, it awakens one to a notion of pride; thus Tukā, with complaints like these, cries out for no gift but yourself.

## 299

O RĀMA, prince of Ayodhya, lord of the lowly and friend, destroy the sin and fever that stand in my way, make me happy! You accepted the berries tasted by the Bhil woman; you are yourself polluted. Tukā says, I am your darling child, but your nature is too deep for me.

## 300

IF you cry to him, he leaps up at once and rends a pillar, who is so clement as this but my mother Viṭhai? If you remember her, she runs and embraces you. Tukā says, As I sing of thee, give me union with thee through thy name.

## 301

HE has lifted up his hand, he has proclaimed his purpose; God sits on his royal throne; if you come as a beggar, he will be your lord. Through his protecting power alone many have escaped out of trouble. Here and in the next world Tukā will not allow him once to be lost.

## 302

THAT deity who tends the cows, will he ask a rich present from you? He is pacified by the language of faith; he is gladdened by imperfect speech. He needs no multitude of forms nor profession of respect. Tukā says, In the company of the helpless he lays aside his greatness.

## 303

ŚANAKA, Śuka and the rest secured salvation for Parīkshiti in seven days. Call speedily on God to remember this; he cannot wait for thee patiently. For Draupadī's sake Nārāyaṇa made haste; he left Garuḍa behind him. God makes great haste, for he delights in his worshippers' love.

## 304

VITTHALA is an unpaid servant who works for no reward. Hand on hip he stands upright, unmoved, he sits not down; he requires no store of merit, he regards not caste or lineage. Tukā says, If you cry to him, he makes haste to visit you.

## 305

WE have a milk cow in our house; the three worlds cannot contain her milk. Her colour is dark blue, her name is Śrīdhara, she grazes on the earth and the fourteen worlds. She has no calf, she will go like a mother with any one, she yields her milk to any who caresses her; her milk flows in four abundant streams, it satisfies Sanaka and the other sages. Tukā says, My hunger is nothing to her, for her love satisfies the three worlds.

---

# X. God's Protecting Love

## 306

YOU need not hand a babe to his mother, she is drawn to him by her own nature. Why have I begun to be troubled? He to whom I belong from the womb will set my burden on his head. The mother unbidden offers her child sweetmeats; she takes no pleasure in eating them herself. When he is busy playing, she searches for him and puts him to her breast. She feels his pain herself, she grows as restless as corn that is parching in a dish. Tukā says, She forgets herself, she suffers no blow to touch him.

## 307

THOU knowest our hearts, though we tell thee nothing. Thou dost pervade the world; there is no need to tell thee aught. But these desires of mine I cannot govern though I would; meanwhile they leave me no energy to subdue them. What do I lack since I was brought into the world? From the hour wherein I was conceived I was strengthened by you. Tukā says, I have governed my desires, and turned them from every object but Nārāyaṇa.

## 308

BY the favour of God, feed on this food, everyone of you that is entitled to it. Brahmā and the other gods can hardly obtain these fragments; despise not you this nectar of Brahmā. The store is full enough to satisfy all; title to the food exists in every soul. Herein the mighty one is inclined to grant our wishes; he fulfils the desires of all. Here the supply is inexhaustible; one is tempted to take mouthful after mouthful for ever. Tukā says, The cooking is done by Lakshmī's hand; God has with him a maidservant incomparable.

## 309

THE gain which is beyond the reach of Bramhā we simple suppliants obtain through that mighty one. By abandoning desires we acquire the worship of him; Padmanābha becomes our debtor through the service. There is no limit to the milk of Kāmadhenu; it flows as the wishes of men flow. In the spot where we sit there is a tide of happiness which transcends the three-fold distinction. We servants of Vishṇu have nothing lacking in the world; Nārāyaṇa is seated at peace within us. Tukā says, This is the grand dinner, where no one remains unsatisfied, or if there be any such, let him be.

### 310

OUR mother Viṭhai is like a cool shadow; her breast is ever filled with love; seated in her lap I shall seek her bosom and drink as much as I desire. O yield the milk of thy mercy and nourish my frame; a stream of nectar flows from thee. My spirit cannot contain this joy; what is the whole sea compared to it? If we go astray she feels herself in danger; with loving desire she protects us on every side. Tukā says, I know not what care is; I am Vithai's dear babe.

### 311

THE mother understands the child's secret, his joys, his griefs and all his actions. He who lends a support to a blind man, he understands his purposes. He who has set a suppliant behind him, he knows how to protect him. If one holds the girdle of a man in the water, he takes him over the stream without fatigue. Tukā says, If a man has entrusted his lip to Viṭṭhala, he knows his condition.

### 312

THOU art our merciful mother, O Viṭṭhala, a shadow to thy suppliant; the milk of love ever flows in thy breast, thy sight is pure and sweet as nectar. Thou canst discern the inward parts and sufferest not hunger or thirst, pain or weariness to vex us. Thou dost chase far away the thirst of desire and illusion; thou givest us a place to play in. Tukā says, Set me with the saints, where the hand of time cannot reach me.

### 313

SUCH is the loving trust of my Viṭṭhobā that God, as he becomes our teacher, assumes a pleasing form, and fulfils our desires; we may hope he will take us to himself. He shields us on all sides; if destruction draw nigh, he averts it. He preserves what we have acquired; he knows what would distress us; he takes us by the hand and leads us. Tukā says, He who believes this not, let him search the Purāṇas with attention.

### 314

PATIENCE makes Nārāyaṇa our ally; he suffers no weary pain, no anxious care, to overtake his servants. Sing then his praises joyfully; with his disc he keeps off the power of Time and Death. When her child is sick, the mother spends her life for him; yet there is no common generosity that is like Nārāyaṇa's. Assuredly my own experience has taught me this. Tukā says, You must be truthful, for no assumption will serve your turn.

### 315

HE who is the repose of his worshippers, he stands and cries to us to hasten. With fond interest he takes and puts morsels of love in my mouth. He fastens us to his waist-cloth and takes us quickly over the stream of the world. Greatly he desires his worshippers, and looks round in every quarter for them. Tukā says, He is a sea of mercy, he satisfies abundantly the desire of all.

## 316

LISTEN to the greatness of love: Rāma ate the berries of the Bhil woman: he hungers after love, he is ravenous to feed on it. He pays no heed to the eight transcendental powers or the ocean of milk; he drinks Sudāma's water and eats his mouthfuls of parched rice. He does not complain that another has tasted it or despise it as small, says Tukā, because of the love that offers it.

## 317

THERE are plenty of poets from house to house, but no one knows the true taste of God's favour. A noisy rogue delights in ornaments; he forgets the trouble they will bring him. Men ought to accept the benefits they can have for nothing. Tukā says, They know this, yet they continue blind.

## 318

I DELIGHT to sing your praises; the mention of your love tastes sweet in my mouth. Two birds were born upon one tree; a mischievous hunter drew near. He flew a hawk near the tree; he fitted an arrow to his bow. Thereupon the birds remember thee. "O run to us, consort of Lakshmī, our mother, and father! If we fly up, the hawk will strike us; if we sit still, the hunter will pierce us!" Hearing the birds' prayer, he assumed with speed a serpent's form; he bit the hunter and flung him on the ground, his arrow struck the hawk. Thus art thou merciful to thy servants, a support in time of peril. Tukā says, No speech in the three worlds can describe thy joy.

## VI

# The Problem of Action

## I.—The perplexing Aspect of the World

### 319

THE fair has begun; the confusion is at its height; the paths laid down by our past spread in every direction. You must suffer as your own place requires the effects of the three-fold rule of action. On you God looks as a witness, you have no part in his plans. He has once for all set you your lesson, distinguishing between merit and sin. Men enjoy the sweets earned by their own conduct. Tukā says, Men are in another's power, because they have fallen into debt; their fetters will be broken, if they entreat God.

### 320

HOW long will you endure the dizzy whirl of time? See, it is every day chasing you. Save yourself from the eighty-four lakhs of re-birth; go and supplicate Pāṇḍuranga. When the body is born, death is born with it; in the same moment it is born and dies. Tukā says, Your line of lives is like a string of vessels on a water wheel, each will be released when its pot is broken.

### 321

THE circles of sin and merit, of joy and pain, spread outwards impelled by each other. I have seen all these marvels with my own eyes; it is time that sets in motion the souls of men. When the soul has visited heaven, then follows hell; the one succeeds the other. Tukā says, My mind has taken fright; O clasp me to your side, Nārāyaṇa.

### 322

GOOD is his name, fair his form, it soothes the eye and drives away the feverish heat. Viṭṭhala! Viṭṭhala! To repeat his name is a present and easy help, a very essence. This weapon is an arrow fit for extremity, for a critical and final hour. Why need a man provide himself with funeral gifts? Nārāyaṇa destroys pain, if you fix your eyes on him. The best of all doctrines becomes ours, for Nārāyaṇa bestows it on us. Go therefore to implore his aid, only this is required of you: this is why I am angry against the world, it is a poisonous snake gleaming before the eyes. O generous one, I have forsaken thee through this enemy; it has made me pass through the cycle of re-births, it has taught me false desire. I am intoxicated by wanderings in "I" and "mine." I have been robbed and put to shame, have suffered the penalty of actions, births without number I have gone through. Now I must cut myself loose. Tukā casts himself before thee, O God!

### 323

I HAVE been harassed by the world; I have dwelt in my mother's womb; I must enter the gate of the womb eight million times; I am born a needy beggar; my life is passed under a stranger's power; I am fast bound in the meshes of my past; the fated influence of the past continues with me, it puts forth its power and whirls me along. My stomach is empty; I am never at rest; I have no fixed course or home or village. I have no power, O God, to end my wanderings; my soul dances about like rice frying in a pan. Ages have passed in this futile strain; I know not how many more await me. I cannot close my course, for it begins again; so the end of the world must set me free. Who will finish this suffering of mine? Who will take my burden on himself? Thy name will convey me over the sea of the world; thou dost run to help the distressed. Now run to me, O Nārāyaṇa, me, poor and wretched that I am; consider not my merits or my faults; Tukā implores thy mercy.

## 324

THIS was my desire and I have gained my uttermost longing. What I have gained is Nārāyaṇa, as it were; a gain imperishable, uncloying. I will not loose my hold of his feet; what a great thing I have gained at the cost of this life! Where can such a shelter be found? My merit has bestowed it on me. An illusion has passed over me; my spirit strayed; I was caught in the snare of the world; it was well that my eyes were opened. Now let me attain to this faith, let no unsteadiness overtake me; to this end I implore thy compassion, O merciful one, O giver of the world. Now will my mind comprehend thee itself; how many a blow keeps it from thee; shame and prosperity stand hostile in the path. These holy men have taken pity on me; they have adorned my speech. They have created in me a love of thy praises; Tukā throws himself at their feet.

325

THOU hast assembled together the five vital elements of the body; thou hast set the spirit of selfish pride to assail them. What comes there of "I" and "mine"? Who can bear this burden? How can we delight in the body? It is itself but a prey to death. The soul does not perish; it quits its old frame and enters a new one; according to its store of merit it passes through a good or evil life. Desire increases the spreading creeper of the world; we should check its growth; this is true wisdom. Tukā says, A hidden treasure is esteemed the more highly.

## II.—The Impossibility of Escaping our Past

326

MEN are subject to the sum of their past; it brings them pleasure or pain. By contact with one who is bleeding we sully ourselves. It is from the bait that disaster proceeds; by shunning that we secure happiness. Tukā says, My soul has taken fright, it has severed itself from everything.

327

DESIRES add to our guilt; the touch of the past cannot be changed. These are profitable words; it is Nārāyaṇa who has pronounced them. You have what your past has assigned you by a fixed rule; exertions will leave you with nothing but exertions. Tukā says, If you embrace peace, it will bestow joy upon you.

## 328

IT is mind that puts the mind in motion; so too the intellect the intellect, from moment to moment. I have learned how to protect myself by the aid of the power that entrapped me; whatever notion springs up in it, by the aid of it I subdue. Thoughts arise in me, and pass away. Tukā says, I have witnessed both processes.

## 329

I HAVE little faith or intellect, a short life and no control over it. I am a molten image of guilt, do thou who art the image of the Vedas, hear me! How shall I throw off my guilt? I am soiled within by actions good and bad. There was a past, there is a present, there will be a future; it is impossible to reach the end. To this body belongs a history of manifold action, the revolution of eight million re-births, the influx of the three qualities; it is a prison formed by our past, with birth and age and death appointed for it. The soul resembles not the body, wherein the five elements are mingled. It is ordered and contrived by the past; an empty worthless ear of corn. Son, daughter, brother,—the whole range of family connections,—they are even as logs of wood that meet in a great flood, and are parted when the waters subside. Therefore I beg this much of thee that thou wilt end my ignorance; thou art the merciful Lord of the world. Tukā clasps thy feet and entreats thee.

## 330

FIRE is kindled, the corpse is burned, consumed already as it is by the three fevers, but your store of merit, actions and destiny, your place in the world, does not pass away. Your destiny goes on revolving like a Persian wheel; the full pots ascend, the empty pots go down. Secure your passage through the world and the five fires, thus you will reach the repose of the Spirit. Let your tongue cease not to pronounce the names of Nārāyaṇa and Rāma; they shall destroy birth, age and death, sin and merit, and all forms of pain. Suffer heat and cold and the solitude of the jungle, and master the postures and concentration of the mind; practise austerities, go on pilgrimage, bestow gifts, perform duties and vows, sacrifice and follow the house-holder's purposes; you will not in these stages of life avoid pain and pleasure, the experiences of birth and age. Then when you have subdued lust and rage and selfishness, seek the further stage and secure the infinite; still, when you study the law, thoughts of pride, with rules and prohibitions, come assailing you; you praise and censure others, incurring guilt, it will cling to you with the strength of adamant. Tukā says, All accomplishments are roots of sin, relinquish these false sources of pain; go and supplicate the saints, and you may pass your life in any shape you please.

## 331

WHEN pleasures drag away the blind souls of men, who will take compassion on them? When we enter the scene of mortal life, faith in Nārāyaṇa is not born along with us. What pleasure is it to cling to wordly life, and to fall into the hands of Death? The ministers of hell measure their bodies, then they drag them about and torture them. Their state will be piteous in the end, when they are parted from life. Millions of births they have passed through before, and they have as many more to encounter. Their eyes are bandaged, they are fastened to the mill, they feel the torture of the yoke and the goad. They cannot tell how far they have toiled; they forget even hunger and thirst in their misery. This is all due to merit or demerit in action and in store; for such as will not with confidence recite Hari's name. Tukā says, They pay no price and yet say that Viṭṭhala is dear; they will not even spend their voice, which costs them nothing; how vastly to be pitied are they!

## 332

SALVATION and perdition are contrived by the mind; send your mind to a solitary spot, to dwell with holy men; watch over it, for it runs a headlong course of its own. Honour and dishonour are the tokens by which the mind judges; but it will concentrate itself if you force it to. Tukā says, It is the mind that carries us over the stream of the world, or binds us to the eight million re-births.

## 333

DO not imagine to bring together things discordant in their natures. What is to happen will happen because it is destined; what Nārāyaṇa has ordained will come to pass. If you kill a cow to satisfy a hungry tiger, will it be called a meritorious deed? Tukā says, If a man is too lazy to think the matter out, his father and mother are asses.

## III.—Nothing is Gained by Works of Law or Austerities

### 334

WHEN I look for some means of escape, I see that my feet are entangled; I am caught in such a strait that my intellect and force are reft away. The stores of my past actions have been mounting up from all time; I am held as in a cleft by rules and prohibitions, they are so compounded that I cannot disengage them. When I sweep them away, they increase again of themselves; I am tortured by the desires that pursue me. Tukā says, Now set me free; I am altogether feeble, O God!

### 335

SO long as the root is left we find pain constantly growing; but surely it should not be the yogi's practice to increase our troubles. Why they choose to do so, I cannot tell, nor what they are like or what the habit of their minds is. Tukā says, It is in vain that we vex our minds.

### 336

HE who casts his body away deceives time and creeps into a corner; such men cast rudely from them the rug they have long worn. They will not get another till the time comes; for the next chance is far out of sight. Tukā says, This is an impediment to service; it is a craving too hastily conceived.

### 337

IT is a student's duty to recite the Vedas; in the second stage a man must perform the six tasks. When he takes to the forest he seeks separation through union; a sanyāsi must renounce his plans. If a man is initiate, know his open secret; he is beyond all caste, religion or family. He who preaches a rule and does not follow it, he is a sinner, as the Vedas say. Tukā says, Every state has its own rules; it is all empty toil that ends in pain.

---

## IV.—Our Faith a Reward of Merit

### 338

A FLOOD of joy is poured forth, with streaming waves of love; I will tie on me a float of Viṭṭhala's name, and swim to the further shore. Ho! people, all, brother and friends, leap in! This will not last for ever, this immeasurable flood of nectar. Tūkā says, It is due to our great merits that it has run along this path.

### 339

IT is well that I was born and came to possess a human body. This was a great acquisition; it has made me fit for happiness. I received organs, hand, foot and ear, eyes, and mouth to speak with; these have gained for me thee, O Nārāyaṇa, and thus the disease of mortal life vanishes. If merit is stored up grain by grain, then this is the reward after many lives. Thy name clings to my speech; when the saints are gathering around me for this spot that I have gained, how can I be grateful enough! All I can do is to lay my soul at thy feet, O mother mine, Pāṇḍuranga

## 340

O YOU who are swallowed up by the world, preserve something true at least; the piteous lord has bestowed upon you a human body, a good surrounding; do not put obstacles in your own path, it is ruinous to talk of stored-up sin and merit. Make haste and sow seed, to increase your store of good seed. Recognize that what you do makes up your store of actions, what has passed your store of merit, and destiny is what remains to work itself out. Falsehood is born of evil habits; disease of pleasures. Tukā says, The uncontrollable tongue voids itself in filth.

## 341

YOUR field has grown ripe; you must watch the four corners of it; it has borne a crop, but you must take care of it. Watch it, watch it, never rest, till it is put up in stacks. Put a stone in your sling, like a vigorous watchman; all the bands of sparrows will fly away, when they hear your shouts. Light a fire and keep awake in another quarter of the field. If the birds descend upon you, you will need both strength and skill. Set up your thrashing-ground, and make all the beggars happy, when you pile up your stack. Pay off the revenue and give everyone in the village his share. Tukā says, Afterwards you need exert yourself no more; you have secured what you want and thrown away the chaff and empty ears.

## 342

KEEP off the forest fires! Your field is devoured by sparrows,—don't put up with such damage; stay awake, though you feel sleepy! If you keep company with thieves, you will lose everything. If you shut your eyes, you will fall into a well, be it night time, day time or lamp light. If you keep a barren cow, how will you get milk or cream from her? If your float is burst, says Tukā, how will it carry you over the stream?

## VII

# The Sense of Sin

### 343

FALLEN of fallen, thrice fallen am I; but do thou raise me by thy power. I have neither purity of heart, nor a faith firmly set at thy feet; I am created out of sin, how often shall I repeat it? says Tukā.

### 344

WHAT pleasure is there in clinging to the world? Tell me, O Hari! All the world is perishable; O you who stand fast, you have left the world far behind; when first I dwelt in the womb, how can I tell the pangs I endured; nine months I suffered, then I was born; my childhood passed in ignorance; in my youth I was harassed by lust; with old age arrived care; I must die; then I must be born again. I have no rest for a moment, ever speeding through the eighty-four lakhs of re-birth. Greedy passions run after me, and throng about me. Cursed be the name of my selfishness! Enough of these encumbrances now; I will be a poor man to dwell at thy door, I will be thy lowly servant. Tukā says, Be merciful to me now!

## 345

A CHILD tells his mother of his hunger and thirst: what does he know of the troubles she takes to relieve him? Even so take all my burden on thyself and protect me. Why wilt thou remember my merits or my faults? I am one heap of sin, O Nārāyaṇa! Void of my service to thee, abject, guilty—why wilt thou consider all this now? When my spirit first followed thy feet, I trusted to this acquisition. Tukā says, Thou hast saved many; O bethink thee of me now!

## 346

I CALL myself his servant, but I do not act as though I were; my inward and outward parts are at variance. I show myself singing and dancing to the people, but the love of Nārāyaṇa dwells not within me. I know nothing of the needful secret; I am sunk in a gulf of pride. Death has carried off my treasure, hand over hand; the length of my days has been numbered. Tukā says, I seem to have wasted my life; every one will laugh at me.

## 347

VOID of works and sense I am nothing but thy lowly servant; O God, protect me and still my agitated soul. Cast no reproach on me; receive within thyself, says Tukā, the million offences I have committed.

## 348

PRESERVE me when I am sinking in the sea of life. Consider me no burden—regard not my mountainous guilt. Preserve your own—what is your title and claim? Tukā says, I am guilty, a heap of sins.

### 349

SUCH as I am I have sought your protection, O Hari! Now you must not belie your reputation. My mind is not purified, but I call myself your devotee. Wretch that I am, who cares for me? Tukā utters your name.

### 350

I HAD fallen into confusion and desire of what is worthless; through pride I had grown false and culpable. It is well that my eyes were opened or I should have suffered anguish. All creation is weeping tears through its own misconduct. My mind is so pre-occupied by gain that I have forgotten death; it will never turn back from its purposes. Tukā says, If a man remembers not Nārāyaṇa, he stores up wealth and dies and leaves it for his children to quarrel over.

### 351

I HAVE become skilful in my own conceit; I have given up faith for idle self-satisfaction; thereafter that I should waste my time is a small thing; lust and rage have come to dwell in me. The world is full of faults; the spirits of men persist in envy. Tukā says, I shall admonish mankind, but I am not free from a single fault myself.

### 352

THE all-pervading illusion has spread its shadow abroad; sincerity is called simplicity, intrigue is called success. Our own mind fetters us. Tukā says, O God, you must unravel this riddle.

## 353

MY spirit is entangled, O Murāri, by wealth; it sets my mind roaming from door to door. It dies in the search unsatisfied; the earth submits to it, yet it is not contented. I see that my own heart is not pure; I have fallen into the destructive power of the senses. My soul is ruined, for wealth brings fetters and the scourge; O Hari, do thou swiftly cut off this evil that clings to me. Other evils too why need I count up;—sinful illusions, evil affections. I am tortured by lust and rage; who but thou can set me free? As we gaze on the truth, sleep vanishes; sleep, sloth and pride are afraid of it. Let them not stay with me, O God; I have no desire except to see thee. Doubt brings on great evils, and shame is too much for me, while truth and devotion are far from me. Do not dismiss me, O brother of the humble; so Tukā beseeches you.

## 354

THOUGH I speak gentle words, yet lust and rage flourish within me; I cannot tell, O Pāṇḍuranga, how it is that I have moved towards thy feet. My spirit is not pure, as the saints describe purity, from the testimony of the Purāṇas. Tukā says, Bring me to experience, O God, and show me the pure truth.

## 355

GREAT men have called me your servant, so protect me, Lord of the helpless, Saviour of the sinful; guard thus these titles of thine. My heart tells me, if my faults be looked into, they are endless. I know not how to serve thee, but thou viewest the inward parts. Tukā says, Thou art a sea of mercy, O sever the net of the world.

## 356

I KNOW not by what means I shall keep my faith ever fixed at thy feet. How can I prevail on thee to come and dwell in my heart? When, O God, wilt thou grant me to contemplate thee with genuine faith? Do thou banish all in me that is deceitful and come in thy genuine nature to dwell within me. Tukā says, Sinful as I am, let thy power save me, O Pāṇḍuranga.

## 357

I WOULD gladly know the truth about the soul, but my mind drags me away, with ungracious obstinacy. I can make no progress because it is so narrow; my conduct is altogether crazy. We can taste nothing till the right time comes; I have made up my mind to this. Tukā says, Your words serve to disclose you: why should I make you speak time after time?

## 358

WHO will support me in my reflections? Who will fortify my mind? I am neither learned nor skilled in debate, nor pure of lineage. In this evil age there are many clever folk, who will torment me when I sing thy praises. I am beset by a doubt whether I shall worship thee, or not, O God! Tukā says, Now to live apart from mankind or to die, both of these resolves are good.

## 359

HARD it is to cross this sea of the world, we cannot pass it; we have drifted far away, we cannot reach the shore beyond. We cannot reckon, O generous one, the cycle of re-births we have seen. We have fallen into a whirlpool, that has drawn us down in its vast eddies. We have grown up, but our intellect is vacant; it has wandered far and knows not where it is. If I let this hour pass, how shall I enquire again? In births unnumbered I have known enjoyment, food, sleep, and sensual pleasure; yea, in childhood, youth and age, pleasure is lord of all. I have passed these regions and travelled here; I have been rambling about. Now I pray thee unfold this knot, with a might as of dawning day. I will leave this worldly path, I am wearied by many a visit I have paid to it. I came to fancy it was all true; I fell into contamination, says Tukā.

## 360

I CANNOT reach him, I feel distressed. There are many who rule over me. I am fast bound and I cannot loose myself; I am fallen into the power of my past. A grievous load lies upon my head, the claims of "I" and "mine." I am robbed by bold thieves in my own house, though I know it all the time. I only ask this of thee, that thou wouldst commit me to the saints; I have broken my voice with entreaties; now do not make me despair. Now is the great crisis; henceforth what can I do? When the day is gone, night will prevail; in the night time a cry of sorrow alone will be left me. Alas! there will be left the power of my past to control me; I shall be in a stranger's power. There is no place for me to hide in; thoughts of heavy care are roused within me. Such is my perilous state, that I cry to the sea

9

of mercy. Tukā says, My strength, my intellect, and all success lie in thy feet alone.

## 361

NOW I shall toil no more in this world of woe; I shall go humbly to the saints and beg of them a place by their feet. I know of no merit of mine that has brought thy feet within my reach. Now, O mother, forget me not, I beseech thee with loud cries. I am harassed by the world. I am caught in the poisonous net of illusive desire. The three qualities of the world foam like venom at my mouth, and I am overwhelmed with misery. Why should I number other miseries? The whole world is an eddy of misery. I cannot bear it; adamant would break beneath it; my soul is filled with trembling fear; I utterly shrink from the tale of this fetid world. I am changed from a sane man to a mad man. I turn to the infinite one, says Tukā.

## 362

GIVE me, O God, a humble condition; for the ant finds a particle of sugar to eat. Airāvata is a huge jewel, but he has to endure the goad. Grandeur brings sharp torments. Tukā says, Know that we ought to be smaller than the smallest of things.

## 363

HOW can I be saved? How shall Nārāyaṇa be merciful to me? Tell me, O ye saints, and pacify my mind. How shall the sum of my past perish? How shall merit and demerit abandon me? I know not the secret, and hence I despair. How shall I keep my mind at rest, beyond the reach of evil? How can I make myself pure?

How shall I see my way to the end? How shall I provide me such a store of merit? I will embrace the feet of God; the lord of the world will gently caress me till my throat is choked with devotion. How it will soothe my eyes to behold that happiness, that various delight! I cannot tell how my lot will guide me; perchance desire will grow up within me. I weigh this thought continually day and night; I am disquieted. Tukā says, I have no strength of my own, to bring me to this final repose.

## 364

IF a man has two wives, sin dwells in his house; you need not go searching for sin; one who wants it need only visit him. No long reflections on the subject are needed. Where there is falsehood, there is a heap of sin; where men speak the truth, there pleasures come welling up. Tukā says, Profit and loss are not far apart.

## 365

NOW make me wake to consciousness. Divert my intellect from this world. O sea of mercy, release and receive me; I have fallen a prey to the turning wheel of time. If thou wilt, what is impossible? A mustard seed will become a mountain, or a mountain a seed. O mother, set me within the trench of thy pity. I have spent my life hitherto in ignorance, through my own natural temper. I know not how, but my life is passed, and I have reached not the next stage of my path. Now I feel afraid, for day after day is passing away from me. I have travelled so far, and what have I done? I have not remembered thy feet. O best of beings, pity my sins, past and future. In thy name let me know thy love; release me from all doubt. Let my heart dwell amid thy attributes; give me a place by thy feet. Thy sweetness I shall taste with my voice. It will be a recompense, says Tukā.

## 366

O NĀRĀYAṆA, pure and good, whose name is a sea of goodness, hear our prayer, protect thy lowly worshippers! we have laboured for our bellies; we have neglected our religious duties. We have left thy path; therefore I urge thee with entreaties. I have become a cripple amongst men; a bounden slave of the world, I know not when thou wilt set me free; I am bound by adamantine chains. Here I never recall thee, I have no rest for a moment, I have fallen into a stream that bears me elsewhere. I see no advantage for me. I have spent my life away from thee, wandering idly in foreign lands; I was cut off from thee by sickness and trouble, and pains and pleasures I engaged in. I am become my own enemy; I have neither son, wife nor friend; why have I increased my earthly ties, O lord of the world? says Tukā.

## 367

WHAT can a feeble man know about right or wrong? He who is mighty has hidden himself from me. I cry aloud at the door and no one hears me; the house is empty; there is no one at home. If a chance guest comes and you speak kindly to him, do you waste your words? Tukā says, O holy Hari, such kindness becomes you well.

### 368

WHEN a little girl goes to her mother-in-law's house, she looks behind her on the way; so it is with my soul. O Keśava, when wilt thou come to me? When a child loses his mother, he looks round him anxiously. Tukā says, I am distressed like a fish taken out of the water.

### 369

THAT a mother should abandon her living child shows something strange in the child himself. Is he mute or deaf? What is lacking in Nārāyaṇa that he cannot understand us? He will not protect me for a moment, so evil a season of misfortune has overtaken me. Tukā says, There is no sweet savour in my speech; it is like bitter fruit.

### 370

MY spirit is carried away by desire; it suffers me not to look on thy face; fain would my heart break for sorrow. Why hast thou made me like a young wife in her husband's house? I have no power, no authority of my own. In the morning when I feel I ought to visit thee, I cannot steal to thee, my desire continues unsatisfied. Thus it seems that all my toils are wasted; all that I have spent is lost, says Tukā.

### 371

AS a fish pants out of the water, so pants my soul; my mind is chafed like that of one who cannot find a buried treasure. When a child is parted from his mother, you know how troubled he is, O God! How often need I tell you what my state is; show me your feet which are the essence of all means! This anxious care has scorched my heart; I cannot tell why I have been forgotten. Tukā says, You know all this, so be merciful, O God!

### 372

THERE is none who respects me; as far as reputation goes I am lost. What service is credited to me possessed of such power, that the house of God should be favourable to me? What purity have I, of descent, lineage or action, that thy secret should be revealed to me? What strength of austerities or liberality, what single source of power have I? Tukā says, I am a burden on the earth; what do I know of the future?

### 373

I FEAR the world, yet I cannot shake it off; so I am distressed and cry to thee. If I think about anything, my mind runs away from me. Tukā says, O God, thought cannot make its way in here.

### 374

TO no purpose have I indulged the world; I have nothing of it and nothing of God. I have imagined that God does not exist; a man who has food to eat knows not what hunger is. My speech is graced by command of words, but the truth does not penetrate within me. I have become a wanderer; I have lost both the world and thy feet, O God! Tukā says, If I had known this long ago, I should not have allowed this frenzy to touch me.

## 375

I HAVE begun to wonder, O God, whether thou wilt accept me or not, whether thou wilt or wilt not let me behold thy feet. My mind is therefore full of agitation; I am fearful whether thou wilt speak to me or not; I doubt whether thou wilt remember me or not. Tukā says, I have no income of my own, therefore I exert myself, O God!

## 376

I SEE my own village no more; a lonely stranger, how much must I suffer? I look for some messenger passing along the road; when will some friend meet me? As I look I find on every side a waste prospect before me. Tukā says, No one, O Pāṇḍuranga, brings me tidings of you; I feel anxious about you.

## 377

THE store of my past is unpleasing to me; my heart is chafed and troubled unwittingly. I have strayed from the path; in the world I have played many a worldly part. It is well that my eyes are opened, that I have found a boatman. Tukā says, If you hear my piteous cry, at once, O Nārāyaṇa, leap across the stream.

## 378

THERE is knowledge of Brahma in every house, but much adulterated; if there be any who has a particle of it pure, bestow it upon me, feeble wretch that I am! If desire and fond hope be mingled with it, there results pride visible afar. Lust and rage are a grievous affliction; when they enter into us, they are poison. Tukā says, We gain nothing in this way; our life is sold and wasted.

## 379

HOW can we constrain you, unless you show us mercy, by any confidence or anticipation of ours! We shall be henceforth as wretched as before, uttering piteous cries. We shall be full of fear and anxious thought; to what shall we attach ourselves? Tukā says, Our life is void of faith and therefore God remains far from us.

## 380

I HOPE nothing more than to call myself your servant; but I do not know the secret of your service; do you be charitable to me. We go on prating with our lips; ostentation is vain without faith. Tukā says, We know how to make a great display.

## 381

THY worshippers dwell intently upon thee; I cannot turn my thoughts to austerities, repetition of names and other means. With piteous cries I have entreated thy mercy. Tukā says, Accept the little I have to offer.

## 382

GOD'S door is shut; all importunity is vain; come now, let us go home; do not keep him waking. God is asleep. What avails it to stand here? God is angry, says Tukā; he will not accept our service.

## 383

O GOD, I have caught the fever of the world in serving my family, so now I remember thy feet; come, O mother Pāṇḍurang, I have borne the burden of many lives; I do not know the secret path of deliverance. I am surrounded on all sides by thieves; no one protects me; I am greatly afflicted, greatly oppressed, and long weary. Tukā says, O run speedily to me; it is thy glory to be called lord of the helpless.

## 384

MY life is altogether wretched; what ground of faith can I see now? I cannot bear to hear of the world; if I call anyone a friend, I find him a stranger. Means of bodily pleasure are poison to me; honour is a snare; dignity and high position are a toil and a burden: my life is weary. Tukā says, I can hear nothing else, I delight in the feet of Vishṇu's servants.

## VIII

# Remonstrances with God

### 385

WHY am I made thus pitiful and brought low among the abject? Why is thy power weakened as it seems, O God! I am ashamed to call myself thy servant; once my speech was filled with a sweetness far different from the taste of these words. Once I could put to shame the utterances of the saints; I know the character of my words to-day from comparing them with what once I said. Tukā says, What is it that has made me speak, except thy favour, O Viṭṭhala?

### 386

WHY has some adverse season stepped in to destroy me with thee? Why have such perplexities arisen? Why will you not visit me and prevent them? Why, O God, have I clung inwardly to this idea of separation? Either I am very sinful, or you have grown weak; you have not your old strength now. Are you indebted or bankrupt? Are you forcibly bound by reason of a debt? Tukā says, Why are you so entangled that you have separated your treasure from mine?

### 387

YOU are a wealthy man; what loss have you suffered that is due to any fault of mine? If you will not receive me, I will declare amid the saints how you have dealt with me. Show me some witness to prove that I have delighted in any other than you. Tukā says, Speak, O Pāṇḍuranga; disclose to me what suspicion has possessed you!

388

I HAVE come to you with varied entreaties, yet you heed me not. O God, why should I form these deceitful hopes of you? You and I are parted; but now contemplation shall bring us together. Tukā says, Shameful is the fluctuating life of desire.

389

WHEN my doubts are dispelled, I perceive a sweet savour, but who can care for what is vapid and tasteless? Now do not deceive me falsely: whither can I go with my entreaties continually? What evil is it if life departs? what good if it linger on? Tukā says, You have created us children to love you, so how can you distinguish between us?

390

YOU know me to be impatient, and you will not disappoint me. Why do you put off the time of my salvation? Bestow it upon me and stop my complaints. If you know I am not to be released, why do you set me praying time after time? Tukā says, O God, O blessed above man, what thought can you take for me?

391

METHINKS you have turned forgetful; but we remember your pledges; you display your title of Saviour, but, tell me, how will you explain it? I am not, like you, hungry after wealth; I shall talk of anything else and chase away that desire. Tukā says, I shall renounce the body; I shall wave it round you together with pride and cast it away.

## 392

IF I should wrestle with you closely, in that moment I must needs abolish your world-wide fame. While it is yet time, keep that purpose from my mind: if the hour of trial comes, which of us will prove stronger? I will tie my neck to your feet, I will not suffer you to move. When I have brought on this fatal moment, all will be decided. Tukā says, We know you well from of old, O Viṭṭhobā; you love to bring things to a crisis.

## 393

I HAVE not disobeyed any voice of authority: why has Nārāyaṇa left me? With undoubting mind I beseech him, for I have not found the peace that knows no care. It is not right that you should forget your servants; for there is perfect justice in your feet. Tukā says, You are not ashamed, though we are sinking in the gulf of anguish!

## 394

SINCE I have ceased to be his servant, I will speak in my lord's presence as my experience directs me. Why do you not answer? I spend my powers in earnest cries. How can the sweetness of trust be born, when there is no pleasant savour of love? Tukā says, O wise prince, bethink thee of this, O Lord of the senses.

### 395

WE are lost in a wood of anxiety: why do you still delay? Come, O Viṭṭhala, our strength is spent in entreaties. Why do you not fear disgrace, thus abandoning your own children? Tukā says, We are full of anxious longing; we have laid hold of God, but he seems to be far off.

### 396

ALL faults are chased away by your name and the song of your praises—this reputation of yours why have you begun to falsify? Perchance you shrink from our sin; but that brings anxious care on us. Tukā says, I am convinced that your service, O God, will conquer Time and Death.

### 397

I HAVE not sought any honour from you, O Viṭṭhala, that you should have exposed me to this public shame. I never cried out for my belly's sake, nor took you by the hand, says Tukā, into a court of justice.

### 398

WE have given him up: why should we quarrel with him? Let him continue as he is; if we make ourselves anxious, we gain nothing but anxiety. If we speak to him, he grows weary; he prefers to hold aloof from us. Tukā says, We have something of our own to keep—patience!

### 399

LET me dwell with those who love you beyond measure, then, O husband of Lakshmī, I will be a trouble to you no more. I will fall at the saint's feet and continue there; I will ask nothing more, I will do nothing else, O Viṭṭhobā. That which vexes you and me will be averted at one stroke; I sit like a debtor laying hold of you, I cry aloud at your door. Tukā says, Attend, O Viṭṭhala, to my speech; you must not wholly neglect me.

## 400

BESHREW the life of him who has a weak patron; death were better for him! Listen, O God; this is proper, that you should protect what is right. It were better to be the dog of one whose words are feared throughout the land. Tukā says, Why have I made these suggestions? You, who know the heart, ought to recognize the reason.

## 401

I AM humbler than the humblest of men, and you are proud of me. I have come to seek your protection, you must give me your true blessing. O sea of mercy, O Lord of the humble, see that you protect your own name! Tukā says, It were not well now if you should cast me off.

## 402

WHY have you counted me a burden?—for so it seems you have. You have given others salvation times without number: is there no place for me even at last? My sin is strong and stout; it can stand even before you. There is something still dragging me from behind; I have seen a strange puzzle. How will the saints believe me, when I say that you are feeble? What! Has

Nārāyaṇa grown old, that he cannot keep his time-honoured pledge? Now do not hide yourself. Do not hold me aloof. Why have you spread a curtain within the house and kept me aloof? Do not tantalize me, O infinite one; why do you pretend who know me not? Why do you not assume your power? Tukā says, Come forth!

## 403

THE saints will laugh at me, even those who have seen thee embodied. I am cast down; I am, it seems, an unprofitable worshipper. How can I meditate upon you, how can I describe you? Your praises have been sung long ago. I cannot forget them and still I cling to hope. Why have you created this path, if it is all fruitless and leads nowhere? It brings misery on us, your children, for we go on following each other. Tell me, whose is the fault? I cling to thy feet and beg you to answer. You are the mother of us all. What is there different from others in me? If I am no use to you, why did you bring me forth? O Nārāyaṇa, answer me, I beg, and teach my ignorance. I have cried to you long, I am wearied with seeking the way. Tukā says, I have spread a dish for you, I know not, O my lord, why you find it distasteful.

## 404

THIS thy knowledge of Brahma I need not; enough for me is the form visible and lovely. A saviour of the sinful, why dost thou tarry? Hast thou forgotten thy promise? I have burned up the world, and here I sit in my yard: is it not in thy mind or heart? Tukā says, Be not angry, O Viṭṭhala; rise up and meet me now.

## 405

HEAR me, O Pāṇḍuranga, I would say something to you by yourself. If our store of merit is to save us, what place is left for you? What sort of piety is it to repay a debt? Will people think the act worthy of honour? If a man gives himself credit for it, he will gain nothing by his concert; we ought to feed a man who wants food. A beggar is the right person to feed and the gift is appropriate. Gratitude is due to a wise liberality, when a man gives where he has no hope of getting back. Be assured that the man is rightly called brave who puts the lowly behind his back and protects him; the merit of that noble act, is boundless. Listen to my words, O Nārāyaṇa! Now what more shall I say? If you save me, then I will call you great. Fulfil your own words, says Tukā, then I shall know you.

## 406

INFINITE in action, who makest all action visible, why art thou dumb to me? O piety, O protector of piety, who settest all in motion and liest beyond all! thou dost not consider the limits of caste or creed; thou dost render to each perfect service. Thou art never ashamed, O Govinda: why art thou silent now? Perchance thy incarnation, whether as fish or tortoise, has wearied thee. O Lord of the world, perchance thou art tired with making and unmaking in the world. O consort of Lakhsmī, how often must I entreat thee and come again and again crying to thee? Dost thou say, "Enough of thy company"? O image of pity, what has happened? How must I deal with thee now?

Why art thou angry? O thou that dost dispel sorrow, O saviour of the sinful, says Tukā.

## 407

WE sinful people throw fetters upon you, but you must escape from the toils yourself. We act without weighing the guilt of our conduct, you must protect us and choose and decide for us. You must protect us without charging a cowry, when we call on you, O God, for your name's sake. Your name is a sea of mercy, saviour of the sinful; such promises we have found. Though we commit millions of sins, you are compassionate of heart, says Tukā.

## 408

WE have paid off our debt by offering you our faith. You now must satisfy our cravings; and make us your darlings. This is our rule, and this the duty you owe to us. Tukā says, We know the service that is required of us.

## 409

TO meet you time after time is misleading, O heedless one! What good can we get from you? We shall simply lose ourselves. If a man does not recover his principal, he may die while he is counting the interest. Tukā says, Such is the character you have impressed on the three worlds.

## 410

IF we are in debt or on evil terms with any one, or are guilty of murder, we cannot escape without paying the cost—so you will tell mankind, but you pretend not to know it yourself. My connection with you is slight, but you should avoid disgrace in the world's eyes. Tukā says, For this very reason, if you don't accept me, you won't get a discharge.

411

I HAVE come to supplicate you with my whole heart, body, speech and mind, O God! No other purpose enters my mind, my desire is fixed at thy feet. I have a heavy burden upon me: who but thou can stir it, O God? I am thy servant, thou are my debtor, thou hast pursued me from afar. Tukā says, I have sat like a creditor before thee; meet me and settle the account.

412

I SPEAK in a resolute spirit; these are not the words of a friend. My mind is thrown into a fever when I hear of the distress of others; now that I see it visibly near me, I can bear it no longer. If you keep Tukā in this mind, the devotees will curse you.

413

I WAIT expectantly for some message or invitation: why cannot you take pity on my trouble? O Pāṇḍuranga, you have kindled my desire, it is you who have set me in motion! What have I gained by being born?—thus I say to myself every moment. Tukā says, We do not receive our true portion; the world reproaches us; this is one profit when the account is settled.

414

WE have lost your presence; this talk of philosophy is dry. Now, O God, I am resolved neither to walk nor talk with any one.

You have found an excuse for absence; you have resolved to leave us. Tukā says, Still my desire remains; I delight to meet you.

### 415

IF the child of a rich man looks destitute, whom are the world to laugh at, O God! Vicious or offensive though he be, yet his father has to look after him. Even so I am a sinful man, says Tukā, but I am thy servant, stamped as thy own.

### 416

IN deceiving us you have entangled yourself! How can you go on cheating us? Why have you taught us wisdom? Why have you assumed name and form, O father? Tukā says, It will not do for you to entrust us to others.

### 417

WHAT! shall we fill our stomachs now and pretend to stir the world as devotees? If such be your intention, declare it; for we have long been wearied. Shall we continue the tradition of poetry by stringing words together? What! says Tukā, shall we open a shop, O Nārāyaṇa, and go on ruining men?

### 418

HARI, you have a vast heap of bliss in your house; how can you be in any want on my account? Why is not a share given to me? We have a father then completely possessed of all attributes. Tukā says, O Pāṇḍuranga, I stand before you; O tell me this!

## 419

HAVE we no right to ask you for our own? Yet we have ceased calling on you, because the opinion of men forbids it. Come now, let us sit down, and cast our accounts up. Tukā says, I will disturb you from your place, O Viṭṭhala!

## 420

WHERE will you hide yourself when I claim my portion? The saints will bear witness to my claims, for they know the signs of just rights. I will sit at your doors like a creditor and will not suffer you to come out. Tukā says, I am imperishable; you have to bear the burden of your Godhead.

## 421

THIS one thing fills me with wonder; my cries for pity have been wasted, as though I had put these up to a corpse. How could one fail to be angry, on seeing you so false? Tukā says, O Viṭṭhala, how can you improve on what I have said?

## 422

WE shall ask you for what you have, for we have not given up all activities like you. All goes well as long as we do not reveal your faults; but how could we publish them? Why do you not give to one what you give to another? Tukā says, While this weakness is yet unknown to the people, take care of your reputation.

## 423

LET be now; how often must I come entreating you? My destiny is strong; you are weak before it. Now, O Lord of Pāṇḍhari, I shall destroy your titles of glory. Tukā says, A strong man will twist the ear of a weaker.

## 424

WE are children of many vows and much desire. Who else utters your name, O God, or offers you balls of rice? Whom have you before or behind you? Who stands near you to talk to? Tukā says, O Pāṇḍuranga, what companions have you?

## 425

WE are known to each other of old; if you will cast me off, you are welcome to do so; you will lose your name for honesty; degradation will fall to me. The deposit I have made with you —is it right you should deny it through avarice? Tukā says, O generous one, do not hesitate!

## 426

HARI, you are cruel and inconceivable, you are stern and heartless; you do what should not be done; what no other has done, you do. You took from Harischandra his glory, his kingdom, horses, and wealth; you caused him to sell his wife and son to a tanner. You brought together Nala and Damayantī, and you parted them; this all the world knows and the Pāurṇas tell the tale. King Śibi, mighty lord, compassionate towards all creatures—at last his flesh was weighed in balances. Karṇa on the stricken field was covered with arrows in the fray; you come up and ask him to take out his teeth for you! Bali, who spared no wealth of his, held forth his hand; Vāmana in his insolence sent him down to hell. Murāri sat as a creditor in Śriyāla's house, and caused him to kill his own son. Those who worship you are brought to such straits as these. Tukā says, We know not what you will do in time to come.

## 427

SHALL we be your servants, and yet ask another for good? Cursed be such a life! What shall I say to you, O Viṭṭhobā? Under the lucky protection of the great any fortune good or bad is agreeable; but we are always afraid of the world. We should be delighted to die: why then does this beggar's condition trouble us? If you protect us, shall we seek protection from any other? Tukā says, Don't you know who is disgraced by this state of things?

# IX

# Prayers

### 428

YOU are the generous friend of the helpless, you set yourself to destroy sorrow, delusion, and anxious care. I have come to take refuge in you ; save me, O merciful parent ! Grant me to serve thy feet amid the saints, then shall I never forget thee. This is the wish of my soul ; O fulfil my desires ; give me faith and love to sing thy glorious name and nature. Deliver me from all that stands between us ; listen to my application ; I ask thee for nothing else, neither pleasure, nor riches nor royal power ; my prayers will not fetter thee with a demand for aught else than faith. With folded hands I lay my head at thy feet ; Tukā entreats the Lord of Pāṇḍhari. Bring to the stage the glorious tale of thy deeds ! Fulfil thou this desire of mine.

### 429

THERE is no limit to thy attributes, but my intellect is weak. O Nārāyaṇa, O thou that knowest all and takest us beyond the world, I lay one prayer before thee. Humble as I am, how can I know the due signs of devotion to thee ? I cannot even wash my face clean, but I spend my time in contemplating thee. Suffer no frenzy to possess me that will lead my mind astray. Take me by the hand and lead me ; make me walk by thy light. I have offered thee my body with perfect devotion, O Lord of Pāṇḍhari! Keep me in chances good and evil; spread over me the shadow of thy favour. If I speak of skill, thou art prince of all skill; of knowledge, thou art prince of all knowledge; in nothing art thou wanting, yet my faith is dull. I have given thee my capital, I have laid my power of speech at thy feet; give me a return according as thou dost esteem it. Tukā says, Thou knowest true from false.

## 430

THE company of great poets would contaminate me; they foully abuse their gifts. Those who delight in pride are blind and deaf; their faces shall be blackened with shame at last. Red lac may be put next to gold, but their properties continue what they were Men fall into confusion, says Tukā, because they do not know the difference between a servant and a master.

## 431

I LAY my head at thy feet in supplication, O Lord of Pāṇḍhari, listen to my prayer! Let me dwell for ever at thy feet; be content to be straitened; give me a little room there! Whether I have faith or not, I have come where thou art. Look upon me with favourable countenance, O Lord of Pāṇḍhari. Tukā says, We are thy feeble and errant creatures; by thy name and with thy hand dissever the meshes of the world.

## 432

TO whom shall I appeal but thee, O Nārāyaṇa? Who will fulfil my desires? Put me to thy breast, O merciful mother! Consider not thy own weariness, keep me not far from thee; preserve the lowly being thou hast accepted; give me willingly the gift of life. I trust I shall never quit this pure draught divine; give me what I beg of thee, a place by thy feet for ever. This was appointed and stored up for me, that thou shouldst show me this path. I eagerly desire this honour; I demand joyfully the gift of thy service. I will entreat thee with piteous cries, for I find nothing else sweet. Sleeping, waking and dreaming, I have fixed my thought and my spirit on thy form. Now though we meet not, we have met: ask me whether this be so or not; this imperishable spring has begun to flow. Tukā says, You have given me help within.

## 433

I HAVE no strength of my own, I know not how you will help me. I am delayed by this clog that is fastened on me. Give me my own, O God,—the store that you have set apart for me; I form no further, no extravagant desire. I do not pursue you like a bravado; I use no language but your own. Call in daysmen to decide between us; it is meet that you delay not. I will not deal with you by violence, O Gopāla. Tukā says, I fall at your feet; O set my neck free.

## 434

BE not vexed at our antique speech; you are our mother and we your darling children. O Mother Viṭhā, give each of us, great and small, tender morsels of your love! Respond to our fond desire! Whether we have faith or not, we have come to thee. Now, O Lord of Pāṇḍhari, look upon us kindly! we are your foolish errant children, says

Tukā; dissever by your name the meshes of this world.

## 435

GLADLY would I compare thee, O best of beings; but when I consider, to whom art thou like, O Lord of three worlds? Take my gross speech, make it sweet, and listen to it. Tukā blithely diverts himself; you must complete his festal joy.

## 436

MY life has been fruitless and passed under deep oppression. Now, then, run, run to me! O Hari, why are you waiting? I have spent my days struggling over "mine" or "thine"; my face is soiled with dirt. My mind suffers me not to trust; it seeks to drown me in the sea of life. Pleasures have beset and oppressed me. Now I have come to thee, O run and save me, says Tukā.

## 437

ABANDON these desires, these wicked cravings, O mind; the intellect is the one idle source of delight in man. In thee I find peculiar bliss; therefore I embrace thy feet in love. Thus with complete faith I have come as a suppliant to thee; for bodily pain made me greatly afraid. There is no other saviour, though the thirty-three crores of gods should guide me. Mankind desire the grandeur of wealth; but it were best for us to find thee. I have abandoned all, says Tukā; I entreat thee, O Viṭṭhala, my head laid up at thy feet.

## 438

DO but this, O God, at my request; burn up my pride, root and branch. Do but this; let me see thee in everything with impartial eye. Let me place on my head with reverence the dust from the saints' feet. Hear but this prayer, O Lord of Pāṇḍhari, dwell in my heart day and night. Tukā says, I have come to thee, O save me, unreasoning as my faith may be!

## 439

O RAKHUMAI, we want something from you; tell us if aught was left when Sanaka and the rest satisfied themselves. We sit without and venture forth a hope, that we shall satisfy each other's mouths. We have travelled thus far, O generous one, hoping in thy name. Deep is the love you have now bestowed upon us. Tukā says, Speak now, O Viṭṭhala!

## 440

HE who forbids his disciples to serve him, and honours them as gods, that man's advice brings forth fruit; others are themselves contaminated by their pupils' faults. His knowledge of God is true; he pays no heed to the life of the body Tukā says, I speak the truth, let men be angry if they will.

## 441

MY eyes are weary with waiting for you: when will you show me your feet? O Lady Viṭṭhali, you are my mother, cast over me the shade of your mercy; I have long waited for you. Tukā says, My arms long to embrace you, let me clasp you, O Pāṇḍuranga!

## 442

AS I look around me, I see that all is worthless: reveal to me the snares of illusion, O God! I do not cling to any of my surroundings; I am pure and enlightened within. Take off the veil of illusion that thou hast spread between us and thee; do not drive us mad, O God! Why hast thou ordained such expressions as "my soul" and "the universal soul", when thou knowest the truth? In thy desire for service thou takest no thought for us; thou sendest us wandering from door to door. Since I have now discovered the truth of this union, keep far from me the notion that we are two. Tukā says, Why should I desire the shadow? The wild geese perished in the starry sky.

## 443

FOR our sake thou didst right easily display thyself in the fish and the tortoise and the boar. When we utter thy name, O Mistress of Pāṇḍhari, run to us with fond affection, give us thy fond breast! We cannot see thee anywhere; leap suddenly into sight. Take our suffering upon thyself and give us joy; set us safe behind thee; there we will fight against Time and Death. Tukā says, O sea of mercy, take us over in thy boat.

## 444

O NARĀYAṆA, annihilate my pain! Keep every wandering impulse of mine at thy feet, making thy home in my mind. Bestow thy caresses on me, and place the fruit within my reach, Tukā says, O thou who relievest the fatigue of the humble!

## 445

TURN not thy back on thy suppliant! Hear my entreaty, O Lord of the world! Answer speedily those who beseech thee! Come running and help the oppressed! Be thou rest for the weary! Take on thy head thy servant's burden! Tukā says, Forget us not, O God!

## 446

RUN to me, O mother; why are you waiting? I have no endurance to wait, I am cast down by the loss of you. Soothe me, for I am deeply troubled. Tukā says, When shall I lay my head at your feet?

## 447

THROUGH the power of faith how small you have become, you whose form was described by the saints of old! Make that form fit for my eyes and show it me, O Keśava! I will declare it when I have seen it; I will embrace your feet; I will stand gazing upon them with folded hands. Tukā says, O Nārāyaṇa, fulfil my deep and earnest desire.

## 448

I HAVE but little sense, therefore I cry to thee for pity; show me thy feet, O Keśava! I have no endurance, O Nārāyaṇa. Tukā says, Have mercy on me and my hapless fate.

## 449

THE magic stone by its virtue has turned common metal into gold; even so, O Lord of Pāṇḍhari, consider not my faults or shortcomings.

The Ganges does not charge with impurity a filthy stream that runs below a village. Tukā says, Common earth is valued if musk has imparted its odour into it.

## 450

WE have been severed from you; we are all laid open to the world. We have no friends belonging to us in this your swelling flood of life. We have renounced the world, we have broken away from the place where we sat; now, O God, says Tukā, do not keep us aloof.

## 451

I HAVE no power to understand anything; I do not know what will become of me. In considering the requirements of the Purāṇas I have worn myself to death. We are bondslaves of the senses; our minds are steeped in the impressions. Even one sense I cannot subdue; how can I control all? Tukā says, Save me, O Pāṇḍuranga, else it is in vain that I have become thy servant.

## 452

IF I desired to serve those around me, I have no strength for such a purpose. O Lord God, carry me to that spot which the saints have reached! Why should I compare myself to those who went before me? I cannot equal them. Tukā says, Fulfil my fond desires and longings.

## 453

ANNIHILATE this separation, the fruit of learning, between us; for it has murdered me. When our food digests, we profit by it; if we vomit it up and waste it, our body is distressed.

A man's riches are well used, if he enjoys them, if they mingle their powers with the vital functions. Tukā says, Save me, O Viṭṭhala, I am better off as an ignorant servant.

## 454

I HAVE only one mind for all purposes; accept, O God, this feeble service which I offer thee! Thou art the source of all; I lay my spirit at thy feet. Tukā sings thy praises from the platform of his heart.

## 455

I WAIT for your favour; O give me the remains when your plate is washed; I will take what is left when your meal is finished. I shall be all alone, if I am parted from you. Tukā says, I have set my mind at rest.

## 456

I HAVE given you my fortune and endured poverty; you may show your gratitude by making me a return in the end. You have found a place for my name and form, or who would call you God? Tukā says, O Hari, I have given you a seat within the house of my heart.

## 457

IF you will give me a rosary, I will fall at your feet: who throws himself before anybody for nothing? When people see a profit in the account book, they believe in it; if a man is liberal, he is respected. If you mean to be liberal in return for my service, pray send me a mark of favour speedily. Tukā says, If you turn miser, who will look after the credit of your name?

## 458

COME, Pāṇḍuranga, lift me up and set me in thy lap; though I have sought this shelter, I feel myself a stranger. Set me free and carry me with thee, O God; there is no force that can thwart thy purposes. Tukā says, O Lord of the senses, why dost thou delay?

## 459

I HAVE come to thy feet with fond affection, which I will offer thee as best as I may. Where else should I go? Here I gladly pour myself out. To describe thee fully we have faith as our only instrument. Tukā says, Satisfy our fond cravings, O merciful mother, Viṭṭhali!

## 460

WHAT are you waiting for? Step forward now; let me set my head at your feet: I stand before you with folded hands. Grant me that goodly union with you; let not our love be severed. Tukā says, Come forward, O Viṭṭhala!

## 461

IF I view it correctly, this is a boat to carry me over the sea of life. In my mind I will embrace thy feet; that which is called happiness is there. The marks which show the godhead are known in my mind; all else is sunk in this devotion. Tukā says, It is well I have found this secret.

## 462

THE Purāṇas call you merciful; to them I trust; I can tell no other means to learn your secret. I cannot make it plain whatever I say, so

I have come to you with a supplication. If you will show me mercy, it is a small thing with you; it will drive away much care from me. Tukā says, Show me your holy face, and the hunger of my eyes will be satisfied.

## 463

O LORD of Pāṇḍhari, thou pitiest the unprotected; I heard this thy fame, and found great relief. O run to help the friendless; make walls of thy name about their houses. Tukā says, The benefit is easy to gain; we shall place our mind at his feet.

## 464

SET me free, O infinite one, set me free! What other is there that bestows life like you? Do you not know who would repent it if I had to seek protection from another? Tukā says, O my friend, O husband of Rakhumai!

## 465

I HAVE pledged my body, speech and mind; I have become a debtor to you to make a profit. I had lost all, my belly sank in through hunger; so I gave up the world and found repose, O God! I have not a tola nor the twelfth of a tola left to give you; you know it already, O Lord of the illusive world! Others mightier than I have incurred heavy debts to you. Tukā says, Take and make your own any being who is heavily on your books.

## 466

WE have come to thee wearied out with suffering in the wood; O Viṭṭhobā, suffer us to fall at thy feet for repose. We have suffered shame and we came to implore thy grace. Tukā says, We have made these great efforts to gain thee.

### 467

ONE may gain distinction and popular honour and fill one's stomach by false behaviour; but a man will not gain his true ends by these means. If I embrace this grandeur of knowledge, I shall be severed from your feet. In cherishing the body the passions break forth; my enemies dwell within myself. Why should I destroy myself by pride and regard for public esteem? Tukā says, O God, grant me this happy rite, to look upon thy feet.

### 468

WITH due affection clasp me to your heart; I have come very hopefully to entreat a gift. When I fix my thoughts on you, permit me to serve you. Tukā's brother says, Send to me an apt frame of mind, O God!

### 469

SHOW me the secret, for what do I know myself, O God? I do not wear the bright colours of other men, therefore I have come as a suppliant to thee. If you give me courage, my mind will grow steady. Tukā says, With your high power you should protect your loving children.

### 470

YOU are the embodiment of righteous conduct; in your hands are actions for good and evil. O generous one, release me from the meshes of Karma. If you will receive me, can I be a burden to you? Tukā says, You are the life of lives, O Nārāyaṇa!

471

WHAT is there you cannot do? Now save me from shame; I am a heap of trangressions, I am encased in the net, head and toes. Protect, oh protect me! Look on me graciously! Tukā says, O God, grant me to serve thee continually.

472

MAKE and keep me your servant; grant me this blessing; let the saints give into my hands the nine forms of worship, as they are named. Tukā says, Through the support of your feet I shall of a surety cross the sea of the world.

473

LET the saints listen to my last request; O God, do not forget me. Why should I continue with many words? It is all known at thy feet. Tukā says, I fall at thy feet, grant me the shadow of thy favour.

474

IT is your part to silence the contentions of the world: who would willingly embroil himself in these? Read the riddles you have set. I have finished the task imposed on me; I have observed and published abroad the duties of religion. Tukā says, Now let your burden rest on your own head.

475

IT is not my wish to have illusive wealth, to take care for the world. To gain thy feet I have composed my spirit; now I want nothing else. Be merciful and accept me, delay not, O God. I have learned that there is nothing real here, so I have narrowed my desires. Tukā says, O sea of mercy, accomplish my hopes.

## 476

I ENJOY no pleasure. I need no honour—this world passes—what shall I do? Luxuries set my flesh on fire; sweet food is poison to me. I dislike to hear my praises when men extol me; they weary my soul. Tell me how to reach thee; let me not be swallowed up in the mirage of the world. Tukā says, Do good to me now, take me out of the flame where I burn.

## 477

ARISE, you are weary, you have stayed awake; O sleep, my Lord! Rakhumai has prepared your bed and stands waiting for you. O best of beings, pardon as ever my prating speech. Tukā's brother falls at the feet of Nārāyaṇa.

## 478

WHILE the serpent is entranced by his flute, the charmer pounces on him; he keeps him confined in a cage for a dwelling place, and goes wandering from door to door to fill his own belly. Such is my state, O Pāṇḍuranga; I am a prisoner, O set me free! Nothing can I do for myself, unless you take compassion on me. The fish gets the hook stuck in his throat because he swallows the bait; when he is drawn forth he strives to take breath. What are his father and mother to him then? A bird is snared by her desire to approach her young; as she looks on them, she is caught fast in the net; while she runs towards them with fond affection, she thinks not of death, she saves neither herself nor her brood. Through his love of sweets a fly is caught in a trap, and then he goes on fluttering wildly. Tukā says, My soul is possessed by desire; O dweller in Pāṇḍhari, take pity on me!

## 479

OH husband of Lakshmī, Lord of the abject thou of the lotus-navel! Set me at thy feet where pleasure dwells. Little is my desire, and thou art a generous prince. Tukā says, I am tormented by this sensuous life, O run to me speedily!

## 480

A VIGOROUS body is the instrument needed for your service; O Pāṇḍuranga, do not suffer my body to be wasted! Shorten my life, but let me still delight in thy praises. Tukā says, There is no loss worse than the loss of these.

## 481

WORSHIP offered in the mind is what the Lord of the senses prefers. He accepts the thoughts that dwell with him; he heeds no outward show. He knows the heart, the impressions left by the past and present. Tukā says, How can falsehood continue before him?

## 482

SPEAK a word for us, O Rukhmabai. If there is anything left, make haste and send it us. We are waiting, anxiously longing, for one morsel. Tukā says, He gave us many a dish of love; cry out the name of Viṭṭhala.

## 483

I SIT at the door waiting for him with my hand upon my brow. My thoughts and eyes are fixed upon the road to Pāṇḍhari. When shall I see him coming? I count the hours and minutes on my fingers. My left eyelid itches; my right arm throbs; my mind in its impatience forgets my body. I have no pleasure in my bed, I forget house and wife, hunger and thirst. Tukā says, Blessed will be the day when I see a messenger coming from Pāṇḍhari.

## 484

YOU have granted all our entreaties whenever we made them. So confess that you are our mother, O Pāṇḍuranga. If you set us on your thigh, we shall never rise. Tukā says, Put into our mouth a morsel of divine knowledge.

## 485

I COME as thy bond-servant to find thee; O do good to me, Pāṇḍuranga! It is thy glory to be called saviour of the sinful; O preserve it for thy own! The saints will call thee the Lord of the helpless; when I heard this I took confidence. Make me not hopeless; be not heedless of me, bestow on thy suppliant the gift of thy mercy. Tukā says, I am a heap of sin, give me a place by thy feet O God.

X

# The Conditions of Acceptation

486

THROUGH repentance guilt vanishes in the twinkling of an eye; the transgressor remains at peace; a good man from first to last. This is the true ceremony of purification, to bathe the mind in repentance. Tukā says, Sin cannot touch repentance.

487

A WISE listener does not aspire to be an eloquent speaker; he clings to faith alone; blessed is he in the world; Brahma dwells within him. You need neither wash your face nor bathe yourself, call upon the name of Rāma continually. One may neglect the repetition of spells, austerities, meditation, and efforts at union, yet if he be merciful towards living creatures, then, says Tukā, be he learned or ignorant, the infinite one loves him more than his own soul.

488

HERE no other effort is needed, to go to meet God; accept him with a mind intent on that alone. Empty your bodily frame. Exhaust your heart of the six passions. Tukā says, Where desire ceases to exist, there he makes his dwelling place

489

TO lay aside hatred is the secret of attainment, other rules of renunciation are waste of words.

All assumptions fall away from us; pure and impure are discerned from each other in the end. True renunciation is oblivion of all objects, we should obey the rules of Scripture so far as is necessary. Tukā says, It is in contemplation I delight; this alone guides us to the truth.

### 490

MISERABLE are all who turn their faces from Nārāyaṇa. They shake their hands clear of him; but they only fit themselves for punishment. Sin and merit may be a provision for our path, but they require the pains of begging. Tukā says, Behold what a stream of vanity flows here!

### 491

NĀRĀYAṆA has shown me a simple path: I need neither austerities of diet nor any other means. I must praise God in this base age of the world, then he will come to me. I need not leave business or public life, I need not take to the jungle, smear myself with ashes, or mortify my body. Tukā says, I deem all other sources idle, save thy name alone!

### 492

AWAY with place and time, with rites and spells of all kinds. Make your mind tranquil and call upon him for mercy. God our Lord will come to the spot where we are sitting, for he occupies every spot himself; it is an unpolluted body that he chooses for his seat. He perceives the subject of our thoughts, therefore regard him with due respect. Gladly he devoured the dry grain offered him, and smacked his lips over it. He desires an offering, but he knows faith is all his servants have to give. Tukā says, The infinite one will merge our soul in his.

493

A MAN is not a Bramhāchārya because he has left his wife; vain is the renunciation which consists in leaving one's country. Lust and fear grow up through desire; we must quit idle prating of renunciation. If a man whose legs are trembling talks about his valour, the right moment will scatter it to the winds. Tukā says, Sin cleaves to the tongue, if it praises what is worthless.

494

YOU must dig up desire by the roots, then only can you be said to have renounced the world. If you will not do so, you should live in the world and enjoy it; you should not make yourself ridiculous. You must strike down desire and triumph over it, then you may escape from all the world. Tukā says, If you are eager for union with God, you must first annihilate the germs of desire.

495

THE speech of some men is sweet and melodious, they are truly manifestations of God, but fate ordains otherwise of others. The words of others are sharp and biting. Tukā says, There are three sorts of men.

496

THE duties of the four stages, if neglected, bring on sin; such is not our simple service, where faith is the key to all, O God! Austerities destroy the powers of sense, and the effect vanishes in a moment; if the form of words is slightly mispronounced, a sane man will go mad. Though you perform austerities carefully, yet one mistake annuls them; you must observe your duties strictly or your labour is all wasted. There is much that interferes with our practising sympathy; be its object high or low, it is ruined. Tukā says, All merit too is hampered by injunctions and prohibitions.

### 497

AS your faith, such is your fruit; violence can effect nothing with God. The men of a caste consort together, for they recognize each other; only the anvil can separate the diamond from the matrix. Tukā says, You had better purify your mind, for an impure mind cannot serve him.

### 498

WHAT is sung for the music's sake keeps the mind interested. When a hungry man sees food, then it is hard to abstain from eating. So keep your mind in an expectant frame to hear God's praises. Tukā says, No one is satisfied till he has eaten his food.

### 499

THIS is the medicine for the disease of life, that heals birth, and age and sickness; no more trouble will follow, it will slay the six enemies. I have anointed my eyes with his purple form, for the six Śāstras, the four Vedas, the eighteen Purāṇas drove me away like a scoundrel. Thus I have made me a garland of Vishṇu's thousand names; give me no food that I cannot digest. If you keep your faith pure after taking it, you may say you secured the reward of doing so. You need not leave your own house, you need not let the wind blow upon you. Do away with much talking, avoid all the company; you need give but one pleasant medicine, it will taste like butter. Avoid the milk that needs much churning, there is no quality about that. Bathe in repentance, clothe yourself with the quarters of heaven, let all the sweat of desire pour out of you. You will become what once you were. Tukā says, We will enjoy the passionless state.

### 500

BE it son, daughter, or brother, you must act yourself free from them. If you find them to be mischievous, you must not touch them and cover yourself with blame. Break the pot! At one stroke make them as dead to you! Tukā says, Unless you renounce them, you will not escape the fruits of their company.

### 501

WHATEVER keeps you from God, be it your father or mother, give it up! Be it your darling son, your treasured money, it is your enemy if it brings you misery. Pralhāda gave up his father, Vibhīshaṇa his brother, Bharata his mother and kingdom. Tukā says, All pious duties are contained in the feet of Hari; other resources bring misery.

### 502

VANQUISH pride, and then you may speak of austerity and union attained; this is truly a noble exercise; this you should practice. Then the process of rebirth stops; the burden of the body passes away. Tukā says, We ought not to retain the tie of regard for honour or dishonour.

503

THE saints have told us an easy secret; to take the cymbal and *dindi* and dance. Wave round him and caste away the delight of absolute union; this praise of God is like a sweet juice of Brahma. Henceforward this glorious service occupies us most and most, it is fully accomplished through the fortune that has made us thy worshippers. No doubt need arise in our minds; the four modes of salvation are handmaids to the worshippers of Hari. Tukā says, If the mind attains peace, the threefold fever vanishes at once.

504

WE have discovered one means to compass Viṭṭhala: then what strength has he against you? He surrenders to you himself; he cries to you for pardon, and performs your heart's desire. Through the power of faith alone you will not reach him, no, not in length of time; but if you join the saints, he will rise up in answer to your call. Tukā says, Bind him to my soul with bonds of love; I will not leave him who gives away all he has.

505

REMEMBER God; make this your resource; give up all other machinations. Awake, awake! Why will you weary yourself in vain? Weighed down by pride of knowledge, you are drowning in the gulf of the world: why will you not rise out of it? Tukā says, You will reach God by faith; through efforts to know him, you will not understand him.

## 506

IF you become a reasoner or a reader, still listen with devotion to the story of Kṛishṇa. As when milk and ghee and sugar are mingled, such is the savour of its sweetness. Learn its worth, O father, and tie it up in your cloth, keep it by you; this sweetness is manifold. If you desire to save yourself, dig up the mischievous root of learning. Wealth of flowers and sandal smeared on the body,—without food to eat, these ornaments are vain, and such is all sweetness apart from the story of Hari. That which the Vedas and Purāṇas intend is all contained in the story of Viṭṭhala. Tukā says, Others are mere granaries of gravel; mere jingle is the chief thing there.

## 507

FALSE teachers assert that Brahma is a delusion; they make other people as wretched as themselves. A vicious man naturally teaches evil doctrine; he follows the inclinations of his own mind as a trained bull follows his master. *Suran* and *rai* are digestible, if you cook them; if you are too impatient to do so, they will make you ill. You persuade a child to take medicine by showing him a piece of sugar. If you seek salvation, first sift the Vedas, discard those sayings in them which are fruitless. Tukā says, If a man cherishes his own body, Nārāyaṇa will not come to meet him.

## 508

IT is a little thing, if your mind helps you. The tumult of passions vanishes, it closes in Pāṇḍuranga. No search is needed; here you have the essence of all means of attainment. Tukā says, Look on all pride as false and quit it.

### 509

WEARY not thyself; search not the forest of philosophy. Come to the house of the milkman, of him that was bound with the rope. Thou art troubled by doubt; thou knowest not the way nor the clue; Tukā says, The doctrine of Māyā is a deadweight; cast off thy sense of self.

### 510

AVOID the world; be at rest; let no stain of affection come upon thee: thus shalt thou gain true union, true knowledge of Brahma; without experience of it all talk is idle chatter. He who has conquered his senses and destroyed his desires, he thereafter forms no designs. Tukā says, It is not knowledge that enters his heart; his heart is a dwelling-place of joy.

### 511

YOU cannot make yourself a saint in the market-place nor get peace by wandering through jungle and forest; this condition is not to be bought for heaps of wealth, it cannot be found in heaven or in hell. Tukā says, You must give your own soul in change for it, else you need not talk about it.

### 512

THE children of cowherds, brought up on whey, were they handsome? Why was God so fond of them? what service, what devotion did they render him? Was God hungry that he accepted the bajari grains of Vidura? Tukā says, The deformed maid Kubja, was she a heap of beauty?

## 513

WE cannot experience his pleasure as long as the soul hesitates over it. If you avoid all grief for past pleasures, he will set you free from association with them. Tukā says, In all ways he is perfectly endowed; the scriptures declare his glory to be such.

## 514

IT is hard to reach the glorious estate of the saints; there is no opportunity for talkative people here. A cow or a buffalo may be a stout animal, but it will not equal the wishing cow. Tukā says, You must be yourself what you ought to be, then you will know what that glorious state is like.

## 515

I PROCLAIM these tidings, since I have power to do so; we are your children by loving service; we speak the language of close affection. By dwelling close to you we shall do away with doubt and fear. Tukā says, There is a genuine taste here; how can we go away?

## 516

YOU say you have no merit; do not talk in this way. Shout out Hari's name; in good sooth do not waste your birth. Your neck will be caught in the toils of Yama: then how can you say "Hari"? Do not, O do not say foolishly, the body is meant for pleasure; do not, like a low wretch, say the body is infirm. Tukā says, How often shall I tell you, your mouth will be filled with mud at last?

## 517

IF you have faith alone, you need strive no more I have learned this through my own faith. If you remember God, you have all pleasures present before you. Tukā says, It is worship of the spirit that Nārāyaṇa desires.

## 518

AWAY with knowledge of Brahma and intuitions of the self in the self! Let me be thy worshipper and thou my God. Show me thy form that delighted the cowherds; I will set my head at thy feet. When I have seen thy holy face, I will embrace thee; I will cast away my existence as an offering to thee. When I have enquired of thee I will declare thy secret; I will sit by myself and tell myself the story of the delights. Tukā says, Now that thou knowest my heart, delay not the hour.

## 519

WHAT is there that we need know or know not? The essential thing is to contemplate thy feet. What is there that we need do or do not? What is there that we need say or say not? Where need we go or go not? All is well if we remember thy name. Tukā says, You make it easy for us; our will turns sinful into righteous deeds.

## 520

GOD himself has set apart the sweet dish of his worship; let some one make good his claim to it and Hari will give it him. In the strength of ascetic repose we must conquer the six enemies. Tukā cries, There will be nothing left undone!

## 521

NOW amid deeds right and wrong is there anything proper for me? I must look to my own advantage. You know that I am a sinner, but I have come to you as a suppliant. Here prince and peasant are alike; there is no difference of persons in your house. I have come to your feet as best I could, so you must not cast me out. It is an old fashion—I speak seriously—that when men fall into difficulties, they begin to praise another. I have laid my burden on your head and sit still; I have given up all traffic with the world; from the first I counted this the highest spot, a place of eternal refuge. Here the one secret needed is patience,—but that too I rejected as useless; knowing that this body shall pass away, I have clung to thy name as the thing essential. Thou hast sent me repose for the hour through all the messengers; I have clung in my soul to that which is needful. Tukā says, Give me at last, O God, that place which the saints have told of.

## 522

IF doctors could preserve men's lives, then who would think of God? How can I tell what sort of balance is left by my store of merit? If vows could give us sons and daughters, what need could there be of marrying? Tukā's generous master knows this secret.

## 523

ALL the steps I have wandered have been wasted; there is but one door to enter by. The secret is to set the feet of Viṭṭhala in one's soul; let no one forget it for a moment. It is easy for all to find this element; no secret introduction in your ear is needed. Tukā says, Here every desire is satisfied; he, the root and trunk of all, is sufficient.

524

MEANS of liberation present themselves in many forms, but consider whether they attain the end; it is the end of churning to produce butter. A bird meets with no obstacle on its way; it flies through the heavens to its goal. You can attain devotion by renouncing the world wholly, you need it not much, little or in moderate degree. Tukā says, If you have merit stored up from the past, to-day, suddenly, you may meet with perfect satisfaction.

525

BUNDLE up honour and dishonour and put them away: where peace of mind abides, there the vision of God comes. Where peace dwells, the lapse of time loses its power. Put down every impulse to move as it arises. Tukā says, It is a little thing to ask.

526

BLESSED it is to be born in a pure family; I shall soon be returning home. This we have heard with our ears and are now digesting in our mind. Let your heart be filled with yearnings, and be awake to your true interests. Tukā says, Whoso has faith, know verily that faith is God.

527

SACRIFICE is ever designed to protect mortal creatures; but it is offered in various forms according to the motive present. If you want to start on the road that leads to the worship of Brahma, there are several modes prescribed. If it is granted you to adopt one, still you will depend for fruit on the seed present in your soul. Blessed is he in the world who not only begins but finishes his task; it is indispensable that you reach the end; what precedes is all peaceful effort. Rare is the man who knows how to follow the path. Tukā has left the perishable and imperishable worlds; he looks into the arts which the Vedas teach and speaks by the favouring grace of Viṭṭhala.

## 528

WHATEVER load we take up, it becomes an evil and keeps us from Govinda. I will sit still and remember your feet; I will gaze up on your dwelling place, O God! The indestructible is one day broken and doubt succeeds to resolution; for the mind creates sin as it makes a serpent of a rope. Tukā says, He who pervades the universe dwells in it; let us attain this conception and rest full of joy in it.

## 529

IF the water is not pure, what will soap effect? Thus if the soul is not pure, what will advice effect? If a tree bears neither fruit nor flower, what will Spring effect? If a woman is barren, what can a husband do for her? If a man is impotent, what can a wife do for him? If the soul has vanished, how can the body stir? Tukā says, Without rain there can be no harvest.

### 530

YOU have your mind for your whole capital; how can you divide it? So clasp Pāṇḍuranga firmly, and leave your body to inherited destiny. Let no other purposes entrap your mind; then you will find the true purpose of life attainable. Tukā says, You must learn that this is right, then you will learn the primal purpose.

### 531

WHY should I cast my body on saws or sharp weapons, or into the midst of fire? Why should I dwell in the forest suffering cold, heat and thirst; why should I sit dumb? Why should I put ashes or dust on my head and wander through the four quarters of the land? Why should I give up food and fast; why should I destroy my life? Tukā says, Why should I adopt such means as these? Give me faith, O Pāṇḍuranga!

### 532

GOD has not told us that *we* should sing, while *you* utter never a word. Cry Rāma! Rāma! strike the cymbals; dance till you sway to and fro in love, seeking your own profit. When the task is so simple, why should you be so lazy? The hand is the natural prey of fire: why do you take such care of it in your indolence? Here is no room for shame or thought of the public voice; here devotion is due. He who laughs at us is guilty of such sin as the slayer of a Brāhmaṇa commits. Let each offer God his faith in the form he chooses, for God has no preference, no consistent rule. Happy are they who listen to his praises. Tukā says, Others are born mere stones.

### 533

IF a man bear Pāṇḍuranga about in his mind, though he love him not, yet Pāṇḍuranga will help him. Let a passion to visit Pāṇḍhari possess you, if you form it; you will doubtless gain your desire. Be weak if you will, be the slave of another, but do not cease to contemplate him. Tukā says, You should die contemplating him, or you will return to the world for this end.

### 534

HE who is bound with the fetters of hope remains a slave of the world; he who heeds nothing is venerated by all. In this matter all depends on ourselves; why should we blame others? Troubles assail the suspicious; the unsuspecting is ready to feast himself. Tukā says, Fear is in store for him; a thief runs swiftly after him.

### 535

CAST thy burden on God's head; wave thy body round him and cast it away. False are the passions and pride that dwell within it; sweep away this burden swiftly when the chance occurs. Cry out at once for pity; let nothing come between you and him. Tukā says, Cease to converse with what is false; then joy will dawn upon you.

### 536

THE servants of Vishṇu know that all is full of him; others have to carry burdens on their heads. All devices and penances are a burden; the only plan is to throw off pride. Pride is hard indeed; even adamant may be broken, but the net of illusion cannot be severed. Tukā says, Through worship we shall discover the secret, all others will find the world a barren waste.

## 537

YOU may seek to attain all gods, but these faults of yours stand in the way, for the two things are incompatible, they will not go together. If you plant sugar-cane and onions in the same trench, their flavour and sweetness are different. Tukā says, Poison and nectar will not go together.

## 538

WHY is man not ashamed to say "mine" of daughter, son, wife, wealth or property? Nothing can release him from the power of death, save the truth of Nārāyaṇa. How often shall I tell you, wretched man, says Tukā, you know not the principle of life by which you live?

## 539

REGARD no words of your Guru that sever you from Nārāyaṇa. Bali pierced an eye of Śukra and made him blind, because he came in his way. If God exerts himself, what may not come to pass?—then why do you struggle in vain, man by man? The wives of the sages broke their husband's orders and took them food; God performed all those women needed; he fulfilled for them religious rites and saved them from shame. God has set fathers against sons; he caused Pralhāda to smite the demon. Many a difficulty his father put in his way, but he never ceased to profess God's name. The wives of the cowherds became immoral and unchaste and committed adultery with

God; but what he gave them he gave to none other, for he became entirely one with them. Unholy deeds we should commit, if they bring the possession of God; proper actions we should give up, if they sever us from him. Tukā says, He is full of compassion, therefore he saved Ajamela.

## 540

WE shall ask him to take us to his own place; act towards men according to their faith; if they are false, treat them as false. Let us not draw any curtain of separation between us and him. Tukā says, God is pleased by sincere faith and truthfulness.

## XI

# The Necessity of Experience

### 541

THERE are three ways of perception: first, as when one carries a load; then, from hearsay; last, through personal experience. A man's reward is according to his faith; it is but water that falls when the sun is in Arcturus, yet it becomes a pearl. It is one thing to see food, or talk of food, and another thing to take food,—a very different thing. Tukā says, A diamond is a diamond to one who can tell it; it is a flint for a fool.

### 542

MILK is sweet itself; but the taste of sugar enhances it; be assured that the knowledge of God resembles this; it is feeble without devotion. Food without salt has no savour; to have the scholar's credit is like the efforts of a blind man to see. Tukā says, The essential part of a *tambura* is its dead wires.

### 543

WHAT good will Kāśi and the Ganges do you, if you are not pure within? If you put hard grain in boiling water, it does not change; it gains no flavour, it will not cook. What will a man gain by garlands and marks on his forehead, if he is vile and void of faith? Tukā says, A man who talks without love is merely barking; his words are ineffective.

## 544

WE find it easy to talk, but it is action that sets the legs trembling. It is no easy thing to renounce passion; if you tell me so, I deem it false. If you talk of eating poison by mouthfuls, he is the lucky man who can do it. Tukā says, The man who can illustrate by action—I set his feet within my soul.

## 545

IT is not the fruit of action nor of contemplation; it is not what men call knowledge, nor a notion of the mind. It is not the foul chatter of one who wearies us with talking; it is not the whirl of objects that surrounds us, nor the naked firmament above us. Tukā says, It is something that the spirit finds within itself.

## 546

THE fevered man cannot enjoy sugar, though others know how sweet it is; in his mouth alone it tastes like earth, though all others eat their fill of it. If you compel him to eat it, you can put it inside his teeth; but the lucky people are those who get it when they ask for it. Tukā says, If one comes to this pass through want of merit, how can any one else help him?

## 547

A GOLDEN plate is filled with sugar and milk, and given to a dog to drink; a necklace of pearls is hung about an ass; musk is plastered on a hog. A reciter of the Vedas utters wisdom to a deaf man,—how can he tell his meaning? Tukā says, He alone understands a thing who truly possesses it; the Sādhu alone understands the glory of devotion.

548

SENDING of gifts, falling at his feet, liberation itself is idle—what avails it? When we have met him and obtained it, all will see how good it is. If we do not meet him face to face, what is the use of dry talk about him? Tukā remains silent; listen to the evidence in your own hearts.

549

BE satisfied with inward pleasure; what need is there of chattering about it? This business of rules and prohibitions is heart-breaking; without the sweetness of spiritual experience both teacher and taught increase their tribulation. In your own mind you think this talk of experience madness, but you do not alter its value. If you would attain to means of salvation, be calm and silent. Tukā says, Verbosity has ruined crowds of Brāhmaṇas.

550

IF a man goes on describing cakes and rubbing his hands to show how they are made, he brings spittle into his mouth, but his speech is insipid, it is like unsalted food that has neither taste nor flavour. One who can only talk and has no spirit within him—what is the good of his words? Curses on them! Tukā says, A talkative and loquacious temper is the root of falsehood.

551

THE mother puts a morsel in her infant's mouth, but she rules her children with authority;

thus knowledge sets us far from God, and puts a growing interval between us and him. The same mother bore both children, but her affection towards them takes a different course. Tukā says, The stronger is separated from her, the infant is laid to her breast.

## 552

WHEAT is all the same in kind, but bad cooks spoil it. To know the secret of an art is the great thing; be it much or little; the secret what to do and where to do it. By honest toil different kinds of grain may be made into different dainties. Tukā says, It is skill that is valuable; words are false and worthless.

## 553

MEN may dispute over arguments they have learned; and yet know nothing of the secret truth. Learned men may preach, and yet never attain their desire, the happiness of the self. Tukā says, They are like men that give evidence for a bribe and know nothing of the facts.

## 554

YOU must pass along the road, if you mean to reach the spot; it is no use listening to mere tales of it. Listen to me, I humbly entreat you; inactive faith will not carry you forward. A virgin and a matron alike have gained their knowledge from experience; it is not acquired by hearsay. Tukā says, Here is needed one immersed in the subject; when the source is cleared, light will proceed from it.

## 555

HE has toiled at the study of books; and the fruit is mere oil. Now he has fathomed the nature of all things; he finds there is no place left for his soul. The tree bends beneath its fruit, when it has produced a genuine crop. Tukā says, Henceforth you must offer faith to God.

## 556

IF you know Nārāyaṇa's tokens, pray show him to me; he dwells with the saints, but others are kept aloof by their own fear of him. Small as an atom, he is filled with light that reveals him. Those who can master the songs, they can understand him; he is hidden by arguments, good and bad, and the reasoning of the logicians. Tukā says, You must anoint your eyes to behold him.

## 557

ONLY the devotee knows the devotee's high estate; it is hard for others to attain to their station. Though they know the secrets of knowledge, they assume ignorance for the sake of that pleasure; they speak not, though they speak with their lips; to increase love and joy in the world they have kept themselves apart, though they are not apart, from God. They beat cymbals, they call upon his name, they proclaim a season of abundant love, to save ignorant shepherds of the people. Tukā says, Well they know all this who have learned it by faith unalloyed.

## 558

WRAP up and put away your knowledge; here faith is what you must trust to. If you follow One, all is accomplished for you, the Lord of Pāṇḍhari assures you thereof. There is no room here for arguments, right or wrong; no room for painful efforts. Tukā says, Unless faith accompany it, whatever men say is weariness.

559

I HAVE not known myself the joys of devotion, how then can I understand philosophy, O God? Do not, I pray, look on me unmoved, when I speak of union with you. The mind alone will not bestow peace upon us, unless we have seen the feet of God. Tukā says, My speech has conceived a passion for your qualities; it cannot be still, though you say nothing to me.

560

BEFORE she has borne a child, if a woman performs joyful ceremonies, she is a silly creature practising nonsense. What is the good of such public display? The mere mention of sugar brings no pleasure. A forced attempt to belch will not make a man fat; he will still look thin and miserable. Tukā says, You talkative men, listen to me; if you have no experience, do not assume the exterior of knowledge.

561

THIS is the impression the world has left on me; if God ceases to speak to a man he too ought to be silent; there is no need to wait, he should make up his mind to that at once. Tukā says, People act very differently,—when God has ceased to speak to them, they go on talking about him.

## 562

TEARS will not come into the eyes, if there be no yearning in the heart; apart from this speech is idle, prating, a fruitless diversion. If the Lord is not attentive to us, our words are profitless. Tukā says, We must wait till we meet him face to face.

## 563

"THE gift of a daughter with her marriage ornaments is nothing less than a gift of the world." So one says, but the foolish fellow knows not the truth; he will know it some day by suffering. If you do your worldly duties, you will fill your stomach, but you will let religion perish. God helps the truth; practise it and you will see for yourself. Food, honour and wealth are a matter of destiny. Tukā says, Enjoy pleasure now if you will; it will turn to destruction some day.

## 564

THE fire cannot burn the string that bears the charmed amulet; everything else is its prey: why need I prove the fact? When a woman has a lord, her beauty is for no other to enjoy. Tukā says, Where there is a fault, the magic touchstone will not let it conceal itself.

## 565

SPEECH may describe him, but experience is hard to attain; our own tendencies draw us in many directions. How can we be still and calm, when death is pursuing us? Our bellies lead us into pride and ostentation; we shall lose our principal at last. Tukā says, O Nārāyaṇa, it is good that you awaken the world with your hand that calms all fear.

## 566

IF we say God is a false conception, we feel a suspicion that we are wrong; I myself have come to know him by serving him. If we feel disposed to make him non-existent, then we make his praises folly. Tukā says, It is our own unsteadiness that prevents us from fixing our thoughts on him.

## 567

THERE is no appointed time for contemplation, it should be practised without ceasing. Auspicious is the mouth that is always uttering "Nārāyaṇa." Delightful is faith in him who excels all; here all pretences are idle. Such is the advice Tukā gives to mankind.

## 568

I HAVE been spreading out viands of speech: how can these be real or satisfy us? When you have gone home, no one will know what disappointment is, though many of you have met and eaten. At sunrise you may conceive both sunrise and sunset, if in your waking thoughts you form an image of them. Tukā sets to work enlightening ignorant children, awakening the rest of mankind.

## 569

IF experience is completed by experience, then the mind grows steady; when gold is burnt in a crucible all impurity is burned out of it and a jewel emerges. So one thing alone remains when body, speech and spirit are done with; that is joy in the three worlds. Tukā says, We have conquered mortal conditions by taking service with Viṭṭhobā.

570

GOD alone knows who secures the real fruit of worship, who can abide by the institutions of worship. Now, O God, you are my hearer and my preacher; let me serve you. The clever and the acute do not end in this; they make idle conjectures at their own will. Tukā says, We have halted in one house; O Hari, there is union between you and me.

571

WHAT a long tale you tell without warrant! As long as you know not the Lord of Pāṇḍhari, so long you will prefer worthless things. Who cares for your dry philosophy? Tukā says, Service is the only thing: lay aside that pride of learning.

572

WHAT will he who honours thee lose? He who will not honour thee, what will he gain? We will see Viṭṭhala in all things; let him dwell in our mind in any form he pleases. Those who are slaves of the world prattle idly from their own point of view; of such, some praise, some blame thee, O Pāṇḍuranga, says Tukā.

# XII

# Triumphant Happiness

## 573

I HAVE found a sea of love, an inexhaustible flood; I have opened a treasure of spiritual knowledge, it diffuses the lustre of a million suns, arisen in thy worshipper's souls. Unexpectedly, without an effort, I have heard the eternal secret, I have learned to know God. The seed of the high reunion has been enfolded in my own destiny I have now beheld him in whose sight is all goodness, a sea of happy augury, the supreme power of mystic words. I have attained him, whose name is nectar, whose nature is pure, intellect free from passion. The very joy of peace and compassion is found in this joy, that accompanies the knowledge of the being and knowing God; this Pundalika declares. Lo! Pāṇḍhari has unfolded the delight of infinite joy! I do not myself know the stage beyond desire that the faithful need; I do not know the universal brotherhood of living things. Tukā says, O Lord of Pāṇḍhari, let me now dwell with the saints!

## 574

IT is well that death has not yet devoured me, I have lived so long; the rest of my life I offer to thee. O Hari, death allowed me a respite; my life has not yet perished; let me use to some purpose the time that is left; the chaff that has vanished—let it go! I was drowned in falsehood till I reached the bank; I struggled hard in the dream of life.

My time of conscious life I wasted, but I have gained something real, a sweet mouthful of food. I have sent a cry to thee, whereby my fears have fled; it seems to be thy fond delight to watch over thy suppliants. The night was passed meditating on my sin; there was light indeed, when the dawn appeared. What fault of ours can survive, when we have thee for our champion? Perish then body, pleasure, pride and honour; I will strive for these no more; I am come, says Tukā, to seek thee, Nārāyaṇa, Lord of the world.

## 575

O GOD, thou art our merciful master, loving to the humble, the guardian of thy worshippers; thou art our tender mother, thou dost lift every burden; all our careful thoughts we pass on to thee; it is for thee to keep us when we stray. Henceforth thou dost deliver us to the saints; if any man neglects us, thou canst not endure it. We have neither care nor fear of life nor death nor anything else. We have attained heaven upon earth, all Vaikuṇṭha has come to us. We know not whether it is day or night, an eternal splendour has dawned upon us. Billows of joy roll upon us. How can we describe that happiness? Through singing thy name, thou hast adorned me with a rich jewel. Tukā says, Through the virtue of thy name, what have I left to wish for?

## 576

MY pleasure in the company of the saints is ever doubled through your name. All actions are burned out of existence; I sit swaying to and fro in a passion of love. So I have no more anxious care; you are my father and mother, sister, brother and uncle, my relatives in all degrees. I have found this resolution in you, that you will never forget me; without, within, and by my side you stand inspiring confidence. I may not even dream of sorrow; delight and liberation are become my servants; you their secret source abide with me in the happiness of love. Where your praises are sung, sin is burnt up and guilt flees away: what is wanting to complete my joy? I drink the nectar of Brahma, says Tukā.

## 577

O GOD, thou art a sea of compassion; mother, father, and brother to me! Thou art an ocean of measures for attaining life; thou dost sever the ties of the world, the snares of destruction. Thou art a wall of adamant to thy refugee; freedom from fear is thy generous gift. It is beyond all gods to perceive thee, thou art unembodied, imperishable; where the highest effort of praise is too feeble for the theme, what can I do with my uncultivated wit? Do not make me wait to know thy purposes. I know nothing of faith, but I call myself thine; I know nothing of devotion, but I offer thee homage. For thy own name's sake, O controller of the senses, it behoves thee to run speedily. O Lord of Pāṇḍhari, I am filled with thy joy; I have vanquished pain; I have laid my burden on thy head, I shall fear no more, says Tukā.

## 578

MY desire has drawn near to me: why need I speak? I am bound up with his name and form; I am done with all discourse about it. I am like a dumb man who sits delighted eating sugar. Tukā says, What shall I say now? Silence is the right thing.

579

BENEATH the protection of a mighty one, we have grown mighty; thus we have struck down the world, we have crushed the six evil passions. We have made to be like stubble kindred, wealth and the body. Tukā says, Now we have attained the source of emancipation.

580

MY desires have been accomplished; I have set my spirit firmly at his feet. I have found peace and repose; my distress vanished when I remembered him. The three-fold fever was consumed away, my soul was delighted by the joy of love. Great is my gain, that Pāṇḍuranga dwells in my speech he never stirs from my side; within me I feel a stream of life; the world is merged in him who pervades it. Tukā says, The measure is filled and heaped up, and it overflows like the Ganges in flood.

581

I HAVE tasted a sweet taste, my stomach is filled, for his name suddenly occurred to me; when the tongue utters the name of Viṭṭhala, sin vanishes. Believe it, O all men; he saved Ajamela; he has saved sinners of the lowest degree, for his name's sake. My spirit has attained bliss and joy and eternal repose. Utter Govinda's name from time to time; he knows this who has felt its power; he who loves this will practise it. Tukā says, O thou, who art formless, show us thy form.

## 582

WHO regards the world, while he continues with us people of Hari? Time is swallowed up in the joy of Brahma; we have an excess of delight stored up. We never even dream of care, as the days and nights pass by. Tukā says, This juice of Brahma is a satisfying meal.

## 583

UNDERSTAND what your own form is; why do you despise the mirror of the self? The life of the flesh will not bring you near it; Nārāyaṇa must be generous to you. Babhru did not expect, when he shot his arrows, that they would hit the vital parts of Arjuna. Tukā says, This tale has been handed down by many lips, but it would not have been started had it not been true.

## 584

I HAVE secured now the supreme union; it is mine for ever; I will not abandon it; the foundation is deep laid; there is nothing further to reach beyond this point. What was scattered is brought together again; the books are balanced, the account is clear. Tukā says, Henceforth I shall stop speaking.

## 585

I HAVE found an inexhaustible capital, with which I will maintain my trade. I have found cheap seed in my house; I have stored it up in the form of speech. In lending or borrowing this capital all are benefited; the rate is the same for rich and poor. One who comes to the sale-room is not disappointed, though he knows nothing of the business. Tukā says, I am free from anxiety; I seek for nothing else.

## 586

I WILL keep before my thoughts his delicate feet, the treasure chamber of all happiness. I will keep on my lips his name, that is like a creeper yielding nectar; my body shall be at rest. I will gaze on his fair and beauteous face—a mine of all lovely charms. I will cling to him like a child; I will sit on his thigh and will never rise. Tukā says, He becomes what we have made him; I have embraced in my spirit the happiness that Viṭṭhobā gives.

## 587

BY this purpose and resolution my body has escaped from death; all cravings have been rooted out, I have found my native portion of bliss. I have found the secret; I see before me no anxious care. Tukā says, Why need anyone pity me? Wherein is my soul apart from him?

## 588

MY spirit is infused into this essential juice of all; my joy is unbounded; in him who pervades the world I have found father, family and bosom friend; I recognize them all under one name; I have cut myself free from faith in others. Tukā says, By his name and form all guilt is purged away.

## 589

LIGHT will not vanish now that I have this gem; I am far removed from darkness. I have been myself a witness of your properties—so evince them, O Nārāyaṇa! By remembrance of you I have forgotten the past; I have preserved the experiences vouchsafed to me. Tukā says, I find my diversion in God; we have not two aspects as you have.

590

I AM not wearied, but I am afraid: what can I do in my ignorance? City and waste are alike to me; anger and lust have become my footstools. O infinite one, I have conquered the six rebels now, through the compelling power of thy name. My chief duty now is like a servant to forward my lord's purposes with ready obedience; therefore Tukā stands gazing on his feet, listening for his word.

591

I HAVE finished a profitable journey; how can I describe it in words? My gain has brought me two-fold gain. My soul is comforted by the right of him; fortune has led me to the company of saints, and given me what I delighted in. Tukā says, The efforts which I made have all borne fruit.

592

BLESSED is to-day, for to-day I have seen the saints. I have broken away from the fever of sin; my misery has vanished. I have found peace; my spirit has sunk to rest at thy feet. Tukā says, To-day the Divāli and Dasara have both visited my house together.

593

I HAD been impressed and dragged far away, with a burden on my head; now I have escaped from the burden, for you have accepted me. How many times I cried to you in time past! Tukā says, To-day my service has borne fruit.

594

CURSED be my destiny; my toil is all wasted; the bold claims I made have not been realized. How can I make myself patient now? It is for thee, O Nārāyaṇa, to inspire me. I have been given wisdom to teach me my faults. I am deeply guilty. Tukā says, O piteous king, it is thou that hast satisfied my cravings, now, at last!

595

WHAT merit shall permit me to serve those who have put away duality from them? Show me this secret, O Nārāyaṇa, by the agency of some inward sign. It is hard to serve the saints; and yet the Lord of the world has shown me mercy. Tukā says, I shall not return to my old disposition, I shall repose in joy.

596

SINCE I have seen his holy face, what two-fold pleasure I have received! The hunger of my eyes never departs. My tongue tastes the sweetness that makes nectar insipid. The path of hearing has been swept and cleansed; the sense of difference has vanished. My mind that was soiled and foul has been swept and cleansed, till it is like a crystal. Tukā says, I have found a treasure, even Viṭṭhala, the life of my soul.

597

I HAVE his strength within me; what can death do? I have forfeited my soul as a pledge, till my soul and God are united. I have applied myself to this; I shall not turn back till we are united. Tukā says, I believe I shall one day be like thee.

## 598

KNOWING the secret faith of our innermost hearts, Pāṇḍuraṅga has dealt with us accordingly. The words I have uttered will not fall to the ground; thou art the mother of us friendless people! Thou hast destroyed my misgivings and any sense of separation that remained. Tukā says, Now I am full of joy; I will sing of thy noble qualities unfathomable.

## 599

HOW can I tell the joy that lies in thy feet? Thou hast no experience of it thyself. If I describe the nature of nectar, how shall I be thought to speak the truth? As mother and child we must testify to each other; thus we both shall discern what that happiness is. Tukā says, We detest emancipation: why do you forget this, O cowherd?

## 600

SEEING nothing I have seen all; I have become one with all men, because I have kept myself far from me. Receiving nothing I have received all; I have found feet for my limbs. Eating nothing I have been fed, my tongue has tasted a sweet savour. Though I speak not I am as one that speaks, making manifest the secret of my life. Tukā says, I have not heard with my ears, yet it has come into my mind.

### 601

AS we utter the name, our minds are quieted, our tongues perceive a taste of nectar; omens of gain appear to us. Our minds are delighted; we repose at your feet; we must know that such is your mercy if we utter your name. We have, as it were, feasted; we have cast a stone upon desire; we speak like men who have been satisfied. Delight has come to meet delight; we have found a treasure that is sweet in the mouth. Tukā says, Now we cannot measure our joy.

### 602

EXCELLENT is the test of thy names, it consumes away great guilt. It has bestowed life on us; we employ it abundantly. Sweet and easy—better how far than nectar! Tukā says, Our benefactor, our tree of wishes, cannot be disturbed.

### 603

THIS is a blessed, golden day! The saints have feasted in a row, an excellent feast in full confidence; uttering the name of Rāma Kṛishṇa they have fallen into a glorious trance of love. Tukā says, This hasty meal has been delicious.

## XIII

# Raillery of God

### 604

I HAVE the support of the saints, but you, O formless being, are alone and helpless. Consider this, O God, and enter into no suit with me. You know not how to plead, but we are well versed in quarrels. Tukā says, The only thing left for you then is to be at peace with us.

### 605

A DECEIVER has come to Pāṇḍhari, bringing snares of love with him. Henceforth he has ruined mankind; he carries people off and leaves no trace of them. He lifts up his arms and pierces them with the shaft of his glance. In his passage from Vaikuṇṭha he has made a halt at Pāṇḍhari; it is Puṇḍalika who has brought this thief here and made a place for him. Tukā says, Come you and I, let us seiẓe him!

### 606

A MOTHER sets her children quarrelling, through fond curiosity; she watches all that happens herself. She calls one girl her own and beats another, yet both are near to her heart. "Yours is a big piece"—"mine a small one"—these desires and grumblings are baseless talk.

Tukā says, There remains in one spot the secret that saves us from all exertions.

607

I HAVE learned well to pay you back in your own coin; you are heedless of me; you may say too, O Nārāyaṇa, I am heedless of you. If a cheat meets a greater cheat, it is certain that some one will gain something. This is a one-sided quarrel; there is no danger to my life, says Tukā.

608

I HOPE to behold you; I cannot bear to be heedless of you. My soul has visited your feet; I am here before you in the flesh. I forget all; I cannot rise from the spot when I am sitting. Behold, while life is yet in him, Tukā is cheated out of his life.

609

THESE cries are raised at your door; we see that you are always in debt. You are a shameless fellow, O God, your worshippers often beat and fine you. You hide away yourself and coolly entangle us in feasting. Tukā says, You are a cheat, you dupe us by giving us one thing for another.

610

YOU are as clean as a crystal; you have cleaned out your worshippers; so people do not come to your door, O generous one, for they are cheated there. Your behaviour is known; you have ruined everybody. Tukā says, When you take a man's property, this is the result you show him.

### 611

KNOW you not, O God, what I can say? I ever took delight in your speech. O pervader of the world, to no purpose you puzzle me by your jests. Do as it pleases you, for you dwell in the heart and know all. Tukā says, When I attain to peace, my mind will be released.

### 612

IF our mind is willing to be still and peaceful, why are we full of restless regrets? Why do we fail to recognize your hand in operation, when you take your diversion within us? You set our souls dancing with many fond desires, you increase our longings for chance objects. Tukā says, In this sportive style you design to establish your honour.

### 613

HOW many are the sources of honour and dishonour,—these are the least of your boons. Go and tempt other poor creatures who can find any taste of sweetness in them. Though you should offer us the height of prosperity, we are not greedy of it like others. Tukā says, You are a cheat; this is how you have ruined people.

## XIV

# Faith and Trust

### 614

WHO asks whether we are faint or weary? Who else but thou asks us, O Pāṇḍuranga? To whom shall we tell our joys and sorrows? Who will relieve our hunger and thirst? What other will chase away our fever and deliver us? Whom should we ask for the morsel we want? Who will delight to caress us? To whom shall we allow authority but to thee? What ally shall we find? Tukā says, O Lord, who knowest all, I throw myself at thy feet.

### 615

I HAVE used up every means of reaching thy feet. If I shall offer thee worship, I want faith; I cannot control my soul for any purpose. If I shall offer thee pious deeds, I want will; if I shall offer thee a present, I want treasure. I know not how to honour Brāhmaṇa guests; I am void of compassion. I know not how to serve a teacher or holy men, to reiterate thy name, to undertake mortifications or ceremonies. I cannot lay aside passion, or dwell in the forest or subdue my senses. If I go on a pilgrimage, my mind goes not with me; if I perform ceremonies, I know not myself the due procedure. If I shall say "God is with me," behold I have not forgotten distinctions between myself and others. Therefore I have come as a suppliant, your servant in all humility. Such an one needs no store of merit; I am resolved now, says Tukā.

## 616

A FATHER protects his child; he shows him his own stored up wealth and all his possessions; even so I have been protected, I have not seen any evil standing in my path. Close to the hungry child is the breast; our anxious thoughts are not far from their remedy. Tukā stands entreating on the bank; his mother Pāṇḍuranga leaps over the stream.

## 617

NOW will I sing auspicious hymns and uplift loud praises to Hari; you will avert all our fears, our troubles, our sin and merit. We will deposit in you all our sensuous life; we will continue in this world, yet apart from it. Tukā says, We are your darling children, we will not leave your feet.

## 618

WHEN the child's mouth touches her breast, the mother yields her milk. Both delight in their caresses, the desire of each satisfies the other's desire. As their bodies meet, their bliss increases through their love. Tukā says, I have laid all heavy burdens on my mother's head.

## 619

IF you remember the Lord of Pāṇḍhari, you will not be subject to time even for one moment. Time is ever counting your days, but it cannot count the days you spend in preaching Hari; hence it is that the praise of my Viṭṭhobā has come to be a high way in the three worlds. Tukā says, You have the true fruit of your birth if you remember Gopāla.

### 620

YOU should make no effort to serve the world, for it leads to disobedience to God. He is the controller of the body; of his own motion he will take care of it, so that time cannot assail you. The mother serves her child in obedience to his will; but she does not lose her dignity by this offence. Tukā says, Abandon all assumption; it is a dysentery that distresses the body.

### 621

WHAT does a child know whether his father is rich or poor? He knows not at any time whether a thing is in his father's power or not. When he sees something, he embraces his father and asks for it. Tukā says, A man's inner nature is intelligible to him alone.

### 622

WE ask of thee, O God, that thou wilt permit us to worshi pthy feet. We desire nothing else though thou wouldst give it—prosperity, perfection—or the four liberations. With the saints there is now a season of abundant love. Tukā says, Thy name fulfils my desires.

### 623

MY devotion is simple, concentrated in thee, and strong in faith. Hari, can I abandon this delight and fall away from thee? Now let there be no hasty change in me. Tukā says, With feet set together I stand upright and still before thee.

## 624

SIT still and think upon him; he who gives food and clothes will give thee all. Why need we accumulate any further store, when God is our debtor and supplies all our needs? He is loving and pitiful; he knows how to return his petitioner's endearments. We need not tell him our desires; he knows and gives us what we want. Tukā says, Put his ornaments on your person; you will become yourself Viṭṭhala in the world.

## 625

I MUST needs declare my mind, O God; how is it you know it not? Appoint me my lot as you will; I shall not change. My mind is lame; I can recall no remedy; so I have embraced your feet. Both enjoyment and renunciation bring pain; why should I go on doing and undoing? I have fallen into a grave doubt. Tukā says, When a mother has lost her child in the wood, she grieves because she cannot find him, O mother Viṭṭhala.

## 626

THE goods of Dvāraka have come to this spot; henceforth the lord of devotees gives us courage. He has bound us to him by earnest-money, he has measured us out our purchases fairly; he does not yet think of returning. The servants of Vishṇu wield the measure; they have not yet laid all the tallies aside; nor can we see a time when the measuring will be finished. Those who have gained by this trade have not changed their plans; they have stored up enough for the life here and beyond. Tukā says, I have got my wages;

I have earned a place of confidence in the dwellings of the saints.

627

WE will honour the dust of thy feet; we will eat the scraps that are left of thy food. We will tie up this infinite treasure in our bundles. Viṭṭhala is fit for such poor creatures as we. All gain is accessible through thy contemplation, and chanting the name of Govinda. Thus shall the vicissitudes of birth and death be abolished; this shall be a sure and easy road. I seek for the path of those who went before me; let us go on following the track. Tukā says, We shall bury this life under a slab of stone; we shall go straight to our own mother's house.

628

WE taste all the sweetness of assurance; we feel a fond craving for you. Now that my faith has settled at thy feet, I shall dance for joy. If I know that my master is watchful, then my mind is delighted. Tukā says, Console us and grant us thy love, O mother Viṭṭhala.

629

MY treasure consists in worshipping thy feet; through this good fortune I shall live on, offering thee my mind, little as it is. God has protected me, helpless soul that I am. Tukā, his servant, stands with folded hands beseeching him.

630

I ASK for fragments from the meals of the saints; I will sweep up every row of dishes. I care nothing for ceremonial cleanliness; I am far removed from such ideas. The highest truth of all none need teach me; for God has taught it me well himself. I avoid every other; I know the signal that I stand and wait for. There is no occasion for any doubt here; there is only one kind of food that I desire. Tukā has taken to this and pounces upon it; Nārāyaṇa has satisfied his craving.

631

WHOSE mind is set on thee, such a one let me behold. What a pure and natural faith is this, whereby I move neither hands nor feet, but have gathered all together for an offering, and fixed my eyes on thee. Tukā says, Hide me behind thee, and show me my fond desire.

632

IT is the defects of a thing that bring shame. We need not trouble about the vessel. The question is whether the contents are sweet or tasteless. We must not put poison to our lips, whether it is contained in a big pot or a small one. Tukā says, True faith is a good thing; pretence is worthless.

633

I HAVE offered my speech to Pāṇḍuranga; it finds content in him. It offers pearls of worship, honey of songs in his praise. My utterance flows on in a stream unbroken. Tukā has offered his soul for the last oblation; his trust is perfect.

634

THE light of the sun vanishes in the night; though lamps are multiplied, yet what are they? Now let this controller of the senses dwell in my soul and in my heart; by this aid the secrets of the world become known. If my master is with me, none can come between us; nor shall I pray to any other. By his aid the migrations of rebirth are closed, because his love is near at hand, says Tukā.

## 635

I CARE for no theme but the Lord of Pāṇḍhari. I listen to the song of his praise, I delight to hear it. Tukā says, The sages may say anything; I think of nothing but Viṭṭhala.

## 636

ALL shelters but this are a mere dream. The feet of God are above all, there I have made my dwelling place. No destruction comes near it. Tukā says, I have found the spot and I strive no more.

## 637

I KEEP company with no other, who will vex my mind. I listen to no speech of any other than Viṭṭhala. I may speak of another to please mankind, but my heart is not in it. I love more than my own soul those who love Pāṇḍuranga. Tukā says, Any saint like this knows what is best for me; I listen to no other.

## 638

I HAVE made no other choice than a resolute purpose; of Pāṇḍuranga I think, on him I meditate; dreaming and waking I have turned towards him every organ of sense; I put no faith in any other. Tukā says, My eyes have learnt to know him again; fair is the form that stands for contemplation on the brick.

## 639

LET me fail to find food or beget children, if only Nārāyaṇa will be merciful to me. Thus my own speech advises me, and I declared it also to mankind. Though my body fall into shame or want, let Nārāyaṇa dwell in my thoughts. Tukā says, All this world is perishable; so far as we remember Gopāla, we gain something.

## 640

I MOVE where Hari pulls me by the string of his love; I have given all to Pāṇḍuranga—body, speech and mind; all authority rests with him, he takes pity on me. Tukā says, He disposes of us; we will continue as he wills.

## 641

FAITH is the due offering of God; faith is God himself. Blessed are the pure; can any doubt of this remain in their mind? Beggar as I am, I dearly love God. Tukā says, This is the truth, the gain is large and all faults are driven out.

## 642

A LAMP sees no darkness; treasure up this faith. Nārāyaṇa is a powerful treasure to have in your bundle. When you have the gem of Paradise, all anxious cares will vanish. Tukā says, This is the true treasure both here and hereafter.

## 643

WE were not vigilant, therefore we lost the blessing; we forgot his name, we cherished the world. We were carried far from him by the swollen flood of falsity. Tukā says, We have found a boat in the shape of faith.

### 644

O GOD, thou dost know my innermost desire; how can I escape, O Lord of Vaikuṇṭha? Hadst thou not encouraged me, I should not have been protected. Tukā says, O merciful one, it is well thou hast given me thy help.

### 645

THIS Goddess becomes God when our distresses are over; she does not continue apart from him; there is no need to describe her separately. Awake now! Chant the name of Hari, the name of God! Ask for your parting gift; let no clogging burden remain with you. Sound the drums to proclaim that we have reached our goal. Close your shrine; accept the honour your officers give you. Tukā says, To-day I have read the riddle well.

### 646

THERE are many paths, but this is the one on which the saints have travelled. "Take no devious path"; thus the Purāṇas proclaim. Our road has been cleared; it is a high road; you need not ask the way. There are banners fluttering and brazen images to guide us, says Tukā.

### 647

FROM birth to birth I continue thy suppliant and dependent; I desire nothing but thee, O Keśava! I sing thy name and praises; I have adorned myself, says Tukā, with the ornament of thy name.

## 648

LET me fix my thoughts on him; that will be good even though he does not visit me. It is well if faith dwells within us; know that such good luck is God himself. Though he delay to visit us himself, yet a state of faith may possess us. Tukā says, In either case our own mind brings about the results.

## 649

IF you desire nothing, O God, why have you assumed any name? Why do you impart to any one the knowledge of yourself? Is not this proof of fraud on your part? If a man dances before you with true joy, then your true form stands before him. Tukā says, Love is a thing that should not be impaired.

## 650

FAITH and fixed affection are all the devotee's duty; a firm resolution is the secret they must not forget. Without desire or motive of the mind they must trust in Viṭṭhala; they must not wait upon other gods. Tukā says, When has such an one ever been neglected? The thing has never been heard of.

## 651

DO not give up food or resort to the forest, but enjoy the translation of Nārāyaṇa. The child on his mother's shoulders finds no weariness; other notions of God's dealings should be swept away. Be not entangled in pleasure nor go aside after renunciation; but trust in everything to God and move forward. Tukā says, Do not raise doubts, no other counsel is needed.

## 652

WE are not people of to-day, raw and weak and driven to and fro; we have roots and rootlets in one place—and well-known art thou! You and we have not been put apart. Tukā says, Wherever I am, I am seen to be yours.

## 653

WE need know nothing but Pāṇḍuranga; all doubtful enquiries will fatigue us. By whatever foolish name we have addressed our father, by them he knows our yearnings. He becomes an ornament to grace our speech, if we praise him with all our powers. Tukā says, Out of our complaints joy is born; let us cry aloud from moment to moment.

## 654

LET the burden of knowledge rest on God's head; it is well for us to be ignorant as we are. As he looks upon us, he enjoys our amusing pranks; on both sides there is a growing delight. His dear little ones feel no painful doubt; their minds are set on play, their thoughts are one with his. Tukā says, Nothing hinders us in any direction; our diversions are known in the skies.

## 655

I SHALL respect what I have often said; of that no doubt arises in my mind. You have loved many; you have endured the complaints of men and appeased men. To many men for their faith, you have divided tender morsels of love; with fond indulgence you have set them sporting. Tukā says, I know this secret of yours; I need be anxious no more.

## 656

BY the strength of his devotion the servant of Vishṇu is kept from perishing. Opportunities and blessings visit his house, all powers come walking to him. Who will deny to a son his father's wealth? Tukā says, We sit on his hip, hence we have full confidence.

## 657

ALL our capital is Viṭṭhala—body, speech and spirit; gladly I have laid out my all on this. The true priṇciple of all is your feet, I know nothing else than them. Tukā says, In the society of the saints I am transfigured by this passion.

## 658

IF a thing is not present in your mind, what good will it do to place it before your eyes? This is why a calf forgets its mother. But if your mind is in harmoṇy with another's, then you delight in his speech and love the wind that blows from him. Tukā says, Without faith all is insipid, like food without salt.

## 659

IF you wash the roots of a plant, you will destroy it altogether. The saints complain that you have stirred up many a dispute. The man, whom God directs towards the goal, he casts out from the common herd. Tukā says, Your qualities, if they were imposed on another, would ruin him.

## 660

SITTING, playing, eating, I will sing thy name I will wind round my neck for a garland the name of Rāma Kṛishṇa. My strength and confidence shall be in his name. Tukā says, He is the life of his suppliants.

661

THOUGH men cut my head off, yet my tongue shall speak of no other. I entreat all my senses, not to turn away from Pāṇḍuranga. Let me hear of no other, let me see no other than thee. Let my spirit rest ever at thy feet, attached to the one God. Come, O hands and feet, be this your task, to salute Viṭṭhobā. Tukā says, What shall alarm you? Our champion is Nārāyaṇa.

662

VIṬṬHALA is my mother; her breast is filled with the milk of love. She caresses and lifts me to her breast; she does not stay away from me. She fulfils my entreaties; she is gracious and tender. Tukā says, She puts into my mouth as a morsel the sweet juice of Brahma.

663

GENEROUS and merciful, Lord of the helpless, thou dost listen to thy suppliants' speech. Thou dost remove all burdens from their heads; I have followed thee, body, speech and mind. When we call upon thee, thou dost stand near us, to grant us in good time what we need. As we travel along, thou dost protect us; with thy hand thou dost remove thorns and stones before us. Tukā says, Thy servants feel no anxious care, thou dost heartily make thyself their refuge.

664

WITH all our might we will embrace Śripati; we have laid our soul at his feet; we have wiped away the source of birth and death. We have handed over our plans to him whose business it is to give; we have escaped the guilt of the fetter. Tukā says, Here Viṭṭhala alone is left; he eats and speaks and dances and sings in us.

### 665

I NEITHER worship nor serve other gods; I honour none but Keśava. When I am at thy feet, what do I need, or of whom else shall I ask it? I neither hear nor speak the praise of others; I delight in none but Viṭṭhala. I gaze on his holy face alone; I never leave the lord of Pāṇḍhari. I do not look for release, nor toil for it; I do not fear the world and the change of life and death. Tukā says, Let me feel there is nothing besides Keśava.

### 666

O SPEECH of mine, utter the sweet name of Viṭṭhobā. O eyes, delight yourself with the sight of his face. O ears, listen to the attributes of my Viṭṭhobā. O mind, run to him and rest at his feet. Tukā says, O my soul, forsake not this Keśava.

### 667

WE shall contemplate the acquisition of the Self; we shall sow the seed in the shape of Viṭṭhala. I have gained a fortune in this place; now I shall throw away my body. In future how can such a thing occur? Many a time I have missed the chance. Tukā says, Now I have reached your feet; I do not forget them for a moment.

## 668

I HAVE found the aspiration of my soul; I see the desires of my heart fulfilled. I know not whether it is night or day. I feel my body thrilled by the power I worship. I have gained what I sought in my vow; in the hour of fruition one does not feel himself far from his wish. Tukā says, His gifts are equal; his image on the brick stands evenly.

## 669

A FORMAL worshipper continues his worship till all the materials are exhausted; it is not so with me. O generous one, you will take all my burden upon you O Nārāyaṇa, you know what is really auspicious. Tukā says, I have offered you the attachment of the body.

## 670

AS a chaste bride values her husband above all things, so we value Nārāyaṇa. As an avaricious man delights in money, so do we delight in Nārāyaṇa. Tukā says, My mind is concentrated, I know nothing but Viṭṭhala.

## 671

NOW I am resolved with my whole heart to think of no other. I will sing thy name with complete faith and joy; all my riches are in thy feet. I will cast myself down before thee; I will look on thy face till my eyes are satisfied. I will put away shame and dance openly; I will let no doubt cross my mind. Tukā says, I am thy branded slave, O God; I am resolved to be such.

## 672

I WILL utter God's name heartily, with pure faith. Vitthala is my treasure, my life in the latter end. The weight of merit and demerit is a trouble to me, I will sweep it away, and exchange it all for the other. Tukā says, I will keep it in the base of the heart, the best vessel for it.

## 673

WHEN I recall thee, what other source of pleasure is left me? Nothing comes between us; the seed has borne its fruit. Vain disquietude and weariness—how can they touch my spirit? Tukā says, All doubt has left me, through devotion to thy feet.

## 674

I TREMBLE not and keep quiet; this merciful one is my lord. He will give me eternal joy in the end of all things, the source of the eight million rebirths will pass away. He will show himself generous to other souls also, millions of benefits he will confer. Thou shalt be exalted here and hereafter; utter the name of Rāma, Rāma! Tukā says, Give up your passion for the world, then you will reach the joy of the highest.

## 675

I KNOW thy faith; I have grasped thy feet. I will not let them go; I will not take anything to let them go. I have clung to them so long that you will find it an old affair and a perplexing one to get rid of me. Tukā says, I will not let you go, not if you give me all else.

## 676

I HAVE taken care of this, making it my own treasure. I look on him as the seed, and keep it safe, for from him has proceeded the world. I have separated the chaff; the grain is what is soluble. Tukā says, God is a legacy of treasured merit.

## 677

HOW can I be born again? I am saved from any such care. I am comforted by this thought, that I need never return. Pāṇḍuranga is a ship that will carry us over, if we trust in him. Tukā says, Good sir, every new turn of rebirth is prevented.

## 678

A HEAP of victuals has come to the cooking place; it would be madness to give up one's meal and go begging. The road is finished; it would be folly for me to go backwards. Tukā says, I shall be still and employ my power of speech.

## 679

IF our actions depart from ceremonial rule, do not thou observe our conduct. Count them as service done to thee; show us mercy in the end. I have enquired for the primal source; here my faith has made its abode. Now Tukā feels no eager longing, no impatience any more.

## 680

KEEP me wide, I beseech you, every moment let love choke my throat, let me cast myself on the ground. Actions of good report are neglected; we forget everything. Tukā says, We should gaze on thee with the fondness of lawless passion.

## 681

WHY should we be styled liberated? Bonds we have never felt; we joyfully celebrate thy praises, our mind has forgotten all fear. I see no harm approaching me. Why need I depend on any other? Tukā says, God who guards mankind is my guardian.

## 682

I AM perishing, O God; I know not how to offer thee service or devotion; now I stand still with folded hands before thee. I know not what to do; I gaze upon thy feet. Tukā says, I will gather up in my cloth the gift thou hast given me.

# XV

# The Moral Ideal

## I.—Purity

### 683

WE shall see with our own eyes the darling of our souls; Viṭṭhala is our only god, all others are vain. He stands hand on hip upright behind Puṇḍalika. Tukā says, We shall bear in our heart the husband of Rakhumai.

### 684

THIS is what we mean by guilt, a stain lingering in the soul. Guilt and merit are creatures of the mind, so are all pure and lofty thoughts. The fruit is like the seed, good or bad. Tukā says, It is well to keep the mind pure.

### 685

A PURE life is the worship to be offered to the saints; you need no wealth or possessions. To satisfy those who worship the embodied form they grant a material peace; they come caressing you. As you sing God's praises, his mercy flows forth in a sweet stream; though you live apart, still you are near to him. Tukā says, I tell you the secret at a cheap rate, apply your mind to profit by

## 686

IF one is to achieve the end, there are two means of attaining it; hold in abhorrence the money and wives of others. If virtues sent of God visit thy house, let that be all thy wealth. Tukā says, Then thy body and thy house are God's temple.

## 687

IF we cast forth pride and desire, the body becomes like the jewel Chintāmani. If we cast forth fraud, malice and a censorious spirit, the body grows clear as crystal. Such an one need not visit holy places of liberation, nor Benāres itself; all men come to him. He becomes himself chief of all holy places, liberation is gained by the sight of him. If a man's mind is pure, what can garlands do for him? He is already adorned with all ornaments. Such men ever proclaim the attributes of Hari, joy dwells within them. Body, mind and possessions they have surrendered to the highest; they desire nothing. Tukā says, He is more glorious than the stone Parisa: how can I describe his glory?

## 688

YOU must cook your food so that it will not create disgust or cause pain; then it retains its sweetness; it is pure and true to its own nature. If any contaminating influence enters in, it will show its effects. Tukā says, That which is essentially pure will not change afterwards.

## 689

O BROTHER, here is a rest-house where food is given free; drinking places are provided everywhere; the road is full of pilgrims who have come to satisfy their desire for a pleasant dinner. All comers may partake of it. Sadāśiva has made arrangements that it will never cease. But to be fit for it you must be holy, so with a pure heart call out "Hari" all of you. This is not an obvious truth, nor true apart from the witness of the four Vedas; it will not suffer you to follow the vanities of your own minds. It is smaller than an atom. It is greater than greatness itself, inasmuch as it is the witnessing spirit of the world. This name of Hari is prepared as a soup to fill the belly of the world; rest in the shade of this celestial tree. It is a food that will nourish all castes; cry then Hara! Hara! Mighty God! Tukā, the servant of Hari, is the headman; the rest are all criers. Come, let us bow down at the foot of the temple spire; now that we have seen Vasudeva, this is the holiest time of spring.

## 690

THE religious rites of our fathers should be sought in knowledge and means of attainment; such things deserve the name as place a treasure in our hands. Such things are devotion and a smooth passage to salvation; through them we shall reach peace. Such things are compassion and the service of mankind; in them is the very essence of the true path; in them are greatness and honour and the attainment of the other world. Such things, says Tukā, show that what we call God is God, if we have faith according to their precepts.

## 691

A GOOD seed brings forth sweet and excellent fruit; let our mouth be filled with words of divine sweetness; let our body be employed on useful purposes. Whoso is pure in every way and has a spirit like the water of the Ganges, Tukā says, the sight of him drives away trouble and brings peace.

692

OF all dwellers on earth those alone are pure and unpolluted who love God with lasting love and faith. Those alone are prosperous who go beyond the love of money. Tukā says, If you serve them, your service reaches God.

---

## 11.—Sincerity

693

ACT as you speak, or you disgrace God. What would sweet food be like without salt? Like a lifeless corpse dressed out with ornaments. The actor's make-up is disgraced without appropriate action; a fine shape is worthless without solid qualities. To perform the ceremonies of wedlock without a bride and bridegroom would be an idle waste of money. Tukā says, So it is in my case, so long as I see not the spirit of love within me.

694

THOSE who possess an open mind and pleasant speech, such men deserve to be called fortunate; a happy life lies before them. One who is humble and respectful and does not change his demeanour, Tukā says, we should rejoice when we utter his name.

## 695

THE sandal tree need not call the other trees together and talk of its own perfume. Its inner quality comes to light through its natural power; it cannot restrain it though it would. The sun need not tell his rays to shine when he would arouse the world. Tukā says, The clouds make the peacocks dance; no one can conceal the truth.

## 696

THE sandal tree is sandal in every limb; the philosopher's stone is not void of power in any of its parts. There is no darkness in a flame within or without; sugar is sweet in every particle. Tukā says, Even so in a good man no evil quality can be discerned.

## 697

LET us offer the worship which is best, the worship of the heart; then what do we want with outward preparations? God ought to know the heart and he knows it; in the heart of the true worshipper is the truth which he accepts. In the last hour the spirit shall reap gain or loss according to the seed it has sown. Tukā says, That worship which keeps us in peace secures its end.

## 698

SPLENDOUR accompanies a prince, he need issue no orders. In this world no one honours another without some reward; God alone gives his mercy freely. Ornamentation will not last on anything; the substance beneath soon shows through. Tukā says, If Nārāyaṇa dwells in the heart, a sympathetic demeanour proves his grace.

### 699

TRUTH brings its own reward, it does not need force for an ally. Contemplate the feet of God; patience is the only resource you need. Assuredly you need not fear. Tukā says, You will do well to proclaim yourself his suppliant with all confidence.

---

## III.—Truthfulness

### 700

IF you will speak the truth, you may get Hari for nothing; yet men neglect this cheap resource, and waste their lives. One truthful word is the best of service you can offer to others. Tukā says, If you purge the mind of its guile, you will give it repose.

---

## IV.—Simplicity

### 701

MEN may be passing wise, and versed in argument, yet have never found Viṭṭhobā for their conclusion. They may heap together countless books, yet know not the glory of Viṭṭhobā. Tukā says, A simple heart is needed; without it knowledge is a weariness, an empty measure.

---

## V.—Humility

### 702

HUMILITY is a good thing, O God; it avoids all enmity; in a great flood the trees perish, the blades of grass survive. When the waves pass over them, they escape because they are humble. Tukā says, The secret is to clasp his feet; no violence can harm you.

### 703

ONE who is humble to all creatures brings the infinite under his control; true valour is shown when a man has vanquished Śriranga. He is altogether successful, but humility was the secret of it. Tukā says, Water penetrates to the lowest depth.

### 704

METAL melts in the fire, but still continues within it; it is purified and survives as threads survive in a cloth. All false speech affects the outside alone; pride and arrogance accompany the ignorant man to his death. When the river overflows its banks, the grass, that yields to the stream, rejoices; the tree is uprooted and riven, but that weed is never crushed. The elephant's foot crushes a hostile army, but the ant lives beneath it; who would venture to accompany the insect? You may hammer a diamond as you will, but it enters either the hammer or anvil; will flint stones hold out like this, though they be far larger? Be modest and humble; this is the secret that will take you over the sea of life. Tukā says, It is the burden men carry that makes them sink.

## VI.—Peacefulness

### 705

HE is truly liberated who feels no misgivings ; shame and anxious care are bound up with fond desire. He is happy who embraces peace and solitude ; he is wretched who dwells in the world and plays the hypocrite. Tukā says, Little reflection is needed over this, but outward shows reduce one to misery.

### 706

MERCY, forgiveness, and peace—where these are, there is the dwelling-place of God. He comes running to that house and takes up his abode there. Like a glutton he continues in the spot where his praises are sung. Tukā says, Where worship is offered, the name of God brings him into our possession.

### 707

PEACE is a mistress that overrules pride ; she secures all grandeur. Men do not know this open secret and thus they bring trouble on themselves. If you allow patience to rule, you will be a hero of heroes. Tukā says, The hardest of steel is a close friend of rust.

---

## VII.—Perseverance

### 708

THE tender root can cleave the hard rock ; steady toil will accomplish its end ; there is no task so hard but patience will overcome it. A rope will cut a stone by long rubbing against it; by practice one can learn to digest poison. Tukā says, Where can a place be found to sit? You will find one, O child, in the heart of him who is supreme God.

---

## VIII.—The Service of Others

### 709

WHOSO makes himself the friend of the oppressed, recognize him for a true saint, know that God dwells in him. Mild as butter within and without, such is the nature of a good man. He who takes the unprotected to his heart, who shows to his servants and to his own son the same compassion, Tukā says, how often shall I tell you, he is the very image of the Divine?

### 710

HE who renounces all is ever clear, even as flame, that clings not to any impurity. He who is truthful in speech throughout this worldly course is like the lotus to which the water clings not. He who serves other creatures and shows them compassion, in him the supreme spirit dwells. He who utters not nor listens to criticism of others, he is Janārdana dwelling in the world. Tukā says, he who knows not the secret is exhausted by ritual observances.

### 711

MERIT consists in service to others, sin is injury done to them; there is no other way to gain anything. Truth is the true religion; observances are false, there is no other secret than this. Salvation consists in uttering his name; destruction in turning away from it. The society of the saints is paradise; the heedless and wanton man is hell himself. Tukā says, Our own gain and destruction lie clear before us; let each do as he chooses.

## 712

THE Purāṇas declare that God is the debtor of his worshippers, this is a solid assurance; show then that it is true. What more do I know? I have heard a story that Kabīr going to the market gave away his cloth; when he got home people brought money to his house, he could not take it because he had given the cloth away. God sent beggars to the house of Nāmadeva; as he had no food, he bade them plunder his granary. What historical proof of this can I bring? God paid the debts due to Venkoba. He ground his seed-grain and satisfied the beggars; Nārāyaṇa had to sow his field. Tukā says, The man who can form no resolution, he is truly wretched.

## 713

BLESSED in the world are the compassionate; their true home is Vaikuntha, but they have come here to serve mankind. They speak no false word; they are heedless of the life of the body. Tukā says, Sweet is the speech on their lips; there is room within their hearts.

## 714

FROM singing the name of Hari we must not hinder any one, nor from penance, pilgrimages, charity or vow Millions of a man's ancestors wait to see his practices accomplished; as often as one hinders him the sin of a Brāmhaṇa-murder is incurred. No efforts can release us from our own sins; what time will be left to cleanse us from this? We ought to help men in good deeds, not to deter them; then we shall have merit freely given us, even as we incur destruction in the other case. Tukā says, Believe my words to be beneficial; pleasure or pain you will have freely given you.

### 715

A BENEFACTOR is still such when he has finished his benefactions; he knows not the difference between himself and others. Take up the task you have found, to benefit yourself; do not count your own toil. Look on the souls of other men as you look on your own; be a heap of pure qualities. Tukā says, God submits himself to those whose long-stored patience is inexhaustible.

### 716

IF one consents to sin, he commits sin; both men are guilty alike. The presence of poison makes butter poisonous; nothing can be gained except you abandon wicked company. When you are passing a field, if you see a mischievous animal there, you should raise a shout and drive it away for the time. Tukā says, If you neglect this, guilt will cleave to you; for you saw the need, and you should think your trouble no pains.

### 717

ONE whose mind is for ever unquiet and discontented,—let me never meet such a man, he is a living corpse. There is a stink in his evil words, his speech is contaminated. Tukā says, He knows not the highest word of all, do good to others.

## 718

THE cow runs after her calf; thus she makes her affection visible. Affection induced by schooling will be barren, though your training may deceive strangers. When the calf is weaned, the cow will not suckle it, though you put it to her udder; she drives it away with a kick. Tukā says, Affection needs no pressure; my own experience has taught me this.

## 719

COME, cultivate this field that costs you nothing, even Viṭṭhobā's name. Here there are no pressed men, there is none to feed, no revenue to pay, no oppression, no laborious toil, you have no partner, you are quite your own master. Instead of ploughing you must call on God's name and live virtuously; there are no penalties to be incurred, no stipulations to fulfil. Here is neither weeding to be done nor a waste boundary to be left; for neither actions nor religious duties trouble you. Take divine knowledge for your drill and you need not sow any seed. No seed of accumulated merit is wasted; the crop ripens from the primal source. Yama cannot steal it away, for you have Viṭṭhala's name as watchman. You may be sure this crop will never vanish; only a madman would be anxious about it. Harvest time is ever present; not a single moment is wasted. There is a crop of infinite love; we have no room sufficient to store it. Tukā says, Whoever fails to make this his own, a miserable wretch is he!

720

WE should use our best endeavours for the afflicted; where fruit and consolation follow, there is good reason for our efforts. Such an one is gratified with a little, that he finds in his house at sunrise. What is gained without asking, that, says Tukā, is the best of gains.

---

## IX.—General

721

IF you treat another man's wife as your mother, what does it cost you? If you are not fault-finding and covetous, what does it cost you? If you sit still and call on the name of Rāma, does it bring any vexation? If you trust in the words of the saints, what does it cost you? Is it any burden to speak the truth—does it cost you anything? Tukā says, The reward of these things is God.

722

WHILE yet you have all these organs perfect, hands and feet to walk with, seek your own advantage Fail not to visit holy places. While death is yet far away, sing and listen to the song of Hari's excellent nature. Be truly faithful to him, be not deceived, stray not from him. If you have found a treasure, do not bury it; honour the saints and the assemblage of Brāmhaṇas. Let your deeds be righteous; show compassion to all creatures; when you have reached the age of youth, do not roam about after pleasures. Abandon lust and rage and greed and passion; fail not to keep company with the saints. In the hour of death no power of yours will help you; your power and wealth will be left behind. Thereafter your actions will go to testify for you. Tukā says, Such is the command of Yama.

## 723

THE mind is the only ruler in the city of our body; there he dwells with his two wives; he has sons and grandsons well endowed; he has shown his royal kindness to us. At his direction I came into this country; else I had lost my way. Of his own generous will he came to meet me, he came forward and showed me a smooth path. His fair son has come too, bringing with him four companions. He came by a side path to avoid the thorns; listen whom he brought with him. Before him went Devotion, clasping his hand; behind him came Knowledge, ascetic Repose, and good Works. To the fitful he gave a calm spirit; he made them steady and set them in the right path. How shall I tell the kindness he conferred, passing the kindness of a father and mother? By good deeds I attained the sight of his feet; he gave me freedom from fear—an imperishable gift. I was a wretched wanderer in the villages; my stomach was empty, I had no dwelling-place. Tukā's brother says, He removed all doubt from my mind.

## 724

COME, brothers, let us first revere Vināyaka, setting our heads at our teacher's feet. My voice shall proclaim well pleased the praises of Hari-Hara. This is my vocation; as a servant of God rendering him service I claim to be above others. By watering places the path is made muddy; take, O mendicants, this lip water of mine, that is cooler, more limpid, than aught else that is cool or limpid. Enjoy, O ye fortunate, this well favoured nectar of love! Conquer pride, if ye will beat down all sense of shame and honour. Embrace the faith of Śambu, if ye will; display him, but display him thus. He will not allow destruction to find a place; if the blows of adversity fall, he will protect you. Keep your faith pure and true. Say "Great is Hari-Hara"; let your voice resound. Look on another's wife as a mother, let not your mind be polluted with covetousness. Consider knowledge as a blade of grass; know that we can call such an one brave in his master's service. Spend your strength in the service of others; it is a false action to spread false opinions. It is truth that will carry you over the stream of the world; I bid you be not idle here. Perform the due rites on every Monday, on each eleventh day, sing praises, offer worship, keep vigil in Hari's name. There is merit infinite in song and dance. Again, you have been told that truly the world is not, is not. It is well to keep company with the saints; best of all is the treasure that consists in the service of praise. Walk along the good path; desire is an idle encumbrance. Tukā carries along this exalted yoke, from which depend the active life and the life of repose. Before him lies a growing sweetness; he fills his pots of worship and joyfully sets on his pilgrimage as the servant of Keśava.

725

DO but this; let the wives and wealth of others be nothing to you; be not covetous, but follow your occupation comfortably. Without any covert struggle live peacefully. Enjoy the sweet and fragrant name; be not slothful in uttering the name of Rāma. Be everybody's friend; speak no word of evil import; avoid the wicked; exert yourself for the saints. If you form any hopes apart from God, they will end in the loss of all hopes. If you foster the thirst for desire, you will never find happiness. Trust and be patient; let God be your stay. God is a source of gain and preservation for such; none will be an exception, says Tukā.

## 726

LISTEN, woman, to my words; if you fall asleep and lose your senses, you will have to wake up again; if you pay heed to me, I shall finish my message in one word. If I tell this to the public, it will not be welcome news. I tell you a means of improvement, a secret of the heart; listen to my words. Sit down with concentrated faith and pledge your hand in mine. The place in family life that has fallen to you is the best. If a false faith comes to light in your heart, no fruit will follow. If you have in your power to procure the fulfilment of one prayer, strengthen your faith by the aid of the four Vedas and eighteen Purāṇas. Be persevering. Seek not after wealth or intellect, thus you will be like one who is a happy wife for ever. This goddess of your forefathers has come to bless your old condition; if you forget her, she will yield no fruit; you will not realize what she is. Tukā says, Enjoy the happiness that belongs to you; awake to remembrance. Give ample honour to those of my company that approach you.

## 727

HE who is awake to his own true gain, blessed are his father and mother. The family that has honest sons and daughters, that family makes God feel happy. They listen to the Gīta, they contemplate Viṭṭhobā. Tukā says, Be it mine to serve them, and my good fortune will be unbounded.

## 728

LET your food and clothing be enough for existence; your dwelling a hermitage in a hut or a cave. Let nothing fetter your mind; store up Nārāyaṇa in your heart. Talk not over much, nor sit in public places; keep your mind wakeful and subdue your senses. Tukā says, We should improve our days, resolving the knot of the three qualities.

## 729

NEED I tell you in detail the rules of piety and right conduct? They proceed all from one source, pure faith in Viṭṭhala. Distinguish what is perishable from what is not; visit Pāṇḍhari. Tukā says, Here the butter of the Vedas has been churned forth.

## 730

LISTEN to the duties laid down by the Vedas; I declare their secret in the presence of the saints. The four castes sprang from one body; sin and merit were divided for their portions among them. At the threshold of the Vedas the path is laid down, that we must make no distinction of beginning, middle or end. The mango, the jujube, the fig, the bābhal and the sandal, all these have divine qualities, but all burn alike in the fire. Tukā says, Till the mind has laid aside its properties as mind, till then it is wise thou follow this direction.

## 731

We should destroy time by contemplation, dwell alone and bathe in Ganges water; worship God and walk round the tulsi; control ourselves in eating and pleasures and master the organs of sense. We should avoid slothful sleep and excessive talk; we should make the Supreme Spirit our treasure, and the feet of God our possession. These are the means to procure true gain; we should offer our body to God and take no burden on ourselves. Tukā says, This will bring us perfect joy.

## 732

Where in the past men erred through ignorance, I pardon them; now I make a rule for them! He who goes with a strange woman is no better than an incestuous wretch. Now that I have made this rule, let me see no more the man who cannot govern his mind. Tukā says, We must take our conscience for our guide; I have sworn that I will obey it.

## 733

Mercy means the protection of created beings, destruction belongs to the merciless. Sin means contempt for law; the haughty man acts after his own will. Tukā says, To keep faith alive, God aroused himself and came into the world.

## 734

SUCH as have stored up a heap of merit, such will importune God to save them; if a man is strong enough to send a weak man to Benāres, when he has gone and come back, the merit will be shared between them. When worship or dinner is going on, a sleeping man should be sound; there is boundless pleasure in doing this. To perform a sacrifice a man must take a loan, and one who is prosperous ought to grant it him; if it is lost, neither of them will be grieved. Tukā says, With full knowledge of the purpose the loan should be asked and taken; there should be no false pretences.

## 735

THIS is the blessed fruit of union, patience is in your power; first learn to control the senses. All blessings come to his house, who has made God his friend; he has a field of inheritance, which yields no worthless crop. Tukā says, Do what is right; why vex yourselves with unwise actions?

## 736

LAMENTATION increases lamentation, but a stout spirit of courage stands firm. What is it that fails in this life, my brothers? Cowardice is ruinous. Men say, "Yes, yes," but no one takes our side. Tukā says, One hour is enough if you employ it wisely.

## 737

MAKE your mind clear; from the mind comes everything that is attained; be it liberation or bondage, pleasure, satisfaction, or desire. It is the mind that creates an image; therein the mind worships itself. It is by the mind that desires are fulfilled; the mind is the mother of all things; the mind is teacher and pupil; the mind is its own servant. The mind, if it is clear within itself, confers on itself salvation or destruction. O holy and learned men, all who read or speak, listen to my words. Tukā says, There is no other God than the mind.

### 738

IF a man attacks another with a sickle and he defends himself with a sword, that is no proper conduct, we ought to cry shame on him. If one snaps his fingers at us, need we fight against him with horses and spears? You need not be a gymnast to overcome a eunuch, says Tukā.

---

## X.—Those are few who Attain

### 739

THE mahura bears not as many fruits as flowers, for there are some that drop off; there are few of them that ripen; and ere the layers are cleared, the destruction still goes on. Few are they that reach the goal, for the last stage is the hardest. Round the master are servants high and low; but he alone knows how they serve him. Few are the marksmen whose arrows reach the shining mark; you may call him your friend who reaches the farther shore. Tukā says, Who would believe in outward show?

---

## XVI

# Life under the influence of Religion

### 740

IN your passage over the sea of the world, why are you troubled? On the farther side stands the generous one, with his hands upon his hips. Embrace his feet; the Lord of the world seeks no price from you; in return for faith alone he lifts you upon his shoulder. Live in the world and enjoy it, but do not give up the two days of pilgrimage; mercy and forbearance shall visit your house with fond affection. You shall not be anxious for worldly pleasure or liberation; poverty and misery shall not vex you, says Tuka, if you embrace Pāṇḍuranga, the generous one.

### 741

SINCE they have God behind and before them, why should the servants of Hari fear? Sing his praise joyfully; let not misgivings rule your minds. What violence shall Time do to God? Tukā says, When our master gives us all, what want can remain?

### 742

I CANNOT describe this pleasure; my mouth is not sufficient to praise him. We will serve him joyfully and clasp to our heart our heart's delight. If we would compare anything to this gain, what glory is there like it? Tukā says, I will not lift up my head; I have laid it at the saint's feet.

## 743

VITTHALA, my friend, accompanies me and dwells in my soul; he pervades my frame; he is a shadow to me. He dwells on the tip of my tongue; I can speak of nothing else. The mind is prince above all organs; he too contemplates Viṭṭhala. Tukā says, Now I can never forget this Viṭṭhala.

## 744

STEP by step he supports me; my life is led on to perfection. I have found an assured place in him, and the world I have left void. My spirit goes forward on the path, I am filled in the flesh with growing joy. Tukā says, In this mortal world I have joined the pervading spirit.

## 745

MY stomach is filled, for I sat down in the row at meat; now shall we need to rely on another for salvation? We have called upon thee, so come running to us now; is there any need for us to be in doubt? What place is left now for song? A flood of joy has passed over us. Possessing the friendship of God, we can find room in it even for our foes; how can any place be void of him? All our sorrows are flown away; love has arisen in our hearts. Tukā says, Surely we have prevailed; does God ever dismiss a servant of his?

## 746

THIS is now my task, not to forget thy name to clap my hands and dance delighted by thy love. I enjoy now perfect peace behind me and before; the threefold triad of knowledge, the power of fate are swept away. How happily the day passes on the pure bank of the Godāverī, where there is God, God's temples, and crowds of saints. Tukā says, I have no cares now, I have set on thy head, O Lord of Pāṇḍhari, my burden of getting and keeping.

### 747

O LORD, thou art impatient to serve thy devotees! I have learned to trust thy feet, hence I have given up all other efforts. Sages and saints without number have learned what thy great purpose is. Imperishable is the bliss thou hast bestowed on those that have altogether ceased to heed the world. Tukā says, The spirit cannot contain that bliss; I have set thy feet in my heart.

### 748

HE has given me choice butter to eat. I enjoy this as the fruit of my past; now I look forward to this essence of faith as a support for my life. It has fallen to one who can appreciate it, no blind man that goes on groping. Tukā says, He who takes to God's service, he gains this end.

### 749

AS we recall the name, our throat is choked with emotion; love swells within us. O bless me with that lot! My hair stands erect; sweat breaks forth upon me; a flood of tears fills my eyes; my eight limbs are filled with thy love. I will consume all my body in uttering thy praises; I will sing thy name day and night. Tukā says, I will do nothing else till the end of the world; there is peace unending with the saints.

## 750

HE dwells in my spirit; I rejoice in his words, now methinks I must go to visit him. Kinsmen pine away for each other; in separation they are not severed in spirit. There is eagerness to meet again, an anxious ear for tidings, eager enquiries after the past. Tukā says, The people of Hari are the life of my life, the close associates of my soul.

## 751

I KNOW not how to withdraw my faith; I have laid my soul peacefully at thy feet. This is the spot whence all gain proceeds, such is the general view in my mind. My capital is trust in thee; once for all I am resolved to be thy servant. I look back no more on the desires of the past; henceforth I long to serve thee. I have offered thee all I have; I have crushed the pride of "I" and "mine". I find propitious the unpropitious hour; every day a holy day; I feel assured of thy mercy. The infinite one is the guiding spirit in the concern; I know no other guide. Thus I feel at peace; the gain or loss in the business concerns not me. I pass through life untouched by it. I have kept my heart aloof from all its shows. The earnest effort of the seed is a true shelter in this life; it protects from all assaults of evil. I stand aloof from the chaos of doctrine, and keep myself holy. I love the form which comes to dwell in my mind; Tukā says, I have made it the ornament of my eye.

## 752

WHAT is said with open eyes is consistent with the precepts of religion. Why should you eat dirt, to make people spit on you? What power is strong enough to consume flame with fire? Tukā says, A brave man enters the field of battle; a coward stays muttering to himself.

753

EXCELLENT, excellent art thou, O God, dearer to me than my own soul; my eyes are delighted with the sight of thy face, my ears with the rehearsal of thy attributes. The threefold fever has left all my frame, while I describe thy features, O God! The mind rises above itself, for the subject is high beyond comparison. Tukā's brother says, I cannot conceive your glory.

754

I HAVE no speech to describe thy glory; I cannot truly tell the limits of thy nature. I have laid this body, thy own gift, at thy feet; now what can I renounce for thee to honour thee therewith? I have no faith to serve thee; if I offer thee my life, behold it is thine; I cannot see anything of my own to offer thee. Tukā says, I have nothing I can rely on, to pay the debt of gratitude I owe thee.

755

IN the company of God men turn into God; they who range themselves with the world perish. Each road will take you in a different direction; will bring a different store of merit or demerit. I have shown you the two, but you cannot avoid your own; you must fulfil and be responsible for your own destiny. Tukā says, It is the innate preference that triumphs; instruction is merely a seed that is sown in you.

## 756

HE who has stored up Hari within the temple of his heart, his journeyings are over, he has followed a profitable trade. When you have gained Hari, what is left of fear or anxious care? Tukā says, Hari leaves nothing to be desired.

## 757

THE God of Pāṇḍhari has accepted me; now what can time do to me? I may count him a fly. He has cast out every source of fear; he has come to dwell instead of them himself. He permits no breath of any rival to touch me; I have learnt that he is so resolved. Tukā's brother says, Nothing need make me anxious now; I am seated on the head of an elephant.

## 758

IN faithful devotion is a mine of jewels; a deposit made by Brahma. A band of children follows their mother as a rope is drawn by a single thread. Whencesoever a king demands aught, it is brought before him; no man answers him nay. By the authority that service gives we can make our master our servant; you need spend nothing of your own. There lies ever a middle point between beginning and end, and there it looks well to have a high seat for a prince. Tukā has been suddenly exalted by faith, he is altogether become God in the world.

## 759

FOR a moment we endured evil, but now we have attained a pleasure that never wearies. In pulling down and building up we busied ourselves, but our efforts led to more and more pain.

Tukā says, There is no more going or coming for us now; we dwell at the feet of the infinite one.

760

WE have found an excellent trade, we have reached the place of desire; we have settled our faith at thy feet, our life has found repose. The happy omen has borne fruit; we have escaped from all misery; now that we have seen thee, we shall live and die no more. Good it is that I came to this place; my legs have done well to bring me here. We have turned from the life of bodily sense, we rest under the shadow of Brahma. We have found a treasure, inexhaustible, imperishable, full of bliss. We have seen even his feet who is form beyond form, the slayer of Madana. This is an old coin of the early ages; it has long been hoarded up. It has been counted strange and laid aside; we have walked over it without knowing it. Now that I have embraced him, for my soul's sake I will not leave him. Tukā says, I am weary, O leader of the world; do not let my eyes rest on another.

761

THE saints have returned me an answer that calms all fear; it has given me repose. Now that I have tasted this juice of love, I shall not abandon it; O give me, Nārāyaṇa, the gift of thy favour. If destiny grants it as our due portion on earth, we shall stand by thy feet. Tukā says, I worship thee with my lips; I sing of thee in stammering accents.

762

WE have such a treasure in the world that I cannot describe the varied joys it brings.

He is fully pleased, O God, who embraces thy feet with desire and kisses them. When thy peace is attained, fever dies away, with sin and sense of separation. Tukā says, In every direction I see no difference of parts, no distinction of "my own" and "others".

## 763

O GOD, listen to my prayer, do not grant me liberation! This joy exceeds that other, desired of men though it be. In the homes of us followers of Vishṇu the happiness of love desires to rest; prosperity and accomplishment stand with folded hands at our doors. Grant me not to live in Vaikunṭha, for that pleasure may pass away; but unspeakable is the sweetness of your name when your praises are sung. O dark as the clouds, you know not the glory of your own name. Tukā says, It is that which makes life sweet to us.

## 764

WE have received his blessing, now let us go; looking within ourselves, we can understand his weariness. Now, O Gopāla our lord, sleep undisturbed. You have fulfilled my desires; I go to my own place. We shall wake thee up through our own fond desire for thee, to save us from actions pure and impure, from guilt and suffering. Tukā says, He has given us a meal of his leavings; he has left no division between himself and us.

## 765

NOW let me contemplate this object; let it be fixed before my eyes. I will clasp it to my heart and lodge it deeply therein; I will wave round it and cast away my bodily nature. Thus shall I crown the edifice; my heart is steady now. Tukā says, Let me fall at Viṭṭhobā's fair feet.

## 766

WE have now a perfect sweetness of joy. What was lost is all made up. Pāṇḍuranga is with us and dwells within us. Now we have reached the bank, we find we have recovered all we lost in the flood Tukā says, The dream has passed away and we are awake.

## 767

NOW we shall eat together and we shall have a provision for the future left. We have made a pottage of Hari's name; Hari is allured by means of devotion. Each mouthful will yield an increasing flavour, the very nectar of Brahma. Tukā says, It tastes delicious; the tongue asks for it more and more.

## 768

MY strength was wasted by the long drag of the senses; but whatever happened I laid all before you. Let this purpose of service continue with me; thus I shall find I have passed on my burden to you. Body, speech and mind to serve you, such is my continued thought; through my faith in you I am dead to the world. Tukā says, If I shall offer earnest prayer, let Nārāyaṇa hear me!

## 769

THAT is the right faith, which burns up the store of our past. From moment to moment, I contemplate the feet of my Viṭṭhala. He suffers not my actions to overtake me, no false path to lead me aside. Tukā says, He suffers no stain, no flame of fever to dwell with me.

770

THOUGH life be sad, yet let Hari's name be proclaimed, and who will be lucky enough to be born? He must possess stores of treasured merit; that man alone deserves the privilege. Why are you waiting, O brothers! Show yourselves active and dance for joy. Eat freely of joy, leave none of it over! The joy which you behold, if we can only drink it up, then, says Tukā, what is this world of Time? A mere nothing!

771

I FEEL an inward sweetness, as I gaze upon my treasure of faith; God is my bosom-friend, the bosom-friend of this helpless creature: according to his glorious might let him adorn us with purity. Tukā says, God eats with us, to give us a share in his love.

772

LET this be my calling now, to remember thee, O Govinda. If thou wilt protect me, what need others do for me? Body, speech and mind, I will dwell at thy feet; this indeed I will do. Tukā says, I will sing of thee, with my thoughts fixed upon thy form.

773

NOW we will settle quietly in one spot; we will not cheat each other. We have given up our store of merit and retired from the world; what annoyance can follow us? O God, do you untie the bundle and see what is in it. Tukā says, I have left the world, now shall I cry out to Gopāl.

774

'TIS well that God should dwell in your house continually, that he should be with you in sitting and sleeping, in eating and stirring about. Then you could give up resolution and apprehension; merit and demerit. Tukā says, You may spend all your time with Govinda.

775

HE comes to destruction who has tormented others; but if a man has set his heart on eternal pleasures, there is an abode of all bliss in Pāṇḍuranga; in union with him is a dish of all delights cooked together. Tukā says, Perfect satisfaction is there an accomplished fact.

776

THERE is no joy like peace; all other joy is pain. Lay hold then of peace, you will cross to the further shore. When you are harassed by desire and passion and tormented in body and mind, Tukā says, lay hold of peace and the triple fever will vanish itself.

777

BE it but a little, take this pure essence that never clogs, then shall you be one with him, as the sprout is one with the seed. Let your own heart be your witness that you desire nothing else. Tukā says, In this true essence you will find your own exceeding profit.

## 778

THIS is genuine gold that was laid up long ago; we have brought to light a great man's deposit. The labourer's hand has revealed it and measured it out; I am nobody here, it belongs of right to the owner. The potter's hand creates vessels and such of them as he sends go to the kiln. Tukā says, Our life issues from Nārāyaṇa, as his splendour travels forth in the rays of light.

## 779

THIS spot is free from fear, here alone is rest; therefore I have gathered confidence, I have continued to be his servant. He has given me perfect happiness; I have tasted sweetness at his feet. Tukā says, His name is in my throat, my body is filled with love for him.

## 780

HE who contains within him the fourteen worlds has become a treasure in my throat. What is there lacking in my house? Prosperity and mystic powers embrace me at the door. He who bound the demons to his feet embraces me with both of his arms. He, who has neither form nor shape nor outline, has assumed a shape in answer to my devotion. He, who contains within him the infinite worlds of Brahma, has become as small as an ant for my sake. If I have lightly spurned prosperity and mystic powers, what should I care for the common gifts of the world? Tukā says, I have become stronger than God by putting desire away from me.

## 781

I WILL take the lot that is appointed me: *that* cannot be suitable to others. Keep to yourselves such a wish as looks for many accomplishments. If I am parted from Hari, men may scorn me. Tukā says, Make me your servant, O God; I shall do your bidding.

## 782

DANCE and song are my best refuge; I shall offer you such faith as I can. When you sleep, I must of course obey you and go; when you vanish, I shall make an offering of my life to you; I shall burst forth into joyful and harmonious song. Tukā says, You generous spirit, that give freely to the world, you in an instant will clear away my burden.

## 783

WHY have you given him away in charity, when he is in your power? Come now at once and set your feet together, I shall not let you wander. Abandon not your place, I shall not leave you free to wander. Tukā says, I shall make him respect my wishes.

## 784

NOW I delight in none but him; who is there that prates idly of another? We have learned that earthly pleasure is pain and merit is truly sin. Tukā says, I have dedicated my speech to the infinite one. There is no need of words any more.

## 785

IT is hard to express what divine knowledge is; whence can we obtain inner experience of it? The pleasure of worship leads us to renounce the world; even the ignorant hear thy praises with awakened interest. I cannot listen to other means; thy song alone I hear and sing with delight. There is peace in resorting to the forest; I am mad with desire for Hari's worship. What agent of Death has any power over us, when all day long we are rapt in this blessed meditation? Tukā says, We shall be like children playing at a dinner party, like simple children dividing up their food.

## 786

IT is good to sing the praises of God, for thus the body becomes an image of him. Through love and joy it dances and sways from side to side, till every mortal sense vanishes. The life of man is bound up in one spot; God is connected with all creatures. Tukā says, When God alone is left with us, at that season all fear vanishes.

## 787

I SEE that men are absorbed in worldly thoughts; they do not remember him. My mind retired, as it looked on the wilderness of difficulties. In this spot resounds the tumult of the sensuous organs; the spirit of selfish pride splits my head. Tukā says, O God, the efforts of desire have ruined men.

## 788

WITHOUT reflection we cannot attain to peace. The body is a mass of the three qualities; there is no good quality in it. Through love to God offer him all your gains. Tukā says, What is, is very sweet.

789

WHATEVER be the source of advice, take it to heart. Do not look at the shell, for it is the kernel that gives value to the cocoanut husk. Your wife or children or relatives may put you in mind of Nārāyaṇa. Tukā says, Admire the precious gem, though you have to thank a rag for preserving it.

790

IN this mortal world there is nothing delights us but Hari's name alone. Our mind revolts from worldly life. Our spirits are sick of it. We count gold as earth, diamonds as pebbles. Tukā says, Women will appear as bears in our eyes.

791

ONE life is now divided between two; there is now no difference between us; we and Nārāyaṇa are one; he has kept and fulfilled his promise. Tukā says, We have received the fruit of our toil; time and death have vanished away.

792

WE are now both elder and younger than ourselves; there is none in front of or behind us. We have learned to enjoy solitude and the sense of union; Hari gives us every pleasure. Tukā says, Let us embrace each other, in a spot where a third cannot come.

## 793

O GOD! where is there any grandeur in me? It was well that I was made lowly. The service of the saints is the best path of attainment; I will sing thy name joyfully. Wherever I am, no one questions me; I have perfect repose with a joyful spirit. Tukā says, Though the world should despise me, yet the Lord of the senses would be my protector.

## 794

WHAT other friend have I but thee, O Pāṇḍuranga? I long to see thy dwelling place; I count the days and nights on my fingers. I can take no pleasure in any employment. Tukā says, I am ever contemplating thee.

## 795

O GOD, I cannot succeed in finding the truth, in serving thee or in any thing at all. We must do some good deed to bring us peace; we must dwell silent in the forest. My faith will be purified at thy feet; so choose out this gift and give it me. I have learned the difference between right and wrong through thy kindly glance, O Pāṇḍuranga. Tukā says, I delight to be near thy feet; whatever thou sayest is acceptable to me.

## 796

I ASK thee not for aught, if thou fearest to be asked. Thou knowest that I look on thee expectantly; we are comforted by thy name alone. Prosperity is the gratest treasure thou could'st give, yet we count it as chaff in comparison of salvation

Tukā says, We shall go walking on to Vaikuṇṭha; we shall sit and enjoy calm happiness.

797

THIS is the task of the blessed, to measure out thy name with their speech. He grows fat upon joy; his listeners are saved along with him. He whose crop has ripened—what a store he has to eat! There is abundance for a row of feasters. Tukā salutes his teachers with reverence.

798

I HAVE entered into my own womb; I have begotten myself. My prayers are fulfilled: all desires have vanished. I have become stout and strong in the very moment when I died. Tukā looks round him and finds himself unchanged.

799

DRUM in hand, I worship thee contentedly; I have cried to mankind, "Be assured there is nothing to fear." Mirthfully I sing and dance, keeping time with cymbals and anklets. Tukā says, There is nothing to fear now; God is coming.

800

A GOLDEN pot may be filled with spiritucus liquor: say, O holy saints, what appearances can we trust to? A vessel of clay may contain nectar. Tukā says, Tell me quickly which would be better for us?

801

NOW, O mind, cease to speak of the impious; be not careless of the name of Hari. Let us never talk of them; their name brings repentance on the tongue. No one, they say, should mention a monkey's name in the morning; no one should even mention the wicked. Tukā says, Let us remember the auspicious one; then we shall be happy for ever.

## 802

I AM the servant of the servants of Hari; body, spirit, mind and speech, with them is a plenteous season of joy, billows of music from cymbals and tabors. All evil thoughts are destroyed; there is peace where the praises of Hari are sung. As he hears the praises of Hari, the impious man begins to worship. How Pāṇḍuranga stands up to behold the delights of the scene! Tukā says, Brahma and the rest possess not, possess not this joy!

## 803

LET us salute Vishṇu, our father and mother, whose image is the world, infinite, immeasurable Pāṇḍuranga; I his servant bow before him; let him listen to this one word of mine. The Veda is wearied with singing thy praise, it has sunk into silence declaring thee "not that—not that." The sages and mystics and poets cannot make an end of describing thy qualities. Tukā says, What is my speech in this matter, that it should glorify thee, O God?

## 804

WE have put off the life of the body and kept still at the feet of Viṭṭhobā, knowing beforehand what will avail us. God is already at work; neither pleasure nor pain therefore possesses our minds, since we have heard his voice. I have become separate, alone, and still; I have cast my burden upon Viṭṭhala. Tukā says, He whose mark I bear, he knows all that is good for me.

805

FOR this end I have striven, that my last day might be sweet. Now I have found repose; the motions of thirsty desire have ceased. I am amazed at the efforts I have gone through; yet they have taught me this auspicious name. Tukā says, I have taken liberation for my bride; now I will spend my life in joy and revelry.

806

LET us taste this sweetness; we have found the joy of love. Let us not waste the time; let us contemplate the feet of Viṭṭhala. Let us make a feast of worship; let us take our fill of Nārayaṇa. Tukā says, O Viṭṭhala, you have satisfied our souls.

807

I HAVE driven forth desire and grown far from passion. Now, O Hari, who can henceforth fear death? Whether I am cast away in misery or mounted on horseback, my worldly state is your province; I am heedless of it. The sense of honour and disgrace is vanished from me; pleasure and pain are rooted out. Tukā says, I have no anxiety now.

808

ONE man gives me blame and blows, another honour and worship. All are alike to me; I am far removed from them. The experiences of the body result from our connexion with it; whatever befalls me is welcome. Tukā has all he wants in Janārdana Nārāyaṇa.

## 809

AS oft as I utter the name of Viṭṭhala, I people the unpeopled world with images of dear ones. There I see my father and mother, Viṭṭhala and Rakhumai; wilderness and town are alike to me; all places are excellent. Tukā forgets pleasure and pain; he dances with fond admiration.

## XVII

# Our Attitude towards the World

## I.—The Problem

### 810

THE body is a store-house of pain, a chamber of disease, a stinking corner; there is nothing so abominable. The body is noble, a heap of delights; it is the body that has found the way and attained the primal spirit. The body is a trench of corruption, a snare of illusive desire. Sin has its roots in the body, destruction pervades it. The body is altogether pure, the treasure of treasures; it is the body that breaks the ties of the world, God dwells delighted within it. The body is a creature shapen of ignorance, a mass of evil qualities; misery dwells within it, there is no good quality found there. Give not the body pleasure, neither torture it or forsake it; it is neither good nor bad, says Tukā; turn with ardour to the worship of Hari.

### 811

BRAHMA keeps away from actions good and bad; he does not unite himself to that company. He alone knows Brahma whose own heart witnesses that he has found him. There is an identity between purity and impurity; the bundles of hay are bound with ropes of hay; there is no room for distinction of sin and merit. Tukā says, All depends on our point of view.

## II.—That we should make the most of the World

### 812

TO use the world according to the divine rules is equal to renouncing it; the great precept of religion is to hear God in the heart, first throughout our course, and last. To go to any extreme is to be deceived; restless conjecture discovers many paths. Tukā says, It is faith that procures the grace of God.

### 813

THROUGH God the whole world is related to us; when a rope is stretched, every fibre of it is tense. The world is not worthless or an object of scorn; see how each life is blended with the life of all. The joy and grief of others penetrate us, and ours them, by the same rule. Tukā says, When this pure principle dwells within the heart, the outward man is radiant with light.

### 814

I NEED not care for my body now; I will be satisfied to mete out the treasure I have. I will employ my sight on heavenly truth: I am wearied by worldly matters. Here there is nothing fit to take with us; there is nothing to spend our life on; all is false. In birth and re-birth there is no removal of pain; we are always wretched in the world. If sitting in a boat brings us to the end of our passage, who could weary himself by exerting his arms? Tukā says, This is the sum of all, pass through the world like one sitting in a boat.

## 815

IF you do what is right for your class and station, you will reach the better world. Do you not know that you can become Brahma in the body itself? If you are a learned man, you will show your learning in matters of speech; if a singer, you will sing according to the rules of art; if a Yogi, you will know all about the systems of worship, as they are laid down in the Śastras—the effort by which meditation is accomplished, the motions of the eyes. Tukā says, You do not need all these things; the saints dwell in the body and yet are free from the body.

## 816

WE are Sanyāsis, bound to one spot, lords of the senses manifest in the flesh. We have not rooted out hope and love. This portion we have received unsought; with tranquil minds we have obtained it from Pāṇḍuranga. Our staff is the erect body; we have replaced shaving by doing without it. For the postures of Yoga we choose a rag round the loins; for spiritual freedom a dwelling outside the town. We secure the chief season of time, within time itself; counting the world impure, we dwell apart. Our conduct is governed by cause and effect; our speech is ruled by the laws of speech. Listen to the rule of our conduct, to remain true to ourselves. Tukā loves not disguises, which govern the exterior, but in vain.

## 817

WHAT do *we* know about divorce from the world? We know but the name of Viṭṭhobā; among the crowd of his worshippers we dance rejoicing and beat the cymbals. What do *I* know about peace and mercy and love?—except what I find in the name and praises of Govinda. Why should I practise neglect of the body, when I am immersed in the sea of nectar? Why should I serve him alone in the waste, when I have this joy among men? Tukā says, Right well I know; Viṭṭhala goes by my side.

## 818

THE body which we possess in this world, lo! the gods covet it. We are blessed in our birth, we have become the slaves of Viṭṭhobā. In attaining this mortal life we have found being, mind and happiness. Tukā says, I shall make our first steps to Svarga a symbol of liberation.

## 819

LET mankind practise austerity and other means of attainment; let one seek the end by self-immolation; we do not follow that path, we dance at the cross-roads of Pāṇḍhari. Let others reach the supreme soul; let others declare liberation, the highest end; Tukā says, we servants of Hari reprove their fancy.

## 820

LET the body be treated with respect, for thereby we attain to all happiness, through the recitation of his name. Where there is a glimpse of Brahma, and duality has vanished, the body has become the image of Brahma. Men may perform every rite of worship, sacrifice and austerity; but they are robbed of all merit by wandering thoughts. Tukā says, Lo! perfect delight is here; cast far away all hesitation and behold it.

## 821

NOW I desire nothing else; I grasp one thing alone, him who carries us over the sea of the world, who breaks through the hard fate of re-birth. I will embrace the feet of God; my eternal wealth is in the highest one. Tukā says, Then I shall have truly used this body; I shall have dwelt in the world with perfect humanity.

## 822

THE right enjoyment of pleasures is renunciation; renunciation leaves room for pleasure; the secret is found in this paradox—otherwise from pious acts themselves would proceed impiety. What keeps God away from us, *that* is sin; so put aside false ideas. Tukā says, All else is false respect; let your heart dwell on true gain.

## 823

GOD reveals himself, while his worshippers are passing through the world; the two purposes from each side meet. By the help of God his worshippers enjoy every comfort, while God enjoys the pleasure that their company yields. The worshippers have given God form and shape; they have celebrated the limits assumed by his nature. Two natures have been created in one body, that of God and the worshipper, the master and his servant. Tukā says, Here there is no conscious difference, the worshipper is God and God the worshipper.

## 824

CHANGE your mind somewhat; it is not easy to secure a human form in your next birth;

you gain nothing by struggling for home, wife and wealth. This is a treasure you have suddenly lit on. You had to endure the miseries of the womb. It may keep you coming and going in future, or cause you to fall into hell. Tukā says, Be mindful how you possess this body, or else you will gain nothing from it.

### 825

I REJOICE that I have found the true source; I have dwelt at thy feet. In the saints' company I shall enjoy bliss; my speech shall resound thy attributes. The body shall not omit to serve thee nor the speech nor spirit; I am a bond-maid of the saints—such as I have resolved to be. I have kept my desire to live, but I have separated "myself" from "me". The image of the five elements goes on sporting of itself. I have secured this as my gain, the faith that each object will know itself. Such was the conviction of my soul, when God had removed me from this world. I have abandoned all worldly hopes in this mortal life; all paths of devotion are easy to me. O Saviour of the distressed, all else trembles through fear of thy power. I am changed into mere joy, because I am thy slave; sin and merit can touch me no more; my own wishes I have forgotten, says Tukā, by a swift motion of my soul.

### 826

NAMES and forms are the sphere that we assign to illusion, but within that sphere we have received all our knowledge of him. Marks are set for the distribution of land, but the land is never broken up; wise men alone will understand this. When a child rolls about in his mother's lap, he does not think anything of her, and his mind is free from insolence. Tukā says, The formless Hari-Hara visits us in return for faith.

827

DISEASES are born in the body, yet how could we call them our friends? Simples grow in the forest, yet how could we call them strangers? Tukā says, Such is the body's relation to us, if we make it a friend, it is a friend.

828

WHAT will it avail to live in a glen or a forest, if inward peace be absent? But are those few that have already gone there, and what have they gained? If you enter the forest, you will fall into pits; what will you gain by that? What good will ashes, mere ashes, do, if the inward parts be impure? The pious deeds of every class or station vanish, when men grow weary of them. Tukā says, These things are all snares; give up your trust in them, then it will be well with you.

829

WHATEVER we obtain should be offered to him in service. Worship in his name is an easy thing; all pride must be discarded. On this condition you may enjoy all pleasure and remain an ascetic from the beginning to the end of your life. Tukā says, If a man has no passion for pleasure, he remains unchanged.

830

WHILE his worshippers enjoy all the delights of the world, they are fortified by Viṭṭhobā.

They have neither fear nor anxious care, for the wheel-handed God protects his worshippers. Guilt and merit cannot touch them, for Śrīranga pervades all their thoughts. They are not liberated from the world; they desire to live in it. God bears all the burden of his worshippers. Tukā says, God is a friend in need to his worshippers; through him they are set free from care.

## 831

THE sages secured liberation, because they were afraid of re-birth; but we servants of Vishṇu count it an easy matter. We have made all the world into the image of Brahma; we see in it the image of Viṭṭhala. The Purāṇas admonish us to seek austere paths, but we have found an easy way to Vaikunṭha. Tukā says, Together will all mankind let us accept the everlasting pleasure of his love.

## 832

AS I have set this diversion afoot, I have not neglected any aspect of it. I find the whole world peopled with relatives; I see nothing to cause contamination of man by man. At one stroke I am made acquainted with the whole world; I see nothing anywhere different from myself. Tukā says, I am not limited by time or environment or laws of the mind; I regard nothing but God.

## 833

HE holds lightly at all times the place of Brahma, whose treasure is still Hari's name. The joys of Indra's heaven he counts not joy, but a sickness of mortality. The empire of the world is useless to him; he esteems the sovereignty of hell an evil; he counts the height of mystic power as nothing, and the joy of liberation as sorrow. Tukā says, Away from Hari he deems all life wretched.

834

LABOUR as much as suffices for your belly, but never forget Rāma; make this your chief object, to set your thoughts on Pāṇḍuranga. The desire of God is your inheritance; service rendered to him is your true gain. Tukā says, You can acquire spiritual strength by casting away all your intellect.

835

THE wife or wealth of another is contamination; he who avoids them is pure. You need not trouble to write prose or poetry; keep your mind under your own control. Bethink you of your own true interests, store up your capital of sin or merit. Tukā says, You need not go to the forest; all the world is the same to him who pervades it.

836

LO! the fruit is found within the seed, without any desire of ours. One who seeks in his folly to treat his guide as a pressed labourer, how will he break his fetters? You may call him a senseless madman. Tukā says, Preserve your body to be useful to you in future.

837

WE have no difficulty about liberation; we have it, as it were tied up in a bundle. As we satisfy our fond curiosity to know it, our soul will enjoy a full feast of devotion. How delightful it is to return anything to its owner! I, therefore, count devotion profitable and practise it joyfully. Tukā says, Bring me into the world if you will, but make it for me a scene of joy.

838

THROW some food to your desires, so far as suffices to keep you alive. This will prove that Nārāyaṇa has entered you; for peace of mind is the mark of his presence. I meditate continually on this theme, duly reflecting on the distinct nature of the self. Tukā says, If we turn to adore him, we shall find that he is near us.

839

WHAT has the body to do except to secure love? Those appropriate duties which have fallen to my lot I will perform. I will call upon Nārāyaṇa, for this act cannot be controlled by the limitations of the body. The Lord of Pāṇḍhari, when he hears, will run. The frame of the seven senses and five activities is formed by destiny. Now that it exists, let it be; do thou, O God, guard it that it may be happy. 'Tis well that we have found union; let us keep our enlightened vision. Tukā says, I take no rest.

## III.—That we should renounce the World

840

THE mind is captured by the tempting world, it goes running after it. He who can rescue it is a hero, the one stout warrior in the world. It surprises or bears us down; I fear for your fate. Tukā says, This enemy has ruined many a wise man.

## 841

WHEN you enter the world, do this one thing—walk gradually in the path of liberation. Sharp are the pains and penalties of hell: how is it you fear not that terrible pit? There is no pity there, when Yama has drawn the soul out of the body. If a stray animal is found in the corn, when caught it is punished like a thief. If you pay nothing, how can you reach the goal? You pass along a road which will bring you back. If a man comprehend not, how can he listen? He will be carried off like a prisoner arrested. He may be one who cannot endure to go barefoot; but if he has transgressed, they will drag him across beds of thorns, and make him embrace hot pillars. He may tremble at the river of hell, but he will have to pass through it; he shall not be drowned as he passes, but Yama's rod will fall on him. Hungry and thirsty beyond endurance, so shall they keep him for ever. They shall keep his body cool that the fire consume it not, yet roll him about on a red-hot floor. So make an effort; resign the world while you can; repeat his name if you can; enjoy the sweetness of faith, says Tukā.

## 842

TUKA takes a stick and fiercely he assaults his body. He has caught it and laid it low in a burying-ground, yea, even a mound where men are burned; he has made it pay for all the luxuries it enjoyed. He felt no fear, knowing that it is God who feels pleasure or pain in us. It was put to this extremity to test the mind. Tukā says, Experience is necessary in all things: a coward is chastised.

843

LET me not pray for children or for wealth for any one. By sharing in these things I should fall into misery, for this is the end of both. Let not my ears covet praise or blame, arising from any heed to such things. Tukā says, They prevent us from finding God; we are snared in the net of desire and illusion.

844

WE are amazed at our undue passion for the world—how have you led us to believe it is genuine? This faith of ours is inconceivable to others: we must make our own souls witnesses of it. We see the many in the one and the one in the many; each receives his assurance from his own inclination Tukā says, You know how to create this belief and dispel it; you are skilled in this matter, O God!

845

WHEREVER you dwell, meditate on his name, publish it widely abroad. My master will assuredly set you free; we his servants have solemnly declared this. In singing his praises we discern no man's merits or faults; it is love that brings the wheel-handed God under our control. Tukā says, I find the world very bitter; my hair stands on end; my throat is choking.

## 846

TAKE not on your head at all the burden of the world; devotion itself compels you to cast away everything. To make the beggar's calling a trade is the act of a fool; how can a man live in the bazaar, and put away desires from him? A poet without the gift is a man of milk and water. Tukā says, Be either a sage or a downright clown.

## 847

WE dress up all the parts for the drama; we assume disguises, but we cannot change the inward man. We have set going this varied game to amuse ourselves; but we know what our primal form is. A slab of crystal remains distinct from its attributes, though it looks as if it were red or yellow. Tukā says, We shall sever ourselves from this world and disport ourselves at peace.

## 848

ONCE for all I have performed a ceremony of purification, severing myself from the world; I have renounced the fault known as selfish desire. I have bathed myself in repentance; I have offered a sacrifice of my body, where the life of the one is lost in that of the many. Thither Tukā is drawn, dancing with fond devotion.

## 849

A JEWEL becomes a woman when her husband sees her wearing it. If a loose woman bedecks herself, every one laughs at her. If a man is a hero, his speech is a graceful ornament upon him. Tukā says, Life without something at stake is contemptible.

## 850

TRUTH is ever welcome; through false notions faith departs; through the gift of your favour we know the pure from the impure gold. If a pleasure seeks me out, I will renounce it forthwith. Tukā says, O God, your service is an ointment to the eyes.

## 851

WHAT purpose remains unfulfilled that I should trouble thee any longer? For thy name's sake I need suffer no loss of life or aught else; it recurs easily to the mind. It brings no pangs, nor inflicts starvation; nor demands wealth in cows and buffaloes. O worshipper, all this you know well: why then do you believe in wordly wealth? Tukā says, People break away from thy feet, through the love of the fleeting world.

## 852

GOD has given us a full meal; the world has turned bitter to us. We shall be satisfied to bursting with the joys of Harihara. He draws men to him, so strong is he. Tukā says, No other appetite can arise.

## 853

OUR curious desires have created the world and bring pain on ourselves. It would be well to end the game; if you prolong it, you prolong the noise. If, to learn what fear is, you fill your heart with fear, Tukā says, O mind, you will be turned yourself into living fear.

854

THESE are all devices of the belly; we must not look upon them wistfully; the object of desire remains such to the end. From things material how can spiritual gains proceed? The heart remains desirous, but it asks in vain from this idle hypocrite. Such men rehearse the life and actions of God; but these are idle arts to captivate others. Tukā says, If secret desires reside in the spirit, then deceiver and deceived go to hell together.

855

A LOW man's wisdom bids him worship his body, procuring wanton pleasure and sweet food. He calls it piety to tend his person; but what control has he over his body? It vanishes in a moment, before he is aware; he may swallow food, but he cannot control his body. Tāmradhvaja sawed his body asunder, Śibi cut off his flesh; Śuka and others retired to the forest. Tukā says, When Janaka ruled, he had one of his legs consumed by fire.

856

DESIRE drowns the light within us; how can doubt fail to be a sin? We should realize this for ourselves; if the mind is quite clear, it will testify to it. What was pure and stainless and enlightened was defiled by imposing on it form and name. A blind man cannot walk like one who sees; this is what Tukā says.

857

IF honour increases, do not repose on it; love of the five elements will make you as one of them. You must torment your own mind, or the organs of sense will drag it after them. When a man mingles with another, he will contract his colour through assimilating his own to it. Tukā says, God dwells apart and unconcerned; in human souls a spirit of change is ever at work.

## 858

WHEN we view the illusion from outside, we set ourselves free from fear or influence; we know no distinction of self or other. If we purchase truth, we get a full return of our money; we do not like an unprofitable business. If we rub the spot outside, we aggravate an inward pain, and we must open a passage by burning or cutting. Tukā says, This is no place to glorify ourselves; God has made himself witness and will decide the case.

## 859

SINCE the three aspects of knowledge accompany each other, nothing can remain with one man for ever. One object passes away and another takes possession of his mind. The power of time lies all around us; we cannot run away from it nor fight against it; but if we cry out, Hari mercifully takes us on his shoulders. Whether a man be sinful or meritorious his powers are directed by Śrīpati. Let us go to this Lord of all powers and implore him. Tukā stands on the further bank, and hence he distinguishes this light. There are gourds and plants and rafts floating in the stream; push them on.

## 860

THEY take a lamp and go looking for darkness The wonder is they believe they have found it. We servants of Vishṇu fear not time and death; we have left the mirage of the world; it never overtakes us. If you raise a cloud of dust, you defile the sunlight; O ill-starred creatures, cannot you perceive this? Tukā says, I am covering up fire with a heap of straw; my words are idle.

## 861

WHEN a man is repeating God's name, he is a low wretch if he suffers anger to approach him. If you wear ashes on your person, then do not stare round you at the world. We are surrounded by the wicked; we have to eat along with them. Tukā says, He attains Brahma who leaves actions behind him.

## 862

TIME governs only the changes of the world; therefore let us clasp the feet of Viṭṭhobā. All merit proceeds from him, with him it lies to destroy all sin. Ere time ceases to be, every soul shall be pleased; families of mankind shall be released. Time and death and the pangs of mortal life shall perish, through the utterance of his name alone. Tukā says, You need renounce nothing; I tell the secret to those who receive it with faith.

## 863

CURSED now be name and form; these are the guilt that I carry bound up with me. Let us take the dust on the saints' feet to rid us of this burden of clay. Pride in worthless claims was bringing me to misery. Tukā says, Our joy in the formless is true and beyond all names.

### 864

LAMPS and drums and dinner are ordered; the bride is arrayed and handed to her husband. The husband takes his bride home; the bridegroom is worshipped and bathed. The father and mother are complimented; everyone begs them to finish the programme. "Let us go on with the presents and bathing."—O why do you forget the spirit within? He besieges the marriage guests with pleasures; he bathes them till they look like vessels dipped in oil. Tukā says, You are collecting spittle; you are making a good provision for hell.

### 865

CURSED be all that severs me from thee; it is thy feet that my efforts seek to gain. Do thou, O God, help me now; set me free from all that holds me and take the service offered thee. Sensual pleasures have inflicted a strange disease on me. Or whence comes this disgust from all these things? Tukā says, Let thy own be on thy own head; I shall mix no more with the affairs of the world.

### 866

IT is only the base who turn back from their words; not so does Nārāyaṇa. He has accepted me now; his strength will account me no burden. I have no longing for the world; for I see God as all in all. Tukā says, I will sing your praises; I will not allow any purpose to come between us.

867

EVERY form is destroyed by time; the name of Hari alone is beyond its power. I have lodged the name of the Eternal in my throat; it is life stored up in my heart. Bodily health is a false impression, a mirage; it will perish. Tukā says, God has made me weary of the very name of the disguises of the soul.

868

IF you whirl round yourself, the world seems to be whirling round you; if you stand still yourself, everything seems to be steady. If you shout in a forest place, you hear a second sound arise. The moon moves forward because the clouds move. Tukā says, The impression is false.

869

HE has turned his back on the world, who cares no more for wealth or wife. He who has ceased to distinguish auspicious and inauspicious joy and anger, he has become Janārdana in the world. Tukā says, He who has renounced the body has nothing further to heed.

870

THE stone must suffer the strokes of the chisel ere the true form within it is brought out; then it will be valued as a genuine article. We must hand over the body to undergo what it has merited, and expelling the power of the past over it. To rise in splendour you must learn to loathe the pleasures of the elements, and you must humble yourself. Tukā says, What becomes then of the world? You must turn yourself into what you esteem.

## 871

I WILL embrace this supreme joy; if I place my treasure in thee, all separation between us vanishes. Thou hast spoken the word; my mind is at rest, my spirit rejoices; two-fold is the delight of thy love. Thou art the ornament of the world; the head of Vaikuṇṭha; my own profit is perfect in thee. I have dismissed the illusion of sense, the life of business and intercourse with men; the world repels me altogether. Tukā says, Let Viṭṭhala be mine; I care for nothing else.

## 872

I SET my heart on things needless; cursed be the robe that I wrapped them up in! It is good now that I have seen myself what was truly worth seeing. I have learned by profit what loss is; let me keep the two distinct. Tukā says to himself, Whence all this vain glamour of the world?

## 873

CONTEMPLATING him, I have stood calm and still; but how long is this to last? Beyond this comes a time for absolute silence, when there is no room for speech at all. I made what haste I could; I allowed no suspicion to remain within me. Tukā says, With renunciation I have renounced all, so that illusion will never return upon me.

## 874

WE ought to call nothing here our own, but this speech of ours is wild, and sets us chattering. This mass of the five elements, this body, is truly not ours. Tukā says, Illusion is ever walking backwards.

### 875

WISE men become as senseless as brutes when they take to chewing bodily pleasures. Setting their desires on objects of desire, they have ruined the spiritual essence of the soul. Solid food they have prepared and handed over to others, like a foolish cook who gets buttermilk for himself to drink. Tukā says, This body of ours is a great danger and source of destruction.

### 876

DESPISE dogs and pigs for their bodies, but show them respect for their souls. By so doing I have learned to sweep away "I" and "mine"; if you love the world you will be caught in the net of re-birth. Despise home, wealth and country; embrace spiritually beasts and trees. Tukā says, Let me utter neither "I" nor "mine"; those are true saints who avoid these words.

### 877

DESIRE and thirst and passion are seeds of dishonour; by destroying them a man makes himself worshipful. An unsteady man wins no honour, though he walks to the homes of others; it is hard to set one's eyes on a man who is steady. Tukā says, I address nothing to others, for my words would be wasted; the wise alone will value my words.

### 878

WHAT was impossible has come to pass, I have seen thy feet; now shall I go back into the world, O God? Long had I hoped for this; now I enjoy the fruit of my efforts. How long shall I live in hope of worldly prosperity? Hereafter let this snare be cut off. Those who succumbed have altogether vanished; what chance of salvation they had they gave up. If I go on crossing mountains of difficulty, I shall never cease to be born again. Tukā says, I shall cling to the robe of Pitambar; O God, do thou carry me over the sea of the world.

## 879

I HAVE crossed over; I have justified my confidence; I have spoken thy name; I have dismissed the world. I am tied to nothing now. Tukā says, There is nothing left now.

## 880

DESTINY has enabled me to reach him; now I do not forget him for one moment. With even feet he stands on the brick; the saints have told us how we may know him. Now we will put aside all worldly affairs. This shall be the end of our diligence. Tukā says, We will destroy the revolutions of re-birth, brought about by sin and merit.

## 881

O PĀNDURANGA, you have destroyed my affection for you, but now whisper in my ear the nectar of devotion. So I have left nothing of the world remaining; I have reached the vital principle all at once. I look back no more; whatever is left of the world has in truth no real existence. Tukā says, If my spirit should be perverted, my tongue will utter nonsense.

## 882

O SPIRIT of mine inured to shame, how long shall I instruct thee? Pursue nothing. The enjoyment of society brings misery. Whether any praise or blame or love thee, care not for the pain or pleasure of this. Is it not because of this nature of thine that the mystics assume one portion and remain still? Tukā says, Consider well, my spirit, and make thyself harder than adamant.

## 883

O MY spirit, why dost thou not enter the assembly of Hari's worshippers? Go where all your bones will be restored to you; you are wasting your life in vain. All things that entangle you here will desert you in the last hour. Tukā says, Consider what is true gain.

## 884

LET me cry Viṭṭhala, see Viṭṭhala, make Viṭṭhala into my own soul. Through this eager longing my soul has found satisfaction; it returns to the earth no more. He has released me from the knot; he came and embraced me. Tukā says, My body is filled with Viṭṭhala; I have emptied the hour of anger and lust.

## 885

SPITTING on thoughts of honour and pride, we sing thy praises. I have grown heedless of the body; I care for one thing alone. Wealth and poverty are the same to me; I have weighed them and set them aside. Tukā remains holy, and far from the stain of the world.

## 886

WE ought not to take any burden away from God; if we remember him through hunger and thirst, it is well even so that we have been made to think of him. To have no trouble in sight separates us from Śrīpati. Tukā says, I look on all prosperity as a source of pollution.

## 887

I HAVE no work; see I have nothing more to do! I will go through such movements as present themselves, sitting still like a spectator. Through their needless appetites, mankind of their own will undergo trouble. Tukā has set himself apart; he lives in the world, yet he lives apart from it.

# XVIII

# The Saints

## I.—Their Character

### 888

THE servants of Hari are like Hari; free from fear, desire, anxious care and hope, they heed not the world; they are girded up with the strength of devotion. They have clasped his feet and abandoned the world; they need not honour perishable goods. His name in their throats is a draught of nectar; they need nothing else. There is infinite room for compassion within him; the lord of the world is like a deep sea. The grip of lust and anger cannot be loosened; these are demons that press us into their service. They are strong enough to vanquish death; humble enough to retire before all men; generous enough to give themselves away; possessing all accomplishments, they claim no knowledge. The world is their servant; liberation waits their time. They send prosperity and perfection wandering; yea, the people of Vishṇu will not touch them. They look on birth and death as a dream; they cannot tell their own from what is other men's. Tukā says, With increasing delight I tell the story of their love.

### 889

SUCH are the saints who meet us on this path that the fetter of the world is broken at the sight of them; they are ever filled with the joy of true mind and true being; we shall honour them as hallowed sources of liberation. Faith is their all-sufficing principle; nothing breaks their repose; they crush the spirit of infidelity. By their mercy to all creatures they destroy the root of hatred; they treat all as brothers,—friend, foe, or child of their own. Purify your mind, body and speech; beholding his form everywhere, salute it Be humble with your whole heart, renouncing all presumptuous pride. Be not greedy of gain, nor scrupulous about honour; desire and love are false. One who knows all, yet keeps as still as though he knew nothing, such a one the saints come suddenly to visit. Be truly faithful, and toil not after wealth, then the saints will ever visit you. Thus says Tukā, sick of pride of learning.

## 890

OH brother! let us bow to those who have ceased to heed the sensations of the body, to those who entreat God, to those who visit holy places, to those who come to those who see them off, to those who trust in the speeches of the saints, to those who serve their teacher in faith, to those who cherish their parents, to those who always speak the truth, to those who perceive the pain and joy of others, who guard them from hunger and thirst; to those who have won merit by service to others; to those who govern the organs of sense. Tukā says, Let us bow down to the servants of Hari, for their every desire is fulfilled.

## 891

THE servants of Vishṇu are the only stout warriors in the world; guilt and merit cannot touch them. Sitting and sleeping, Govinda is with them; he is with them in their thoughts. They wear the widening lines on their foreheads, fair garlands on their necks; time and death humble themselves before them. Tukā says, They wear the ornaments of the shell and the wheel; in their mouths is the nectar of his name.

## 892

WE are stout warriors, we shall maintain a sturdy fight; we have dealt heavy blows to sin, we have crushed it. There is a loud uproar, the warriors march shouting on; they wear the shell and wheel for ornaments, with tulsi garlands on their necks. Their arrows bear the name of Rāma; they have smeared themselves with white Gokula clay. Their standards and ensigns wave gaily; their poles bear the image of Garuda. Tukā says, We have conquered time and found repose; we have received all the delight that is due to us.

## 893

WE servants of Vishṇu are softer than butter, yet we can cleave adamant; though dead we are alive, sleeping we are awake; we will give you whatever you ask for. We are generous enough to give away the very cloth from our loins, yet we will put a knave to confusion. We are more loving than father or mother, yet no enemy can deal out such destruction. What do we care for the sweetness of nature? Even poison is weak against us; what bitterness is there in it? Tukā says, We are all sweetness; we satisfy the several desires of all men.

## 894

BLESSED are the pious, for their heart is pure. The saints worship the visible God, they testify that they have faith therein. They know nothing of rules and prohibitions; their hearts are filled with devoted love. Tukā says, O God, you must take a form responsive to their faith.

## 895

THEY dance and clap the hands and roll on the earth in a transport of love. My friends are the saints, the simple and faithful people of Hari. They feel no shame; they have no concern with this world. Tukā says, They feel their throats choking; their eyes are filled with tears.

## 896

WE pretend to possess the source of all happiness, but we have no bread to eat. We talk as though we had pillows, mattresses and bedding, but we have not a loin cloth to put on. If you ask us, we tell you we live in heaven, but we have no dwelling of our own place. Tukā says, We are lords of the three worlds, but we cannot give any one what he needs.

## 897

WE servants of Vishṇu have no hopes of any other; we know not why these wretches continually censure us. Wherever we be, our minds are at peace in themselves. Tukā says, O God, we will make thy service our calling.

## 898

WORSHIP those for whom worship is meet; the people of Hari who stand up to serve him. They are moulded into images of him whose praise they sing. They have forgotten their bodies; joy has entered into them; pride is vanished; they have bidden farewell to shame and honour. There are no tidings with them of lamentation, desire or anxious care. Tukā says, They are friends of Viṭṭhobā; they are all like him.

## 899

THE dwellers in Vaikuṇṭha watch and wait for your worshippers; they feel no pangs of birth and death; they have no future world to think of. Blessed are the servants of Hari; mortal birth they can easily bear, while Brahma and the rest still desire their presence, and all sacred places long to see them. Yama desires earnestly to hear thy praises; he stands with folded hands waiting for them day and night. Prosperity and perfection seek out the worshippers of Hari uninvited; liberation and union are waiting for them. Wherever they stand they are comforted by the joy of love; many too have been saved by them, who were low and guilty wretches. All beings long to see them; while they themselves are unmoved; blessed, says Tukā, are all they who behold him.

## 900

THIS self-controller is the elemental substance of their frame; their life is a boon of love from him. The embrace that unites the saints to him is a delicate bond. In this they find auspicious seasons, achievements and wealth. Tukā says, Night and day he is the food on which they feed.

## 901

CYMBALS and drum in hand, they dwell in Vaikuṇṭha. If you will go with them, make haste and get your provisions together. Where they pass along shouting, there let your spirit dwell. Tukā says, They go along crying "Viṭṭhala."

## 902

WE wear the jewel of Kṛishṇa on our necks, to be a light for the world. We will divide our portion with each other; there is true order in the devotees of Vishṇu. We will look with mockery on Brahma and the other gods, but joyfully on our fellowmen. Tukā says, Among the company of men, we are stout and strong warriors.

## 903

BLESSED are they who delight in God; they enjoy bliss and ever growing happiness, the very height of love; I salute those who possess salvation as it were a treasure tied up in a bundle. Tukā says, All my hopes are centred on Hari's servants.

## 904

IF you have nothing, still offer him anything you can. If you are called his servant, no one will impress you. Get yourself styled a servant of this great master, in any post whatever. Tukā says, In this way you will make yourself master of many.

## 905

THEY will play rejoicing on stringed instruments and drums; for they have conquered the spirit of selfish desire; they have made their head the footstool of God. There is no room left for destroying time, no place for anxious care. Tukā says, Now they will easily go forward to Vaikuṇṭha.

## 906

IF he be absent from the mind, he must be so; still let him dwell in our speech. Let life end in the name and praise of Viṭṭhobā. By dissimulation or any means whatever let me gain the name of a servant of Hari. Tukā says, Hari will some day take care of me.

## 907

AT a meeting the speaker is entitled to respect, to sandal-wood and rice and articles of worship; among the audience, though there be an ascetic, yet he has no right to these things. The head is the highest member of the body; hands and feet come in their appointed place; let all observe the established rules. If a son takes charge of the throne, his father must obey him; this is a rule for all and all should accept it. If a stone be placed on the highest seat, it should not be treated as a common stone; though the instruments of worship be of gold, yet compared with it they are humble. Sometimes anclets are made of gold, sometimes crowns of alloy. That which is the source of power, that is the centre of grace; servants are honoured for the sake of their master; they enjoy his name and his wealth. Tukā says, Understand this is why the saints should be respected.

## 908

A MIGHTY man may be caught in a snare and laid in prison; such an hour may come; all things are in the hands of time. He who gave alms may come to ask them, may beg a beggar to protect him. Tukā says, You know it, O Nārāyaṇa! why should I tell it you?

## 909

HE is not fatigued with guarding the three worlds; what matters our burden to him? When a toad lies in the hollow of a stone, who puts food in its mouth? Birds and serpents gather up no store, yet the infinite one protects them. Tukā says, If I lay my burden on him, my sea of mercy will not disappoint me.

## 910

HE who worships truly, what fear can touch his soul? As he converses with his lord, his joy increases more and more. If you perform the duties of religion, then critical seasons can be endured. Tukā says, It is the great Viṭṭhala who controls my speech.

## 911

IN the village of the saints there is a full harvest of love, there is no pain or disquietude. I will live there as a beggar; they shall cast a morsel to me. In the village of the saints there is an excellent treasure ,Viṭṭhala is all their wealth and store. The meal of the saint is a draught of nectar; they sing his praises continually. The business of the saints is to keep a mart of good advice; they buy and sell the delight of love. Tukā says, There is nothing to compare with this, so I have gone to them as a beggar.

## 912

IN song, in thought, in sleep, sitting, lying, eating, waking, dreaming, whoso forget all but Viṭṭhala, whoso make Viṭṭhala their ornament, their jewel, their sources of delight and the stay of support, Tukā says, they have become Viṭṭhala themselves; all notions of being others have vanished.

## 913

STOUT and sturdy are Viṭṭhala's followers; time and death fall at their feet. They raise a shout of triumph; mountains of guilt are burned up. Grace, mercy, and peace are the arrows in their hands, invincible. Tukā says, They are the only true warriors in the world.

## 914

IF a diamond survives, when you place it on an anvil and strike it with a hammer, that stone will fetch its price; while a false one is crushed. That is a real gem, which, if you bind a thread upon it, will not suffer it to be burned. Tukā says, He is truly a saint who can endure the blows of the world.

## 915

THERE are drills of Europe and iron sickles, but their property and worth are various. Footsteps and images are alike of stone, but they differ in degree of honour. Tukā says, Even so the orders of saints differ.

## 916

WHO is there mightier than Hari, the infinite one? We have acquired the might of this mighty one; we can wield authority over all men. Tukā says, We are prodigal of our lives, therefore we are dearly loved by Govinda.

## 917

WHEREVER I may go, my destiny will not be changed; that supreme gain I shall only procure in the company of the saints. If I had had perfect merits to help me, no source of disunion could have arisen. I need neither fortune, wealth, child, nor wife; the best thing is to dwell close to the saints' feet. Tukā says, Give me this for a freehold inheritance; let me sacrifice my life to win the company of the saints.

## 918

WE beggars are lucky folk; thieves are frightened when they come near us! When we go to beg for a morsel, the dogs look after the houses. Let us be proud of such a career, otherwise our labour is in vain; we must find our dignity in it. By our toil we have built ourselves an imperishable house. Our house needs the castor oil and wild cotton tree—no other timber can bear the load. We have wealth and grain in every house, for we live on charity. Who would be at the trouble of keeping cattle, when he gets everything without anxiety? Cowdung makes our walls bright enough; we can build stands for the tulsi plant. Tukā says, O God, you have driven out all desire.

## II.—Their Services to Men

### 919

WHERE the servants of Vishṇu dwell, the country is blessed, the region is full of merit; the messengers of Yama tell him that if it were wanted as medicine, sin could not be found there. The earth feels the weight of pillared images; it resounds with shouts of victory. Unbidden springs up amid the people the fond love of Govinda. There are groves of tulsi plants, and store of paintings, and all the happy store of Vaikunṭha. Tukā says, No season of want ever visits that land.

### 920

IF I wish to invite the saints, I can find no materials to entertain them; O thou who art the soul of the universe, tell me how to serve them fully. It needs an ocean to contain an ocean; how can I become vast enough to receive one? Tukā says, It were well to call oneself sincerely a suppliant.

### 921

SINCE we should be merciful to all creatures, we should treat each other mercifully, yet honour the saints with your whole heart. If you disdain my preaching, you will enter the path that leads to hell. The diamond, the parisa, and the moharā exist along with other stones, but there is no such kinship between the saints and common men. None is baser than he who esteems alike a village stream, the Ganges and the sea. There are constellations without number; but they cannot be counted equal to the sun and moon. Tukā says,

That which is not malleable is not Phirangi iron, it is cast-iron.

922

IT is well to remember how short life is; the speeches of the saints are like flowers, gentle, soft and pleasant in flavour. When you have heard them with your ears, they are easily digested in the mind. Tukā says, A desire for them is immediate gain.

923

THE servants of Vishṇu by their company have cleansed me from sin; who can look them in the face? They are brave and stout. Impurity grows pure before them; heaps of love and joy spring up; you could not find sin though you needed it for medicine. Tukā says, They have made the earth into Vaikunṭha.

924

THE sun, a lamp or a diamond shows visible objects; objects invisible are revealed by the saints. My powers are too feeble to describe their glory. Brahma and the rest do not truly know it. As sandal cools the fevered frame, so their company drives out the three qualities. Our parents cherished our bodies, but the saints drive away from us illusion, age and death. Sweet food drives away hunger, but the speech of the saints dispels the pain of birth. Tukā says, We should draw near them, though they summon us not, to approach their feet with faith.

925

THE pleasure which the saints feel reaches God; therefore, I serve them. What powers have I to describe this glory? He who is void of form has assumed form and shape in them. I throw myself down in worship before them. Holy floods desire them continuously, to purify themselves. What to them are the eight miraculous powers worth? He allows nothing to stand in their way. Tukā says, They are a jewel of glorious power; I will dwell close by their feet.

### 926

IN holy places we find water and an image of stone, but in the society of good men we have the actual presence of God. Meeting with such, if we offer them our body, that body is blessed. At holy places it is faith that yields fruit; though the ignorant are tempted to visit them. Tukā says, When our sin vanishes, as it vanishes, we learn what a fever it was.

### 927

HOW can I be grateful enough to the saints?—they keep me continually awake. How can I pay off this debt, O God? If I gave up my life at their feet, it would be too little. Their conversation is always edifying; they instruct me at the cost of great toil. Tukā says, As a cow keeps her calf in mind, so they watch over me.

### 928

BY embracing the saints, salvation and union with God are attained; such is the glory of the saints; speech can go no further in describing it. All holy places and seasons are at their feet. Tukā says, The service which is done to them reaches God.

## 929

UTTER the names of the saints and gain merit thereby; I bid you depart not from these names; they bring great gain without toil. Faith in the feet of the saints is a haven of repose. Tukā says, Call on the names of the saints, and your sins will disappear.

## 930

IN this cause I will spend my breath; listen to my message! I love the people of Hari; to converse with them is perfect peace. As for the tales of strangers, I ask not who or whence they are. Tukā says, These are true heroes, pure in spirit every one of them.

## 931

IT is a blessed season when you have met the saints and embraced their feet. The knot of doubt is unravelled; there is calm within the heart. There is a ford through the stream of life established, cross over by this gracious favour. Tukā says, What can surpass his glorious generosity?

## 932

NOW destiny breaks into light; all anxious cares are chased away. The sight of the saints has brought this gain, I have seen him of the lotos navel. I will store this up as a treasure in the casket of my heart. Tukā says, It is a buried treasure, which I have gained by this faith.

## 933

AMID a pile of pots, one is used for cooking, another to hold filth, such are the different lots of men, as destiny appoints them. There are diamonds and common stones in one mine together; but how could the other stones possess the lustre of the diamond? Tukā says, The one is set on the head; the others are used for a staircase.

## 934

I HAVE roused myself; I have entered this company of Hari's worshippers; there the crowd of devotees make the song of triumph resound. The sinful impediment of sleep has vanished. Tukā says, In that spot is the moist shadow of his mercy.

## 935

IF thou wilt meet any one, meet the saints, O mind; think of nothing else. With complete faith they deem God their treasure, they talk of nothing else. If thou wilt live with any, live with the saints; if thou wilt sit anywhere, sit with them; if thou wilt go anywhere, go to their dwellings; there thou shalt have repose. Tukā says, The saints are a sea of joy; O mind, satisfy thyself with them for ever.

## 936

MAKE me a servant of the servants of saints; then, O Hari, I will gladly return to the womb till the end of time. Let my station be humble, but let thy name be ever in my mouth. Tukā says, Let all my thoughts be employed on service to the saints.

## 937

WHEN shall I hear the saints tell me "Pāṇḍuranga has accepted thee"?—after that my spirit will be at rest. Therefore, I gaze upon their feet and faces; this is my great hope; this is what I trust to; I practise no laborious means of attainment. Tukā says, I shall be confident, I shall feel assured that I am saved.

## 938

I PRAISE you more than I have any right to do I cannot see what my own worth allows. I am your feeble servant, O ye saints; keep me at your feet and preserve me. In uttering the spell of Rāmakṛishṇa—Hari, in the feet of Viṭṭhobā is my delight. Tukā says, I eat the morsels you have left; because I trust in your forgiving nature.

## 939

TO-DAY all joys have turned to visit us; we have seen the lotus feet of the saints; we remember them continually; this reason has satisfied our longings. Tukā says, Our speech is confounded; henceforth our busy minds are hushed.

## 940

ONE is safe when he calls himself a servant of the saints; a ready and comfortable alms awaits him. It takes toil to form a deep impression; a slight error of principle brings destruction. To cook a meal, there must be materials ready; when these are well arranged, the dinner is pleasant. Tukā says, It is easy to make up tales, as long as the battle-field of impressions presents itself before the eyes.

941

WE will turn these asses into horses, as long as they stand in our presence; behind our backs they will tear our shoes like mischievous dogs. Yes! we will convert hypocrites into honest men. Tukā says, We will purify dirt, if only it will show itself before us.

---

## III.—The insignificance of Caste in Comparison of Virtue

942

A VAIṢHṆAVA is one who loves God alone, who puts no trust in anything else; body, wealth and his fellow-men are but a straw to him. Though he be afflicted, yet he fails not in his purpose, because he is thoroughly resolved. Tukā says, His caste may be anything at all.

943

WHAT is akin to the devil? A cruel heart; a cruel and grasping spirit in man. The source of virtue is in the inner parts; caste and family cannot ensure it. To taste poison, to distinguish brass from pure gold, you need no evidence but a particle of it. Tukā says, How good it is to come in contact with the truly well-born! there is nothing but butter stored up in them!

## 944

ONE who sells his daughter, his cow or his sermon, he is rightly called a low-caste wretch. The standards of goodness are merits and demerits; God considers not a man's caste. Tukā says, They who do unlawful deeds, these are they who go down into hell.

## 945

THE water of the Ganges cannot see pollution, yet it may do when carried in a pot; what is lofty and what is lowly are not the same, it is pollution that shows the difference between them. Is the world divided into parts to hold the various castes and low castes? Tukā says, Various grains of corn are distinct only till they have been fried.

## 946

SHAME on a Brāmhaṇa who is void of devotion! Blessed is the Vaishṇava who is a *chambar*; his lineage is pure on both sides. So the Purāṇas have decreed; this is no private opinion of my own. Tukā says, Cursed be their self-conceit; may I never behold a bad man of that kind!

## 947

THEY are my friends and comrades who remember the feet of Viṭṭhobā; others I respect only for form's sake, because they are God's creatures. I am become a servant of Vishṇu's worshippers; I will set my desire on the morsels they have left. Tukā says, Such honour as the servants of Vishṇu pay me, I cannot hope to have from others.

## 948

LET me keep company with the saints in any guise; let me lie at their doors like a dog. Then I shall hear the name of Räma; I shall feed on the scraps they leave behind. To be a slave with them, a bond-maid, and a servant, yea, to be humble and wretched with them is good. Tukā says, I shall have perfect joy with the saints; if it is granted me to sit with them.

# XIX

# Appeals and Exhortations

## 949

WHEN we are thirsty, we are delighted to come across water; let the company of the saints be as dear to us as that. When sweet food is placed before a man, he sometimes forgets to say "Enough." Tukā says, A mother yearns over a child when she meets him.

## 950

THOUGH you know these things, how is it you know them not? You will suffer for it in the next stage of your course. Awake, awake, O woman! If you sleep, a thief will ruin you and run away. Don't let men plunder the goods you have. Tukā says, When you see what others have suffered, why are you not afraid?

## 951

THERE is time enough if you will but run after Viṭṭhobā, when you have done with the knots of the world. Take and fill your house with him; then you will come back to life no more. Puṇḍalika made him stand upright and quiet as long as he wished. Tukā says, Such has become the common path.

## 952

A MEAL is delightful, if it be eaten in peace, be the food rich or poor; like a fountain playing by art, it is a source of gratification. Let your thoughts be set on God. Tukā says, Then you will procure that peace which all living things bestow on such a man.

## 953

NOW I give you this advice, do not waste your lives. I cast myself at the feet of all, beseeching you to purify yourselves. Make this your gain, the contemplation of God, with a mind centred in him. Tukā says, Practise a trade that brings true profit; why should I teach you incessantly?

## 954

TIME after time I beg the world to utter the auspicious name of Viṭṭhala. We will utter this auspicious name sitting in rows together. Minute after minute flees away; you must strengthen yourself. Tukā says, Be not faint-hearted, be not idle; these are impediments on your path.

## 955

THE mirage looks real, but it makes the foolish man's heart break with disappointment. Why do you knowingly destroy yourselves? Pray, consider your true interests! A treasure of merit is a companion, an escort for the soul; when it is secured, it yields fruit. Tukā says, You may boast yourselves till you reach the grave; you will be brought to the cowdung cakes and the fire.

## 956

AFTER many a re-birth, you have secured at last this gain; you have entered a human body, so grasp the feet of Viṭṭhala. You have wandered long, and but here you have found a resting place. Tukā says, The simple and wise know this.

## 957

NOW open your eyes; if you cannot see even now, you are a mere stone produced from your mother's womb. Since you have secured such a treasure as this human frame, whatever mystic power you seek you will attain. Enlightening others, many saints have been saved themselves. There is a boat on the bank of the Chandrabhāga, it stands at the door of Pāṇḍuranga. He who stands there hand on hip delays not to protect thee. Tukā says, It costs you nothing to embrace his feet; salvation follows at once.

## 958

NO effort will bring you back to this same life again, to the pleasure and pain you have once passed through. When you know this, why are you blind? You must pass through eight million re-births, through the grievous pains of the womb. You will enter the city of doubt, you will writhe in the nets of illusion. What do the beasts know of sin or merit? They live their lives more or less happily; they are born and die; they grow deaf, blind, lame, and dumb. If the treasure of human life is delivered to you, it is the highest and choicest state. O be calm for a moment, awake and open your eyes! Listen to the words of the Vedas and Purāṇas; Tukā entreats you.

### 959

IF hunger vanishes at the odour of food, then why is there this cooking in every house? Bring a blessing upon yourselves; remember even in your speech the name of Rāma. If thirst vanishes at the sight of water, then why is it stored up in every house? The sight of shade brings no pleasure till we sit down beneath it. You are blessed in singing and listening, if your faith is firm within you. Tukā says, Faith will bring you liberation, then why take the intricate path of knowledge?

### 960

TAKE his spirit for yours; continue your efforts; to him belongs a stout ship; he conveys to the further shore all who seek him; they need not fear the river of the world. Blessed are those who trust in him, for God dwells with them. Tukā says, God is the true servant of the simple.

### 961

PĀṆḌURANGA will bring you to your goal, if you meditate on him; you will find a cell provided for your mind. To attain this fruit there must needs be strength within you. Tukā says, All powers will then wait on your feet.

### 962

DWELL not on rules and prohibitions; remember in your heart Pāṇḍuranga. When you have eaten your food, do not complain that there was a fly in it; for it all goes down at one mouthful. You can make this acquisition easily, but you will find it hard to keep. Tukā says, Spare no labour to obtain; without a poultice of neem-tree leaves you cannot dispel pain.

## 963

LET not want of faith replace your faith; to this name, be assured, belongs much guilt. When the showers of rain stream down, they do good or harm according as the ground is soft or hard. When good things are distributed, if you set your heart on a worthless portion, the wishing tree will bestow that on you. Tukā says, Life is very short; in future look out for what is best.

## 964

BE quick and take your share; you have stayed a long way behind; if you collect worldly riches, the essential portion will be taken by others. Others, like you, have been scared away; I cannot tell how many. Why do not men perceive the favourable moment but go on carrying their burden on their heads? Run! make haste, before it is all spent. What you have tied up in your cloth you have got for your own. Poor-spirited creature, says Tukā, cannot you venture one effort? without that how will you gain this happiness?

## 965

IN the rear of riches comes the assault of this evil age, therefore their society is treacherous. Leave behind you this source of hell, when you have, in good time, set the praises of God before you. To-day is your opportunity to appropriate this gain; henceforward cast your burden upon God. No cravings will change your appointed destiny; this madness of desires is vain and foolish. Tukā says, Wait and take this treasure; listen with reverence to the praises of God.

### 966

HO! some one of you, receive God! He has come unbidden, asking for your house. Those who want none of him are stuck fast where they have stored their treasures. God is tardy; faith has sunk out of sight: what shall we do? Receive God without price: you need pay neither cash nor goods for him. Tukā is feeble through loss of faith; he has bought God on credit and fallen into debt.

### 967

THE mother feels her chief joy in the caress of her child. Gladly she gives him a morsel to eat and satisfies his longings. She puts ornaments upon him and directs her glance towards him; she takes him on her lap and humbles herself before him. She lifts him on her shoulder, and lets no evil eye fall on him. Tukā says, Fall on him for your own gain; visit him of the lotus-navel.

### 968

GOD'S favour shows itself in a loving answer; joy is multiplied in joy. Luckily for many our ship has reached its harbour; come, make haste and take what you want. A thing unattainable has been brought freely to your doors; make no mistake about it now. Tukā says, Through the doors of tongue and ears fill the measure up to the brim.

### 969

YOU must know what is right; the chief duties come first; the mind has to be purified and the spirit made steady. You must not follow the promptings of the mind; you must love the teaching of the saints. If you trust to these precepts, you need no further admonition, says Tukā.

## 970

THE story of the Purāṇas is like a sweet juice; these poems are not idle words or empty chaff. Receive them in faith; go once at least to Pāṇḍhari. By good fortune you have entered into a human body; then visit Viṭṭhala; he will sweep away your store of sin and merit. Take in your hand the cymbals and sing his praises. Tukā says, You need no skill in dialectics; you need not search for the path.

## 971

ALL trouble is unprofitable as long as you do not utter the name of Rāma. Awake, awake, set your mind free from desire. You will recover what you have renounced; if you persist as you are, you will be punished by time. Tukā says, Surrender to Pāṇḍuranga what has fallen to your lot.

## ९७२

YOU have no power of your own to assure yourself in future what you have now. So take what is within your reach; sing his name joyfully. The store of our past is powerful; our actions run on ahead of us. Tukā says, If you behave like an owl, you will return to birth as a pig.

## 973

THE embodied gods could not overcome the world; how can we feeble creatures stand against it? You will soon be ensnared by pleasures, if once they make you their victim. I cannot conceive when they will set you free. You will exhaust yourself with carrying this burden—I too carry it; in vain do we renounce it. Tukā says, How is it you are not ashamed of it? The saints have secured the controller of the senses.

## 974

WHAT the yogi gains in glory is renunciation and peace; in both worlds he secures the delights of festal praise and honour. What men have borrowed from each other they have to pay off in the hour of prosperity. Exert yourself and you will find the original treasure; the cravings of thirst will wear you out. Tukā says, We shall find our true account in activity; we shall enjoy in our souls union with Śiva.

## 975

WHEN you have kept the principal, why need you care about interest! Seal up your own bundle at home; you cannot avoid the attempts of the strangers. Robbers will assault you not far on the road; your business takes you through the swindlers' quarter. Tukā says, Appearances are all false; you will be caught by secret wiles.

## 976

THOSE who attain no mastery in anything have wasted their lives. Listen to this easy secret; contemplation needs no anxious toil. If this resource be neglected, then the shadow of death falls on a man. Tukā says, O mankind, lend your ear to this.

## 977

YOU have all the gifts of fortune, hands and feet to walk with, a mouth to speak with, ears to listen to God's praise, eyes to behold his image. How many blind have been robbed of these, how many dumb and lame! If a house catches fire, a waking man cannot survive unless he runs away. Tukā says, Awake now to your own interests.

## 978

GOOD men have attained liberation in the flesh; abandon the company of the wicked. If poison like a mustard seed enter a mass of food, it will turn it all to poison. Tukā says, Do heedfully such deeds as will bring your own gain.

## 979

THE body is not; "I" comes to an end; Viṭṭhala that was left before is still left. So raise a cry; sweep away time by contemplation. Think not of maintaining yourself; there is a place empty for you within God. Tukā says, If you give up your own soul, God will enter your body.

## 980

SINCE you have an excellent tongue, why do you not repeat ' Viṭṭhala " ? Let your heart turn to him who will rescue you. What gain is there in putting gossip together? Tukā says, All skill is vile save skill in God.

## 981

LOOK not even on your teacher's son, if he be impious, more than on the face of the incestuous. To avoid such it were well to seek solitude, where nothing can interrupt our devotion. Consort not with a fault-finder, for his evil heart is full of enmity. Tukā says, Never speak to one whose sight increases sin.

## 982

IT is a foul life that scorns the saints; shun it as an enemy of mankind. If a woman leaves her husband, she loses family, beauty, and all worldly comfort. How can he be short of fruit who preserves the root? A wise man knows how to observe the due signs. Tukā says, Let all your efforts be directed to one spot; if you have a lamp in your hand, all is well.

## 983

WE destroy a seed and then we reap an ear of corn; all men know this, and appreciate small things as well as great. The gain is not without its price; we must offer our own souls to buy it. Tukā says, If you sacrifice your life in battle, you gain twice as much.

984

SPEECH brings its own evils, but a silent man is like a dumb post. Avoid too much and too little, this is the wise plan; let your speech and your silence be both appropriate. When darkness sets in, day vanishes, and night comes on. Tukā says, The seed lies hidden in the earth and yet it shows itself.

985

SOME men temper and eat the root of aconite ounce by ounce; while others cannot bear to look on it. Some will charm a snake and grasp it, while others tremble to see it. The unattainable may be attained by toil; yes, practice will bring it about, says Tukā.

986

IF you are a god, you can make others like yourself; you need not doubt it. If you are a wicked man, you can do the same. Tukā says, Whatever is reflected in a glass does without doubt penetrate it.

987

IF a man ties a broken gourd round his waist, how can he reach the farther shore safely? He brings destruction on himself, if he listens to no remonstrances. If a hungry man seeks to eat poison, he destroys himself. Tukā says, There are guides preceding us; if you miss the way they point out, you will go wrong.

988

I HAVE suffered much before now in my ignorance; why should I be blind any more? We ought to commit ourselves to one God, and not go groping about from one to another. Whoever it be that keeps the world in motion, he will answer your call. Tukā says, We dogs were put on this search after God; for had no desire been excited in us, we should not have been stirred to the search.

## 989

CRY out "Hari" all of you, and the snares of illusion will be broken. Do not be swallowed up by other vile desires; they will bring much misery with them. Fold your hands and offer with true faith water and a leaf of tulsi; call yourself a sinner once and again. Tukā says, He is an ocean of mercy; if you utter his name, he will carry you to the goal.

# XX

# Rebuke and Admonition

## I.—The Evil Age

### 990

WE have begun to find out by experience the truth of what the saints declared. Mankind are contaminated in this evil age; good deeds are weak and sin is powerful. None observes the rules of his caste or avoids pollution; men create one vast heap of impurities. Those who have learned the Vedas take strong drink; they observe no distinction between things; they are all degenerate. Tukā says, How often shall I make you ashamed? These cravings are numerous and ever present.

### 991

OH! brother, to him I address my recitation of praises; come now, you the Kali age—foul and untidy! Spit upon his face! All speech of self-praise is idle; cast it away! He is a slave to his wife, heedless of his parents; he bestows no charity on beggars. He uses his education to torment people with discussions and he breaks up the parties of other harmless people. He does not revere his village god; Brahmans and beggars never come near him. He is always finding fault. He never remembers Govinda even in a dream. He shuts up his wealth in a pit. He tightens his waist band to keep off hunger; he does not know what charity is. Tukā says, He goes about with affected airs, but he does not let devotion touch him.

## 992

THE saints have described the age of Kali long ago, as the time when the twice born shall forsake their rules. We see this now under our eyes; they forsake the rules of religion and resort to impious deeds. They find it wearisome to practice rites and austerities; they enjoy looking after themselves. They say they are gods themselves and do not visit the temples; but if they are gods, how is it they do not live apart from the world? Tukā says, If I show any respect to these people, some of them will be going to hell.

## 993

SUCH is the nature of the evil age that piety has been ruined. The Brāmhaṇas have given up "Rāma-Rāma" and say "Doma-Doma." They wear black and blue clothes, which they ought not even to touch. Tukā says, They abandon their own calling and cry out vociferously for a boon.

## 994

SUCH is a good name that one can never keep it, O Lord and Master, O saviour of the sinful. If a man takes care of his family, people find fault with him; if he renounces it, they call him lazy and selfish; if he goes through ceremonies, they call him ostentatious; if he discards them, they take him to task. If he lives with the saints, they cry "A disciple!" If he leaves them alone, they say he is an ignoramus. If he is poor, he is born to be a beggar; if he has means, they charge him with pride. If he speaks much, he is over-talkative; if he speaks little, they cry out on his pride. If he stands aloof from men, he is cold-blooded; if he moves amongst them, he is said to ruin his family. If he gets married, they say he is lustful; if he does not, they say he is impotent. If he has no children, they look down on him; if he has a tribe of children, they say it leads to hell. I am sick of mankind, I cannot contain my disgust of them; a worldly man cannot stomach the company of the saints. Tukā says, Listen to my words, leave the world and practise devotion.

---

## 11.—The Obstinacy of the Wicked

### 995

IF a man has faith, a stone will save him; but how can a good man help a wicked one? Though you straighten a dog's tail, it will not stay so: what can the magic stone make of a potsherd? Though you dig a trench and fill it with sugar, yet the seed planted in it bears fruit like itself. Tukā says, Even adamant is sometimes broken, but these wretches are harder still.

### 996

WE may beat a thievish dog on the head; he howls, but he does not give up his tricks. Such, O God, is a man of bad character; he destroys his own soul. To him the loss of his nose brings neither shame nor reflection; he carries the disgrace from house to house. Tukā says, The prints of a man's actions are strong and powerful; they do not suffer him to stir one way or another.

997

IF you wash a donkey in a sacred stream, it will not turn to an Arab steed; even so, whatever advice you offer a scoundrel, you cannot purify his mind. You may feed a snake on sugar and nectar, but the poison within it will not vanish. Tukā says, If you offer a dog milk, it is all the same to him as vomit.

998

WE have to suffer mountains of sorrow; every body knows it; yet men neglect their own advantage, they utter not the name of Hari. Our comforts in the present tell us what our past lives were like—good, bad or middling. Tukā says, If you close your eyes now, you will know what you have to meet when it is dealt out to you.

999

PEOPLE like falsehood; truth they cannot digest. Such is the effect of pride, but they will learn by experience what misery is like. We see men fostering their love for the world, till the agents of Yama seize them. Tukā says, Such are obstinate monkeys and will not listen to advice.

1000

THE monkey seizes the grain within the pot; he does not understand that his hand is caught. I need not explain his mistake; he does not understand what to do for himself. A parrot gets his feet caught in his perch; he forgets all about his two wings. Tukā says, Some men are just like animals; you can do nothing to help them.

### 1001

WHAT! does not even a tree bend? A madman forgets who and what he is; the man who bears no fruit by admonition is like the dry stump of a tree. What! are there not stones that are as mute as sages? Tukā says, You may look on fools as hard corn that will not cook.

### 1002

WE should approach the saints respectfully; it is heart-breaking to deal with low people. A vagabond goes about braying like an ass and gets beaten on the back by Yama. He talks like a fool and does not understand the occasion; the honour he gets by his faulty conduct is mere discredit. Tukā says, His behaviour is foul and offensive.

### 1003

IF you smear sandal powder on an ass, the creature will mingle it with ashes. No being can easily change its own qualities. If you hang a jewel about the neck of a monkey, he bites it off and throws it away and spits on it. Tukā says, A worthless fellow rejects a benefit to himself; his ignorance confirms his folly.

### 1004

THOSE who will not leave their faults, who count the divine secrets folly, what will they do when they suffer for it? when their heads are crushed by Yama's rod? When they show the account of their merit and demerit, they will suffer grievously. Tukā says, O Vitthala, they feel weary at my words.

---

## III.—Ill Temper and Want of Charity

### 1005

HE who is soothed by another's misfortunes, know him for a sinful man; he who is quick to anger is a dweller in hell. He who opens his ears to slander or speaks it himself, Tukā says, he cannot control his tongue, he is a quarrelsome fellow.

### 1006

HE who employs the same mouth to praise and to censure another secretly, he is a vile creature; he loses his gold and eats dirt; he eats sweet dainties and voids excrement; hell takes hold of him. Tukā says, He is like a scorpion that carries a mischievous sting.

### 1007

THE man who calculates the merits and faults of the saints, closes the roll of his own good deeds. He is a fool who crushes a flower to look for its fragrance, or cleaves a plantain stem to find its fruit in it. Tukā says, He who attributes impurity to the Ganges and to fire, he is a miscreant and shall suffer for it.

### 1008

THE world is full of Vishṇu, such is the guiding rule of his worshippers; discussions on the unity of God are an evil. Listen, O ye devotees of

Vishṇu; in what you do seek always your true interest. Put from you all censorious spirit. This is the secret of worshipping the highest. Tukā says, There are many limbs in one body, but one soul feels pain or pleasure.

### 1009

IF a man entertains the low caste creature anger, he ceases to be a Brāhmaṇa. What atonement can he make? It avails him not, if he quits the body. Do not touch this villain; he is all uncleanness within. Tukā says, He who associates with him makes himself of the same caste as his.

### 1010

THE mother rejoices to see a male child; she says, "A son is born." Then he grows up quarrelsome, slanderous, thievish and vicious. Wherever he goes he injures men; he gains nothing but contempt. It is all a sad mistake; why was he not smothered at his birth? The earth shudders beneath his weight; he and such as he are creatures of hell. His speech is cruel; his gaze is evil; his mind is foul; his evil ways make him a pollution; sin and contamination go with him. Tukā says, He is a vile thing, meet to be avoided.

### 1011

ONE like a dog, one swift to anger, he destroys himself, he is a sinful wretch. He has neither respect nor self-control; the milk of good advice does not agree with him. He barks against mankind; other men spit upon him. Tukā says, His mind is filthy; let it be put to shame.

### 1012

YOU may burn rice and sesamum seed, but a fierce and greedy temper will remain as villainous as ever. Why do you weary yourselves in vain, forgetting to worship Pāṇḍuranga? You have spent your time on words and the fruit is hypocrisy and pride; you have practised austerities and pilgrimages and increased your own conceit. You have distributed your wealth to others; you have cherished your self-conceit. Tukā says, You have missed the secret; all your conduct has been impious.

---

## IV.—Pride

### 1013

WERE its parents like the snake or cat, that eat their offspring, then their child would not enjoy their company. Gallows of sandalwood or fetters of gold,—therein is no pleasure, but death and misery. Tukā says, If our learning ends in pride or arrogance, our self-conceit will cast us down to hell.

### 1014

TO sit on a seat side by side with worthier men is a crime no less than incest. I am declaring the rules of righteous conduct: listen to me for your own welfare! If you desire to be worshipped as though you were saints, you will fall into an eddying whirlpool of ruin. Tukā says, If you suddenly desire the highest place, it will not become you and you will disgrace it.

## V.—Deceit

### 1015

THE child of a liar chooses the company of liars; he prefers appearances to reality. The fruit is like the seed; when the plant comes to maturity, it scatters abroad the fragrance of its kind. A jewel round a monkey's name is nothing to him; a vagabond leaves his true wife and goes roaming about the streets. Tukā says, The mother of such a one is an ass; shame waits to overtake her.

### 1016

IF a man displays gold that contains copper and seeks to sell it as pure, a good judge can discern its inward nature, and distinguish the two elements. How perfect seems the mixture when milk and water are mingled; yet a good judge can distinguish them by the taste. Tukā says, The liar has degraded himself in vain; he will come to great distress.

### 1017

THOSE who forsake the truth and point out courses of their own, they shall go to the lowest pit. When a thief is caught, he gives a false name; so both parties are fettered, hands and feet. Tukā says, This is settled in the Purāṇas; it is no idle chatter of mine.

### 1018

THEY make up a bundle of stolen leaves and show off these stale dishes as their own poetic skill; such wicked people stay in hell as long as the sun and moon go round. Tukā says, Accept Nārāyaṇa alone; in other pathways distress will meet you.

---

## VI.—Greediness

### 1019

"WHAT can we get out of him? Who can go on singing for ever? The praises of Hari have beggared us; even sleep deserts us. This troublesome noise interrupts our work and occupation." Tukā says, This is what brutes and scoundrels think.

### 1020

A GREEDY man loses judgment in his haste; he goes on talking nonsense. He shows the hue of his nature, just as poison brings on spasms. Men have gone mad through their passion for wealth, so that they cannot stop talking of it. Tukā says, Both vices end in experience of hell.

### 1021

HE who sells merit commits incest; the wealth of a pander is polluted; you may call the lustful man a suicide; he does whatever he is bidden to do, he cares not for any penalty. He ruins himself for a slight gain; he barters the magic stone for a bit of glass. Tukā says, He has washed his hands of heaven; he reaps nothing but toil; he has only forced his ears to listen to teaching.

### 1022

WHY are you not ashamed to call yourself a servant of Hari, when you are willing to call an ignoble man "Mahārāja?" Is your stomach unsatisfied or what else do you need that you go on wagging your tail in public? Tukā says, It is our belly that brings scorn upon us, that makes a man abject and sets him calling for pity.

### 1023

IF the spirit is at rest, it counts gold as poison. Covetousness is a sinful thing; know this, O simple men; what shall I say to you? If the mind is disturbed, sandalwood will not cool the raging of the body. Tukā says, If the spirit is not at rest, any remedy or ceremony increases affliction.

### 1024

THERE is one that makes his wife play the part of his mother, and puts himself in the place of his fore-fathers. Poor wretch, you have spent too much over it!—with all your tricks and perversions. You have wasted your life feeding on pleasure. Tukā says, You knave! God will have no mercy on you; it is a stone that you worship.

---

## VII.—Worldliness

### 1025

THOSE who acquire incomes, land, power and wealth, know that God is absent from their thoughts. A quarrelsome man carries a burden about with him, he never gains the essential truth; he may purpose to worship God, but it is one stone worshipping another for the sake of gain. Tukā says, They honour God for reward; their crafty thoughts are like the love of a harlot.

## 1026

IN the bond of desires, what does any man know of God? He serves him with his person, but he looks toward the things he desires. Like the ravings of a delirious man are his notions of what is right. Tukā says, He is like good food spoiled by poison.

## 1027

THERE is no peace for the servant of the world; his occupation is never absent from his thoughts; the service of God is entirely deserted; a riot of self-indulgence goes raging on. Toiling night and day he cannot satisfy his family; it is hard for him to gain a sight of God. Tukā says, O destroyers of yourselves, your action is suicide; you have altogether lost Nārāyaṇa.

## 1028

HE follows a path he has not travelled before; he seems to be worldly wise, the wretch! How shameless he is, he never utters the name of Rāma! He stares fiercely on his worldly foes, yet he weeps when he is handed over to Yama; for all that he repents not. He fancies he shall never have to deal with Yama; he is a low wretch, who thinks so! So he is silent still. Ah! why do you behave so? says Tukā.

## 1029

DO they not know what has happened to others? Why must we tell them about it? They may see and hear it, and they know what the Purāṇas have said. They know the question whether the body is real or perishable; why cannot their own experience answer it, as they pass through childhood, youth and age? Why do they delight in wife or child or wealth; who has ever at any time found these help him? Why has the excellent gift of life been given them in vain; why do they not utter Rāma! Rāma!? Why when they know all do they forget it, though they see others die before them? What will they do, says Tukā, when death with his adamantine chains seizes and binds them?

## 1030

I AM astonished at these people; they will not think of their own true interests. What resources have they to make up for this? Who will help them in the latter end? What notion keeps them free from anxiety? What answer will they give to Yama's servants? Feeble creatures that they are, how have they forgotten death? To what pleasures have they given themselves up? With nothing in their hands, what will they do? How can we learn what has happened to them? Why do they not remember Devakī's son, to escape from the trammels of the world? Does he need to be purchased with a price? Why do their minds not admit him? Tukā says, Why will they pass through birth and death again? why have they forgotten the wheel-handed one?

## 1031

IF the secret were known, what would be impossible? But we are entangled in errors. Yet knowledge puts an end to everything; hear, O God, this sentiment of mine. For the sake of the bait the fish gets his gullet pierced by the hook;

even so, greed of wealth ruins men. Tukā says, Something false must happen, for destiny is huge and strong.

### 1032

THEY in whom personal interests and desires dwell, who look on the body as their own, they need provisions for their passage as they go along. Tukā says, He who follows a false path to protect his faith, he suffers for it; one who is fevered by the sun seeks the shade.

---

## VIII.—Sensuality

### 1033

HERE they enjoy sensual pleasures; before them lies the grievous chastisement of Yama; the stern servants of Yama beat and cut and thrash them in countless ways. They make them pass over the edges of swords, over glowing coals of khaira wood; flames shall issue from the heated oil; see, they roll them on the burning ground; they make them clasp fiery pillars. Therefore, Tukā cries, enough now of these agonies and the life that brings them on.

### 1034

IF you mean to ruin yourself, devote all your powers to gambling with dice. Then what becomes of Hari's name? While you are asleep, Rāma is awake; you have acquired for yourself pain and degradation from one birth to another. For the greedy and impudent whoremaster there is a road that leads into the pit. If you choose another way to hell, then be it your delight to speak ill of the saints. Tukā says, Make your mind mad after Rāma, or your labour will be lost; you will be deceived and disappointed.

## 1035

THE rich man who does no pious deeds is robbed by the king; when his mother bore him, would she had been barren! He who sleeps at the time of preaching, but wakes to satisfy his lust, like a dog; who is ashamed to gratify his own wife, but shares the coverlet of a whore, Tukā says, know that he is a man viler than an ass.

## 1036

IF a man has renounced his family, whilst he has not put away passion, his devotion is worthless, he goes to hell without fail. Though he bestow labour on forms of words, if he thinks evil of the saints, Tukā says, his foot returns backwards to that evil spot.

## 1037

BEHOLD, pleasure is like a grain of barley, pain like a mountain. O remember, remember! Heed thou the word of the saints! Night takes away half our lives, together with childhood and old age. Tukā says, After this they are fools who pursue pleasures, like oxen yoked to an oilman's mill.

## 1038

WHY do you make a slave of yourself, an ass loaded with the burden of the world? Sweet viands are pleasant on the tip of the tongue;

but they lose their savour when the stomach is filled. If you pile up sensual pleasures from every organ, still they pass away and leave no trace with you. If you gaze on Viṭṭhobā's form till you are satisfied, you will feel no further thirst of desire. Tukā says, Why do you sever yourself from God to gain what is perishable ?

## IX.—Hypocritical Professions

### 1039

IN this evil age the infidels are turned poets; these quarrelsome people are skilful indeed! In his heart he delights in wealth, wife and children; with his lips he continues his dry prating. He assumes a proud exterior to make men honour him; he talks of renunciation but his heart is not in it. They do not seek their true profit by obeying the Vedas ; they do not sever themselves from the body. Tukā says, That man will endure the pangs of hell, who does not act as he professes.

### 1040

HE displays the pompous air that he has learned; but how can a flint look like a diamond? You luckless fellow, learn where the truth lies; all images of God resemble him. Why have you lent yourself to illusions? Why do you throw away your true greatness? Tukā says, Destruction is visible ahead of you; this is why I make you ashamed.

## 1041

CLEVER people are buried under prohibitions, contentious people under talk; how weary they grow, in the embarrassing straits of pride! What have they gained by their winnowing? They have lost their world and the next. Tukā says, What butter can be abstracted from whey that has once been churned?

## 1042

CURSED be the outward show, that vanishes like a butterfly. The daughter-in-law weeps for her husband's mother, but her inner feeling is different. A hypocrite is smooth tongued, but his inner purpose is different. He is like the Vṛindāvana fruit, which looks handsome, but is not safe to touch. A heron assumes a contemplating attitude, but his object is to catch fish. Tukā says, Like a serpent waving his head, he pretends to be delighted with the service of God.

## 1043

IF your hand trembles when you offer a gift, your words therewith find no acceptance. If your speech of devotion be idle prate, it is like assafœtida mixed with milk, vapid and worthless. If your feet move not to holy places and you say "Why should I spend money on them?" Tukā says, you will accomplish nothing.

## 1044

KEEP me far from talkative men, far from those who condemn the saints and forget thee, O Govinda! Cursed be the face of such a one; let me not set eyes on a quarrelsome man! Tukā says, O God, keep me far from them.

### 1045

ONE whose speech is uncertain, whose mind is unstable, go not to visit such a one; it is a pollution to sit at meat with him. He who reviles holy men and honours the base for private gain, Tukā says, he has one thing on his lips and another in his heart.

---

## X.—Indifference to Religion and Churlish Conduct to the Saints

### 1046

I CARE nothing for his speech, who never speaks of Viṭṭhala. He is my foe, and I shall call him no friend of mine, who has firmly turned away his face from Viṭṭhala. If a man finds the name of Viṭṭhala displeasing, know him for a base wretch, says Tukā.

### 1047

HE who gives not a spoonful to the saints, who asks them for water, but pours out a bath for a maid-servant; who turns his back on the saints, but kisses a maid-servant's brat; who ridicules the saints when he sees them, but cheerfully washes a maid-servant's bodice; spit in his face, says Tukā, he goes to find what hell is like!

### 1048

THE man who shows hospitality to his friends and produces a rod for the saints, who belabours a cow when he sees her, and is glad of a horse's service, who gives fruit and flowers to a harlot freely, but never a morsel of betel nut to Brahmans; who cherishes his wife's family and drives out his father and mother, Tukā says, spit in that man's face; he goes to find what hell is like!

## 1049

THE sluggish mind resembles the lazy body; it takes a good judge to discern them. Some men contemplate God and utter his name; others lie down and go to sleep. Some renounce all; others are all alert to fill their stomachs; some profess love for the sake of their stomachs, others seek true union with God. Each has his own principle within him; but the fruits thereof are diverse, says Tukā.

## 1050

WHOSO torments the servants of Vishṇu, ill-omened is his speech; let him not approach you; his evil conduct brings misfortune. He who loves not the praises of Hari is born of an adulterous woman. Tukā says, His lineage and his spirit are alike impure.

## 1051

TELL me whose protection you have sought: you have made indifference your great crime. Who has given you this advice, "Do not go for protection to Viṭṭhala"? When Yama lays you prostrate on the earth, who will shield you from him? Why do you rob yourself? Time eats up your life; your strength decays from day to day. Tukā says, Explain to him, some one, that he has forgotten his parents.

## 1052

TO dishonour the saints and then worship God is a sin. If thus you act, it is in vain you put flowers on the gods' heads uttering Vedic spells; they turn to stones. If you dishonour your guests while you offer cakes to God, Tukā says, you make a distinction between the saints and God; your worship is an insult to God.

## 1053

TO say "We are God's" and to show no respect to God, this seems to me a strange thing. Yet why say this to other men, who bear the burden of the world on their heads? To give up the world, and yet to seek its honour and treasure, this would be unfair to the world. Tukā says, This is seeking indolence for a friend; see how such men rush to ruin!

## 1054

HE who observes not the eleventh day, know him for a living corpse. Death is measuring out his life, and gnashes his teeth with rage against him. He who keeps no tulsi plant at his door, know his house for a burial-ground. He who has no worshippers of Vishṇu in his family, his raft for crossing the sea of life is foundered. The mouth that speaks not the name of Viṭṭhobā is verily a tanner's pit. Tukā says, His hands are wooden sticks, that goes not to hear the praises of Hari.

## 1055

THOSE who observe not the eleventh day's fast, I know not what their state shall be. What hall I do? I am quite disheartened; men are blind and look at the outside. Those who offer not an inch of wick to Hara and Hari, those who have no love for Nārāyaṇa, Tukā says, I know not what their state shall be.

### 1056

THAT man is a mere corpse, a charnel house, who is a clown void of divine love and service. Such fellows feed like dogs and open their house to the spirits of hell. Where no image is worshipped, refuse thou to dwell; it is an abode of thieves and scoundrels. Tukā says, If a man knows not his true position and powers of the mind, he is a retainer of Yama, beyond reform.

### 1057

SEARCH the Śrutis and you will find that he is no Brahma who does not love to sing the praises of Hari and dance amid Vaishṇavas. He is a vicious wretch, incestuous and vile. Tukā says, If you think differently of him, your mouth will be attacked by leprosy.

### 1058

THEY are hard-hearted listeners whose mind is bent on praise or blame; a luckless fool is he who is absent from service while he is present. He spends his ears, eyes and speech on a profitless purpose; he is an associate of sin; let his negligent mouth be filled with dirt. He is truly profited who has learned to forget the wants of the body. Tukā cries fie on such; he renounces them and shaves their heads.

## 1059

THIS is no pleasure to me—why do they bring their ill-omened faces here? The flavour of my thoughts is spoiled, O Nārāyaṇa, when I see a row of scoundrels before me. A dog goes about with a mouth as filthy as hell; he defiles sweet food. Tukā says, He who shows no deference to the saints and abuses them, abuse him for a guilty scoundrel.

## 1060

WHEN the body is heated by fever, milk tastes like poison; so it is with him who has banished God's truth, a raving fever fastens upon him. When jaundice affects a man's eyes, he sees the moon of a yellow colour. Tukā says, When a man loves spirituous drinks, he cannot taste the sweetness of butter.

## 1061

ONE who is lazy by nature and has moreover his teacher's advice to confirm him, what will prevent him from taking his own way, what will stop him? He cannot practise religion, or obey the rules of conduct. Tukā says, He is an ass; he runs where his mind leads him.

## 1062

A SOW relishes ordure continually; what pleasure has she in savoury food? Thus the irreligious delight in false doctrine; they find no pleasure in the highest truth. You may offer dogs nectar, but their heart is set on bones. Tukā says, Though you feed a snake on milk, it vomits forth poison in return.

### 1063

IF a man destroys the source of milk, what will he gain by doing so? He who finds fault with the Vedas is a low and sinful, a polluted wretch. If a man sets fire to his own house, where will he find a place to live in? Tukā declares the secret; the rest are led astray by error.

### 1064

IF you mean to sing, then sing Viṭṭhala alone; if not, remain silent where you are. If you hold that absolute union is the end, then you will not need speech; you are wasting your efforts on knowledge in vain. Tukā says, How often shall I put you to shame? The shameless man does not know what shame is.

## XI.—Various

### 1065

HE goes off to Kāśi, leaving with his friends his cows, horses and buffaloes. "I shall be back before you know I am gone; honour the confidence I have placed in you. Do not take the corn out of the pit. You may eat the chaff and waste Take a stick and chase away the beggars. You will be cutting my throat if you ask Brahmans to dinner. I have never spent a penny to cure any sickness of mine. You may eat the butter milk, but keep the butter and ghee for me. There is no room in my heart for plundering women and children." Tukā says, The wretch speaks out his notions plainly.

## 1066

HE who eats his food without due ceremony is a dog; what avails his manhood? He is a draught animal, a bullock! He knows nothing of right conduct; he is a burden to the earth; he is a foe of his ancestors and forces pollution upon them. He whose speech is foul, who never speaks the truth even in his dreams, there is none more guilty than he. He who looks to his stomach alone and has no compassion on other creatures; if a beggar on his rounds draws near him, who drives him away, who never worships holy men, visits no holy spot; he is a dowry of hell, he shall come to the worst misery. Tukā says, They destroy their own manhood who forget God and cry out "I" and "Mine."

## 1067

IF you bring a crazy old man to a marriage hall, he will use vulgar language of the bride and bridegroom. He does not understand the occasion; what use is he at such a time? Tukā says, He is an ass; take him away!

## 1068

WHEN a vicious child is begotten in a family, his ancestors cry out with horror. Why did he not perish in the womb? Why did his mother conceive him? She has brought shame into the world; she is a sinful woman. He is swift to cruelty and lustful. His mind is active in evil doing. If he feeds not on censure and scandal, he feels hungry. He gathers up every chance of blaming others. Kindly and virtuous deeds disagree with him; he is like a worm that lives in poison and dies in milk. Tukā says, He is the embodiment of filth; mercy, kindness and peace are far from him.

## 1069

A FOOLISH man gets angry with the oil-merchant; to gratify his resentment he eats dry bread. A woman gets vexed with other people; she renounces her husband, she shaves her head, and loses his affection. Another is angry with her neighbours; she leaves her house and the dogs occupy it. A man is worried by fleas, he burns his house; he loses it, but he does not care. A woman is annoyed with lice; she throws off her clothes and shows herself naked to the world. Tukā says, Think of these; keep your true interest in view; do not be short-sighted.

## 1070

WHEN a man is madly fond of his wife, he keeps on saying "Yes, yes," through deference to her. She makes idle complaints to her husband, as it suits her—"See, you cannot understand my sufferings. I cannot digest my food, though I have eaten eight pounds of wheat and six of flour. Last market day you brought me ten pounds of sugar and a half; it lasted me only a week. I have pain in my stomach continually, though I doctor myself with rice and milk and sugar and ghee. In the middle of the day I have spasms; I lie down on my mattress quite senseless. I cannot get to sleep, though I put flowers on my bed; I cannot bear the children near me. I put sandalwood paste on my brow, yet I have fever in my head continually. My bones have disappeared; my body is nothing but flesh; no one can describe my sufferings." Tukā says, She makes an ass of her husband while he is alive, and when he is dead she drags him down to hell.

### 1071

THE friendship of the vile is like the bright hue on the moth's wing; it vanishes in a moment; its value is lost without service to any one. He is filled with poison, like a snake, in his heart. Tukā says, O God, disclose such villains to me speedily!

### 1072

A BLIND man thinks all men are blind, because he has not himself eyes or sight. A sick man finds sweet food bitter as poison, because his mouth has lost its power to taste. Tukā says, He who is unrighteous himself believes the three worlds are full of falsehood.

### 1073

CURSES on the wretch who is subject to a wife; he has neither honour here nor life hereafter. Curses on the wretch whose mind is set on gain; he cannot welcome guests with due devotion. Curses on the lazy and sleepy man, on the greedy and intemperate glutton. Curses on him who cannot distinguish truth or renounce passion; who gives up spiritual attainments for worldly honour. Tukā says, Cursed be all such people; the censorious and contentious go to hell.

## 1074

IT is not your garments or your speech but your faults that I have censured; perchance you will be angry, good people, at my words. Who knows not that food is the life of the life? Yet if you mix poison with it, it grows poisonous. Who knows not that gold itself is pure? but a mixture of base metal degrades it. If a man be of pure descent and yet bear the inner traits of a low nature, he is rendered useless by his insincerity. Tukā says, A true man meets with honour, but others are beasts of burden carrying ornaments.

## 1075

A DEPRAVED taste will eat cowdung for the sweet roots that grow in it; though food were offered such a one, he would not have it. When he is rebuked, he deems himself praised; he looks on a thrashing as a compliment. A depraved taste follows its dirty inclinations, and gives not up its base habits. Tukā goes on shaming the wretch, to make him quit his vile ways.

## 1076

A SNUB-NOSED man is ashamed when he looks in a mirror; he is vexed to see his nose as it is. Thus, where bad qualities stand in the way, what is true seems hostile to us. What is a diamond to a blind man? It is just like a flint. Tukā says, A dog goes on barking, because he does not know the right time to bark.

## 1077

A HINT is enough for a mettlesome horse; one must take a thorny branch to a rough pony.

What else can I say? Lay this one thing to heart. I am no quarrelsome fellow to seize you by your garments. Tukā says, You turn your backs on me and let your heads hang down in silence.

## 1078

IF a flower is fragrant, that is no reason to crush it in our hands; if a child is handsome, that is no reason to eat him. If a pearl is lustrous, that is no reason to lick it; if we hear a musical instrument, we must not open it to find the source of the sound. If the past has made us what we are, we must not pursue pleasure. Tukā says, Let us show the secret truth to mankind.

## 1079

WHEN man has really eaten, he shows it by belching, otherwise there is nothing but idle straining. One may talk of food, whether he has eaten it or not; but without some real taste words are dry chaff. There are many dainties made of wheat; but let us not merely pretend to eat them. Tukā says, If you have a bracelet on your wrist, it would be absurd to look at it in a mirror.

## 1080

IF a thief counsels a thief, he will teach him his own trade. If a woman goes after a whore, she will become like her. Tukā says, I fear for what will follow, hence my anxiety.

## 1081

A BAD man stinks like poison: avoid him! Hear my words, you that are good: avoid him! Speak not to him! A bad man is filthy within; his speech is like the impurity of a woman. Dread a bad man as you dread that; he runs about like a mad dog. A good man dwells not with a bad man; I bid you flee from his country. Tukā says, How often must I tell you? A bad man is hell incarnate.

## 1082

CONCEIVE one at dinner holding his nose like a man at stool! If a man acts so, it shows he has no sense of his own. People go on making plans and upsetting them—why? Nobody knows. Tukā says, You are weighing milk against butter-milk!

## 1083

IF one wears the jewel of Kṛishṇa at his throat, and his speech be impure, be he man or woman, his true name is whore. If she brings no gift in her hand, if she wears not the bracelet of a stout spirit, such a whore is cast out by the saints, they shave her head and put her to shame. Tukā says, She fails to reach the standard and sinks into misery.

## 1084

IF a man loses his courage, a woman may strike him; then no efforts can recover his authority; it is vanished. If the spirit is crushed, it cannot be renewed by any exertions. Tukā says, If a man's courage is crushed, there is nothing left for him but lamentation.

## 1085

IF a Vedāntin rejects the existence of his own soul, he is guilty of slaying his teacher; the lesson that was taught him is in vain. That which was whispered in his ear he proclaims to be his own shape. If he still harbours enmity to created things, then his knowledge of Brahma has been stolen from him. If he repeats the words he has been taught, but nourishes self-will and anger and speaks the language of praise or censure, then, says Tukā, he wastes his speech.

## 1086

WHAT pleases us is death to the world. Others reject faith and live by appearances. They never heard what truly profits them; therefore they go drifting from door to door. They praise or blame according to fashion; they follow other people's lead. Tukā says, They will not listen when they are taught, they go running to hell.

## 1087

ONE who duly bathes and prays oft destroys his merit by the food he eats. His gain and loss are equal; his income and expenses are the same. The labourer's capital remains just his rope and sickle. Tukā says, A wasteful man will never procure God.

## 1088

A VICIOUS husband will not trust even his wife's brother; he will not trust his wife with him. A man of evil intentions is a thief himself and says other people are thieves. Tukā says, A man's confidence in other people depends on his own desires.

## 1089

AS a prostitute has pimps to go before her, so the companion of the base is base; when one such man rubs against another, then fire breaks forth. Tukā says, We shall cut off their noses, or they will teach others to be like themselves.

## 1090

AN unlucky man will mistake a treasure for snakes and scorpions and bits of charcoal; where there is a blemish in the eye, a bright object will look dirty. When you are dizzy yourself, you will see trees and rocks whirling round you. Tukā says, It is your own sin which bars the way to your advancement.

## 1091

HE who takes his part is like him. He comes to sorrow and gains nothing by it; he imprisons his ancestors in the gaol of hell. The king who hears of it, and punishes not the wretch, is a scoundrel himself. Tukā says, His food is like the lqiuor of drunkenness.

## 1092

HE who speaks thus is surely the son of a shameless mother; he utters not the name of Govinda, he is ever blaming others. How shall he fail to repose in hell? Tukā says, How shall the knave fail to be punished?

## 1093

HE who is void of moral conduct and of faith; who brings evil on others or cavils at them with superior wit; he, like a dog, pollutes sweet food when he touches it. Tukā says, Would that he had died on the fifth day!

## 1094

VAINLY his mother bore him in her womb; she brought forth the handle of an axe; why did she not stifle him at his birth? She begot a mischievous being, a pollution to his forefathers. Tukā says, The mother of an impious man goes to hell.

## 1095

DO not jest with me; I am no weaver or spinner. Sit still and renounce your pride; go and blacken your face for shame! Your jest will not pass here, nor other low tricks of yours. Tukā says, The servant of Hari knows how hollow pleasures are.

## 1096

OFT-TIMES there are children born in a family who ruin their forefathers, whose treasure is idle talk and thievish habits, and the family shares it; the earth is full of pain beneath their weight. Tukā says, They waste their lives like brutes.

## 1097

LET them go on barking, if they will; we must not learn their ways. A man of true faith should refuse to believe in the wicked. To the best of our power we must make the scoundrels ashamed. Tukā says, It is no sin to harry them.

## 1098

THE father shows his gold; the brokers settle the price of his daughter; such is the fate of religion in this age; the holy are degraded and the unholy are strong. The twice-born have forgotten their rules; they are turned slanderous and thievish. They conceal their books and the marks on their foreheads; they put on trousers and shoes. They sit down on their trestles and harass the people, if food is not given them. They write accounts at bania's shops; they live by dealing in oil and ghee. They become servants to the lowest of men; if they fail in their duties, they get beaten. The Rāja oppresses his subjects; the warrior class oppress the wretched. Vaiśyas and Śūdras are naturally a low race—but what of these? They are all mere show; within they are black, without they are bright. Tukā says, O God, why sleepest thou? I cry unto thee!

## 1099

"HE has killed a Brahman; he has killed a cow; he has committed other sins." Such are the praises bestowed on him, the empty fellow who has sold a daughter. He has taken the price of human flesh, therefore men cry out against him. His lust of gold is equal to all sins together. It is a sin in me to name it; my tongue trembles at the words. Tukā says, Why does not the pander beg a piece of dry bread?

## 1100

THE man who reflects not is like an ass; he carries his knowledge like a log of wood. He loves disputation; he loves filth, and leaves the high roads for it. Possessed though he be of wealth, honour or age, he does but scatter the filth that clings to his feet. Birth or family will not redeem a cut-throat. Tukā says, Why do you vainly carry the marks of religion stamped upon you?

## 1101

IF a man has a wife and child dying of hunger and gives himself out publicly as a great man, what could he show people if he took them home? He would have to creep away ashamed. Tukā says, We can tell a fellow like that; worldly people may be deceived but not we.

## 1102

A REVILER of the Vedas is not of pure seed; know him for a low caste man. He who credits not the Vedas nor heeds the speech of the wise, Tukā says, his pleasant words are like sweet food mixed with spirit; touch him not.

## 1103

A DOG cannot tell a guest from a thief or a beggar; when it catches sight of either, it barks wildly at him. It is no use teaching the creature, your words are wasted. Milk makes him sick, but he eats filth; he will not give up his own habits. Tukā says, What use is it to praise or blame a scoundrel for conduct which issues from his own thoughts?

## 1104

THE foal of an ass changes its form every instant after it is born; even such are vile men; their minds are unsteady. It looks well when it is born, but as it grows its shape is spoiled. Tukā says, As it goes braying about it cannot tell the right time from the wrong.

## 1105

A KANARESE woman has married a Maratha, neither can understand the other. Treat me not thus, O husband of Lakshmī; grant me to live in the company of the saints! She calls to him, "Illi bā" (Come here); he runs away, saying "She is swearing at me!" Tukā says, Where one is unsuitable to the other, there pleasure is turned to vexation.

# XXI

# True Worship

## I.—Referring to Outward Observances

### 1106

COME to meet him, if you will; follow me, follow me! To-day, we will feed you till you say "Enough." Come softly, come softly; do not speak to each other. Tukā says, Leave the husks; don't fill your bellies with them!

### 1107

LET us wave lamps round the Lord of Pāṇḍhari; with devoted faith I have come to seek protection at his feet. He who pervades the universe, whose form passes comprehension, he has come to dwell in the house of the cowherd damsels as the child Kṛishṇa. He whose original form is void of qualities, he has displayed himself; he is the Pāṇḍuranga who stands on the brick. O wonder! for his worshipper's sake he has assumed a shape; he wears an anklet to make known his claim and boast. We have waved a lamp round him to beseech a gift. We have exhausted speech in singing his praises. Through the spell of faith and devotion, thou art rendered merciful, O God. Tukā says, We cannot comprehend thy ways, O Pāṇḍuranga.

## 1108

THERE is a pleasure, the very essence of pleasure, standing in the courtyard of Vishṇu's worshippers; there stands the altar of the tulsi plant; the enclosure is washed with cowdung, and painted and hung with garlands; he looks on the ceremonies, and dances. He wears his jewels unchanging, his sacred emblems, and garlands of tulsi about his neck. His name is a stream of nectar in the mouth; the dust of his feet sanctifies the head. Tukā says, Liberation never enters the worshipper's mind, for it seeks to take hold of him.

## 1109

I HAVE seen thy form, standing hand on hip; therefore my spirit is at rest; I am minded not to leave thy feet. I sing of thee with my lips; I clap the cymbals; I dance in thy temple full of happiness and love. Tukā says, In comparison of thy name all this world is worthless.

## 1110

TO-DAY is a holy and welcome day; the Dasra is here; observe it well; it is an auspicious season. Raise a cry of acclamation; take Hari to your hearts, great and small; I bid you not to be slothful. Come, women, come; Hari has stepped forth to cross the frontier. Run and take lamps and wave them round him. Let us wave them round his holy face; let us place his feet upon our heads. Good fortune has visited us in our own houses. Ere we quit this body of ours, there is open to us a happy season, that cannot wither. "Then", says one, "seeing what a time this is, let no one stay to look round her. Leave every other task and accompany Hari." Take these words to heart in every way; do not neglect what you hear; you will never see nor dream of such happiness again; if you neglect it, there will be nothing but lamentation left, nothing but a legend of what is lost. Those who lose him will be infinitely wretched; you may be sure of this; never will return this chance of immortality; be it known to you, or sad destruction will follow. He for whom Brahmā and the rest went mad, to secure whose leavings of food the gods entered the water, and became fish; he in half of whose frame dwells Lakshmī, the mother of the world; he, says Tukā, has come without an effort of ours.

## 1111

WE have laid foot cloths on the earth, and the garlanded one walks thereon, imprinting in red hues the tread of his delicate feet. Adore, all of you, the dust of his feet, who made the bridges of stones swim in the water. Make room for him, stand silent in your places; be dumb and utter not a word! Tukā proclaims the season; halls and porches and doors are opened.

## 1112

HARI has entered; pause a moment; be patient; the fruit will follow. Be not in haste; listen to me; sit still for a moment! The god is shampooed, water is brought along, he is bathed, and Bhavānī dries his person He is clothed in a vesture of golden stripes. Rakhumai supplicates him; now the feast is served, let him go to his seat. The feast is over; he has cleansed his hands; Nārāyaṇa gladly reclines to rest. Tukā says, I tell you the tale now, as many men have told it before me.

## 1113

NOW the time has come for the final prayer; be vigilant all of you! Raise a shout, cry upon him with sudden speed, clap your hands for the Lord of the world! If you die without doing this, you will not reach his feet. Tukā's brother says, But little time is left us.

## 1114

TUKA has risen and gone to his own place; God remains within the temple. O wondrous consummation! The master's orders confer repose on the servant that obeys them. Hari sleeps on the eternal serpent; there no desire is left unfulfilled. Tukā has sent every one outside, telling them that god is asleep.

## 1115

I HAVE waked you with noisy cries, for I know not how to dance or sing. I am no more ashamed or afraid or anxious for my belly's sake. Sit down, for you are tired. We will rub your feet, O generous one; your body is hot. We will make you feel the wind. One delay follows another; how can I describe it? A mother should feel no anger against her child. Tukā says, We will call together all the children and the cowherds and meet you and cry upon you.

## 1116

LET us take lamps and wave them round the consort of Lakshmī. To-day my vows are fulfilled; blessed is this day! Attend, young maidens, all of you! Tukā clasps his hands as he stands near him.

### 1117

DO you go into your own temple; I return home. O Viṭṭhobā, love me still! I will continue at thy feet. My spirit serves thee, though I return to my own village. Tukā says, Perchance I shall miss the way and come wandering back to thy feet.

### 1118

ARISE, all of you; Nārāyaṇa is arisen; the sages of the three worlds rejoice. Raise a shout of acclamation, with the sound of drums; make a noise of tabors and cymbals and stringed instruments. Fold your hands and behold his face with reverence; lay your head at his feet. Tukā says, Ask whatever you desire; tell him your own joys and sorrows.

### 1119

THEY, who eat and take betel on the eleventh day, enjoy as it were the excrement of dogs; such an one is the vilest of all men. There is no ordinance supreme like this; they who observe it duly, who sing and listen to the praises of Hari, they become like Vishṇu himself. He, who eats betel on that day, eats an unclean thing; he shall fall into the power of destruction, he shall find no escape. He who dallies in bed with a mistress shall contract wasting illness, life-long and violent. He who attends not the service of Hari's praise and keeps others from going, know that Meru is a mole-hill compared to his guilt. Tukā says, They fall into Yama's power, and he torments those who heed not the eleventh day.

## 1120

WE will sing and clap our hands at the scene of thy worship; we will dance with spirit, careless of the world. Mightiest among the mighty, you are our champion; from you proceed worldly wealth, salvation and mystic powers. We will shoot an arrow of speech unerring, irresistible; we will crush all impediments. We will break the head of time and death. Tukā's brother says, We have no fondness for life, not even for our own life, much less that of others.

## 1121

YOU do not lose anything by listening to the praises of Hari, or uttering them yourself; by visiting the temple and worshipping God; by pilgrimages to holy places or observances of religion; by visiting the saints or by purity of conduct. Tukā says, Whether you have faith or not, you do not lose anything by exerting yourself.

## 1122

IF you make another observe due rites, half the merit is yours; if you deter him, both of you go to hell together. If you and your friend are righteous, men will honour both of you; if you consort with a thief, no one will spare your life. You give the weapon yourself, you cause your own destruction; you should know the folly of this and avoid it. Send men on pilgrimage and pay the cost; give no imaginative sympathy to thieves. Tukā says, Do not depart from the path of pilgrimage, observance, sacrifice and devotion.

### 1123

WHILE you are worshipping God, should saints visit your house, you should put the gods on one side and worship the saints. The Śālagrāma is an image of Vishṇu; a saint may belong to any caste. Tukā says, Vishṇu's followers increase the opportunities of devotion.

### 1124

I WILL become a beggar, a pilgrim of Pāṇḍhari; this is my chosen path, Viṭṭhala's name alone. Even thus will I worship, by falling at the saints' feet. Tukā says, O God, I will perform that simple service.

### 1125

THE crowning pinnacle is set upon your work. I worship you under the thousand names. Truly the harvest is ripe; it stands thick and plentiful. Nārāyaṇa, the final gift has fallen to our lot. Tukā says, Our bellies are filled; we are saved from the cry of need.

---

## II.—Inner Qualities are more than Outward Observances

### 1126

EVERY action should be offered to God; this is the only worship that reaches him. Every action is perfected by this rule of conduct, that the worshippers are members of God. This is the one secret; this is the message of religion. Tukā says, It is true; it is true; three times I say it is true.

## 1127

WHAT true worship is performed with earthly pomp? Let us light lamps, to show the way to Vaikunṭha; all treasure is stored up there. Why should we perform an idle task with perishable things of earth? Tukā says, Be my escort the people of Vishṇu.

## 1128

INWARD contemplation is the chief worship that should be paid him. All materials of worship are sinful; to relinquish all plans is true sweetness. In obedience is true piety; O knowing ones, know this secret. Tukā says, This attitude of the mind never wearies and is easily maintained.

## 1129

THE platform is filled with seats; we have sent for the ancient mistress of our line; the mistress of Vaikunṭha comes running swiftly—Come to the scene, dear lady Viṭha, with your purple lustre and keen eyes; when shall I behold your sweet and holy face? We offer thee for incense our faults of ignorance and passion; we dedicate to thee every power of our souls. Make thyself all ready, and come running speedily. We will slay thee our own hearts for a victim; we will offer thee the thirst of desire and passion. We have prepared our loving faith as a portion for thee to eat; we have filled the dish and called loudly upon thee. For drums thou shalt have the sounds of the heart in holy rapture; come thyself and enter among us; take the presents that are offered thee; heal Tukā and make him whole.

## 1130

I HAVE purified the temple in my house; pledges are my store and sincere faith. I have made for thee a garland of the mind's three elements; I tell you my vow and my desire. My God is present at the scene; he dances amid the crowd of Vishṇu's followers. He pervades my frame, yet he keeps our two beings distinct. O man, you have your own treasure within you, but you have forgotten the place of it; the foolish inmates of your breast have spoiled and corrupted it. Now no one knows the truth save my God alone. We must be blind and forget the place before we need to search. She gives eyes to the blind; limbs to the lame; children to the barren; our lady Viṭha fulfils every vow. How many are the feeble of the time gone by whose riddles she has unravelled! Tukā says, It needs no time, no time with you; fulfil my desires and then lead me to perfect bliss!

## 1131

I HAVE framed my desire, do you attend to it; let your hand set me free from fear. If I am afflicted by other and evil spirits, my duty will be to repeat your name. Come to this unequalled scene, which I have prepared for you. The name of Hari rises aloft, mingled with cries and the clash of music. We bow before thee, God of Gods, Lord supreme; come running, O merciful one, O master of delight, in whom I delight! Delay not, for all is prepared! Tukā says, Come thou, who art our ancient goddess!

## 1132

THE temple in my house is pure; it belongs to no other than thee; no one need seek the like of it in the three worlds. Come throw yourselves down before her, put up some prayer to her! She will sweep you clean and drive out the demon of the world. Amid the tumult of lust, the prison of the three qualities, if the name of Hari falls on the ears, she stands up. Though the spirit of self lay hold of a man, with lust and rage and spite, yet they flee away when love fills him; they vanish altogether. Though affection and fondness have harboured within you, yet they vanish with one impulse when they behold this scene. Tukā says, If you give him faith, all doubts will be cleared from your mind; you need not go wandering elsewhere.

## 1133

WHEN raw thieves go forth to steal, they behave in strangers' houses as though they were in their own. They gain nothing and get themselves into trouble; they lose their ears and hands and feet. A foolish fellow succeeds in nothing; to him the injuries he receives are pleasures. Tukā says, If men know not the secret, the fruit of their actions overtakes them.

## 1134

ALL my religion is the name of Viṭṭhobā; I perform no task save to utter it. What knowledge have *I*? The saints have been sent by God; therefore they show their kindness to me. Tukā says, What authority have *I*, to make known this path to men?

## 1135

VITHAI steps forth: let her influence travel on; cast out the deities of the past; wrench your neck with a jerk. The only warrior goddess has entered your body; she will drive out all disorders. "Tell my devotee to worship me with faith; if you slay for me a shaggy ram, you have offered me complete worship. If you are obstinate, I will not visit the spot." Tukā says, She visited our ancestors and has come into the family; worship her, all of you, waving round her a tray of lights.

## 1136

I HAVE made him jewels of speech to adorn his person, thus I have worshipped the Lord of the universe. I have made a dainty meal of faith, thus I have fed Nārāyaṇa. I have given him the activities of my body for water to wash his hands; for a purification of the mouth I have offered him my mind; I have given him choice betel nut of my delighted senses; I finally have crowned him with tulsi leaf. I have made him a lamp of devoted faith; I have given him my body for a seat. Tukā serves his feet in silence; he has laid god to rest within his house.

## 1137

BABHAL and rui plants are not trees of wishes, for they grant not the fruits of desire to mankind; there are many cows and buffaloes and goats, but the wishing cow is different from them all. Tukā says, If God will show himself, it will be a supreme merit to have met him.

### 1138

I HAVE no desire to make a request; I need not restrain my tongue. I will not praise what is worthless, through any private desire. We ought to take our share on the books, as every body knows. Tukā says, What sort of service, O God, is due to the master here?

### 1139

WORSHIP ends in peace; we exhaust ourselves by seeking something more. You know this, O saints; you have pronounced the true rule. We must endure cheerfully whatever happens from hour to hour. Tukā says, I place my head at your feet, O saints.

### 1140

I HAVE supplied the needs of all creatures; I have given away all my estate. All times are pure to me, day and night. I have seized the holiest of all moments. I have visited holy places, with ceremony and sacrifice; I have duly observed all pious rules; I have received the reward in full; I have offered all to the infinite one. Tukā says, Now, I speak the unspeakable; body, speech and mind have vanished from me.

### 1141

THEY are worshippers who are heedless of the body, and have foiled the snares of desire. They have sought their pleasure in Nārāyaṇa; wealth, people, mother and father delight them not.

At the end of all things, Govinda is behind and before us; he suffers no trouble to oppress us. Tukā says, You should forward those good actions which help mankind; if you terrify men, you will go down to hell.

## 1142

HE is God's darling who knows the delights of adoration; I will heed no other, be he wise or learned. Whoso poises his thoughts on God's name and form, his slave am I. Tukā says, He is pure who knows the nine forms of worship.

## XXII

# The use of Images in Worship

### 1143

JUST beyond us we see that purple lustre—how glorious! with his noble crown of peacock feathers stitched together. As you look upon him, fever and illusion vanish; adore then the prince of the Yādavas, the lord of Yogis. He who filled with passion the sixteen thousand royal damsels, fair creatures, divine maidens, he stands upon the bank with the lustre of a million moons; it is fastened in jewels on his neck and merges in the lustre of his form. This God who bears the wheel is the chief of the Yādavas; him the thirty-three crores of gods adore; the demons tremble before him; his dark blue countenance destroys sin. How fair are his feet with saffron stained! How fortunate is the brick that is grasped by his feet! The very thought of him makes fire cool, therefore embrace him with experience of your own. The sages, as they see his face, contemplate him in the spirit; the father of the world stands before them in bodily shape. Tukā is frenzied after him; his purple form ravishes the mind.

### 1144

THEY form the Lord of creatures in clay, but what other name can they give to clay? The worship of Śiva reaches Śiva; the clay remains within the clay. Thus the saints worship us, but God receives the worship. We are the servants of the saints; we desire not the rank of saints. We have formed a Vishṇu of stone, but the stone is not Vishṇu; the worship of Vishṇu is offered to Vishṇu; the stone remains in the form of a stone. We have formed out of bronze the mother of the world; but the bronze is not the mother. She takes the worship which is offered to her; the bronze remains what it was. Tukā says, The highest bliss exists in the perfect alone; O sir, he to whom worship belongs by right, he must take it; we remain no more than stone images.

### 1145

IF men are habitations of God, we should fall at their feet, but we should leave alone their habits and aims. Fire is good to drive away cold, but you must not tie it up and carry it about in a cloth. Tukā says, A scorpion or a snake is a habitation of Nārāyaṇa; you may worship him afar, but you must not touch him.

### 1146

BRAHMA dwells in all things; there is no place void of him; then how can you say an image is not God? If men have no faith, how much explanation is needed to move them? They are infidels by their own inclination. The faith which inspired the utterances of the saints finds no approval from contentious men. Tukā says, Possessing not the strong faith of the saints, wicked ones have brought charges against God.

### 1147

DESTINY has brought and bestowed on me the heart of this world. Heartily have I embraced him, with firm and concentrated faith. I have induced him to reveal himself; he stands upright, close at hand, and easy of attainment. Tukā says, I have made him my servant; he has descended at my speech.

## 1148

THIS merciful God will show himself to each in a form that each can comprehend. I have embraced the feet on the brick, where the embodied and unembodied gods dwell together. He is like sugar that is altogether sweet; if part of it be set aside, it is not found defective. Tukā says, Whatsoever I do, it is Hari on whom the experience rests.

## 1149

I HAVE sought out every sign; I have brought him before my mind. I have beheld the prince who dwells at Pāṇḍharpur. If we follow him, what shall we lose? I have seen those even feet; they are set within my soul. There is no ceremony needed save to see him; meditation will effect all; you need observe no holy seasons. Tukā says, All foulness is cleansed away at once; men are purified and dance on the pebbly shore.

## 1150

IF the mind remembers the father of wisdom, the consort of Lakshmī, what does it need more? Who would share his mind with any other thoughts? Pāṇḍuranga is the perfect sum of pleasure. We will sing and dance in time and clap our hands; there is bliss among the company of

Vaishṇavas. In a single pore of his body there are infinite worlds, yet we simple people have brought him upright before us by faith. We have treated the world as false; before us are no more fetters but true liberation. Tukā says, I have found repose through the might of him to whose name I hold myself subject.

### 1151

WE can now satisfy our desire to sing his praises and gaze on his form. Excellent is Pāṇḍuranga, our dark blue god, lustrous and lovely. He is the essence of all bliss; his face is a treasure of perfect attainment. Tukā says, Doubt not there is no limit to his joys.

### 1152

NEITHER the Vedas nor the Śrutis know thee, nor any save us faithful worshippers. We love to see thy visible form; this is our reward, O Lord of the senses. Faith gives us strength; we will set you in our hearts. Tukā says, You stand watching; you will come to our cry.

### 1153

WE do not ask for milk, with the strong elements in it; but give us at least butter milk to help us; we ask not for food, but give us at least water freely. Tukā says, Give me something visible to pray to; let some one fulfil my helpless desires.

## 1154

THERE is none but thyself can describe thee, none in the three worlds. The serpent of the thousand mouths grew weak and weary over the task; every one of his tongues was split into two. O Nārāyaṇa, inapprehensible, invisible, unlimited; infinite, unembodied truth and intelligence! Thou dost assume name and form at thine own desire; thou dost assume name and shape responsive to our own faith. Tukā says, If thou wilt show thyself, then, O Nārāyaṇa, we shall know thee.

## XXIII

# False Religious Observances

### 1155

WITH their straining eyes and painted features they dazzle the beholders, they tell their disciples they have attained union with God; it is all a false uproar, they are cheating them. They light lamps and close the room about them; they convey their instructions in the night time. They adorn the floor of the yard with pictures and spread a clean covering, and describe their mystic figures; they hang up a curtain and set lamps in the four corners; they sit in quaint postures and go through motions with their hands. He says, "You must offer the gods a dish of rich food, many kinds of delicacies; the discourse is over; eat now a morsel." They rinse their mouth with liquor instead of water. He has made his living by his false doctrine; he ruins the faithful; he calls upon them for a vow, and bids them cry, "O teacher, O teacher." The pure truth he has drowned; the noble character of a teacher he makes a means of self-indulgence. He has extinguished all the rules and drowned the Veda; the admonitions of the Śāstras he has swept away. He practises not the concentration of yoga, nor control of the breath; he abandons all rules of conduct and austerities. He has done away with renouncing the passions, and confounded the worship of Hari;

degenerate wretch, he has increased sin. Tukā says, He and his office descend into hell; he brings his ancestors down into the pit.

## 1156

ABANDONING Hara and Hari, they put their faith in worthless deities; listen how they have brought God and piety into contempt. They wear strings of cowries on their necks and carry a filthy wicker basket; they wander from door to door with their chains about their necks; they are dogs in human shape. They paint their faces with vermilion and gnash their teeth; they carry Satvi's lute. They worship the monstrous belly of Gaṇeśa and the elephant's brute trunk. Their idle desires have led them from the path; their faith and worship are false; such are they, says Tukā, who worship any other than Vishṇu and Śiva.

## 1157

IF we love the Lord of Pāṇḍhari, whom shall we call God? I feel deeply ashamed to call any other God. Who would throw away the diamond and pick up flints? Tukā says, So it would be, to abandon a leader like Hara and Hari.

## 1158

MANY have been lost through not worshipping the Lord of Pāṇḍhari; they worship the greedy and false gods that beg and pursue men for food. They have forgotten the lord of all men. Tukā says, They fall at last into the hands of Yama.

## 1159

THE mother of the Śāktas is a sow, that eats ordure in the street; it is her nature to do so, and she runs after it. The mother of the Śāktas is an ass, braying from door to door. Tukā says, They are the children of an adulteress; it is culpable even to speak of them.

## 1160

HE who worships the female energy is verily moulded out of sin; O Pāṇḍuranga, let him not contaminate me! He is lustful and wrathful, a drinker of spirits, delighting in every vile offence. Without hesitation, says Tukā, he commits sin of any kind.

## 1161

PRINCE and subject alike are perverse, where a Śākta makes his dwelling in a land. There is a rank crop of misdeeds; piety is a beggar in the village. The land bears no harvest, it trembles beneath its burden; the winds disperse the clouds. Tukā says, Suffering of every kind comes joyfully to dwell there.

## 1162

IN a region where an ass of a Śākta dwells there is a heap of sins. He has blown good conduct to the winds, and bidden the senses rage unchecked. If he conceives a passion for a woman, he repeats her name with fierce incantations. He is a drinker of spirits, a low wretch; his mind is a pit of uncleanliness. He is not ashamed, for all his beard, to sing the praises of a harlot. Tukā says, The cursed woman will take him to herself at last!

### 1163

TO procure intelligence of past, present or future is an achievement of worthless people. We servants of Vishṇu ought to contemplate him; what is already ensured comes to pass in the course of fate. To practise magic, to trade for reputation, it puts a distance between us and Nārāyaṇa. Tukā says, This world is overpowering; the eight mystic powers are a grievous burden.

### 1164

IF any speech leads you into error, you are deceived in making friendly or affectionate use of it. If the Vedic rule enjoins it, then it is necessary; but much of it is an evil. The fetter of fluent speech is altogether mischievous. Tukā says, It is well to put it far from you.

### 1165

THEY cut the throats of others, there is no end to their cruelty; poor wretches, they are running into debt, they will have to taste of hell They paint a red stone to make a god; they promise an offering to it. Tukā says, This is mere child's play; they would cry out, if others hurt them but a little.

### 1166

SOME are helpless through ignorance; others are carried away by knowledge. It is clear that a dumb man cannot speak; but what use is a talkative man? There is a hindrance in each direction—a well on one side and a tank on the other. Tukā says, Your past history keeps the truth from you.

## 1167

YOU pay entrance-money, and store up sin, in looking on boys disguised for the stage. If you listen to Hari's ministers singing his praise, there merit is secured in growing measure. If some one in Hari's part steals boy's clothes to show the theft of the cowherd damsels, the sin is that of incest. Tukā says, Such is the world now-a-days; people love the outward show, they have renounced service and piety.

## 1168

NO one has ever praised a vicious character, for we have venerable rules descended from the past. If we cite in our defence examples of man's weakness, we employ a false agreement. "Spirits" and "honey" are names similar in form; but the name of the one does not justify us in drinking the other. Tukā says, I borrow these thoughts from others; I scatter them abroad like rain, to fall as they may.

## 1169

THESE gods and goddesses smeared with vermilion,—who could worship such masters? They cry out for their bellies' needs, and demand a handful of sin. They worry others like beggars, for their own sakes; what can they give to men? I have known what it is to wait on them;

it is in truth a base and vile inclination. A slave can only promise hospitality, but a master will offer it with his own hand. Words of compassion, designed for the moment, are all an empty show. How much water can there be in a rivulet?—not enough to wet the lips or satisfy the desires. It is all weariness, from beginning to end, even if it ripens through long penances to fruit. They keep their faces covered with red paint, and wear a heavy garment upon them; they punish themselves with cracks; only beggars call such things gods. Such is not Nārāyaṇa, nor Janārdana, who pervades the world. Tukā says, Meditate on that God, all others come to worship.

# XXIV

# Our Attitude towards Traditional Forms of Worship

### 1170

AMID all the elder goddesses whither should worship be directed? If you embrace faith, they vanish away. Things may look like each other, when they belong to different purposes; if you go to the bottom, you will see that these beings can bear no strokes from above. The chief honour belongs to one at the head; the rest are esteemed according to certain rules; there is a scale, as when large and small vessels are arranged in a pyramid. Tukā says, Go on worshipping them: no one can be angry with you; they will diffuse light in their own proper places.

### 1171

YOU should not even listen to unholy words. Whoso contemns the story of Hari, a wasting pain shall fall upon him. His caste may be high, but he is a vile and sinful wretch. Tukā says, He is as sinful as an unfilial son.

### 1172

THIS way leads to every stage of salvation; the highest worship is that of God manifest. The form that is cherished in our hearts displays himself when he perceives the purity of our faith.

The name of Hari is seed and fruit; the perfection of merit and pious conduct. It is the key of all accomplishments, it dispels anxious care. Where thy name is repeated and thy praises sung and the servants of Hari lay aside shame, there a delicious draught is poured forth, the snares of the entangling world are severed. The signs of his presence dwell within us, God stations himself there; his powers come to visit us unbidden; there is no more birth and death in store for us. You need not abandon your own order of life, nor the pious ways that have grown up in your family; trouble not over anything but the one sufficient name of Viṭṭhobā. Nārāyaṇa, the Declarer of the Vedas, the unembodied Brahma of the Yogis, to the emancipated, says Tukā, he is the primal and perfect spirit, to us simple people he shows himself incarnate.

## 1173

YOU cannot perfectly observe ceremonial rules, and if you fail in aught, you bring about your fall; but the list of names you may recite at any time; it is easily mastered by the simple and faithful. All forms of repentance lie at men's feet when they glorify the Vaishṇavas. Tukā says, Repeat his name joyfully; it brings no guilt.

## XXV

# Against False Teachers and Impostors

### 1174

FALSE teachers have set upon me; now therefore what shall I say, O Viṭṭhala? They are like an eater of onions who wishes for musk, and forgets that he is as poor as a beggar. They torment me with questions of things they comprehend not; though I fall at their feet, they will not leave me. I know nothing but thy feet; thou alone art all in all to me. Tukā says, Would a nail were driven through their lips! how often must I speak to these quarrelsome disputants?

### 1175

A HERETIC may find God in his own soul, devotion in feeding himself, salvation in death. People are ruined by these servants of the flesh; they have made out the Vedas and Purāṇas to be false. They reason in their own capricious way, declaring that there is no re-birth. Tukā says, The penalties of hell leap upon their back; these rogues forget guilt and merit.

### 1176

YOUR dress may attract compliments, but which of you is a true Brāhmaṇa? Confess this to me, then I will present you to the saints.

You may be experts and skilled to perceive the merits and faults of people's looks. Tukā says, You are guilty of sin, if you conceal the truth.

## 1177

LISTEN not to such an one; the wisdom he discourses is like chaff, void of devotion. He extols the doctrine that seeks absolute union, he sets aside devotion; this is grief and weariness both to speaker and listener. Saying "I am Brahma", he nourishes his own person; we should not speak to such a disputant as he. If one turns from the Vedas, and talks heresy, the knave's face is blackened when he meets the saints. If one denounces the love of God and the saints, he is viler, says Tukā, than an eater of dogs.

## 1178

THERE is no greater hypocrite than he who listens to the voices of the crowd. He will attain the dignity of strayed cattle; the servants of Yama will beat him on the back. Some in their own judgment are skilled in words, yet they interpret the Vedas differently. Tukā says, They do not concentrate their faith, hence their mouths are filled with dirt.

## 1179

WHEN a man has learned to use blustering words, his speech is like dry bread without moisture in it. Who will attend to such an one? We hear him as though we heard him not. He goes from house to house professing knowledge, wasting his labour in pounding chaff. Tukā says to himself, How empty and hollow their minds are!

## 1180

A MAN who prates excessively and draws a single line on his forehead, while he is as tricky as an actor, such a talkative fellow is not a follower of Vishṇu. He declares this and that man out of caste; he honours one and harries another. Tukā says, Such an one has nc compassion in him!

## 1181

THERE are men whose speech is sweet to hear; they talk philosophy, but in their heart they are worthless. Such cheating rogues are fit neither for this world nor the next. Listen, for I tell you, you must not let this dust defile you. Tukā says, A bone sets the dogs quarrelling.

## 1182

THEY call themselves saints, but no one sees it in their actions; who would put faith in such men? Their purity vanishes with the hour of trouble. In the rains, brooks look like rivers; when the flood passes, not a drop remains. A pebble, says Tukā, may look like a diamond afar, but it cannot stand the anvil.

## 1183

THERE is such an one as says, "Study my songs!" This he cries as he goes from house to house; yet he knows not the outskirts of his own village; he feels ashamed if he leaves his own corner. He collects fragments from others' songs; by poetical devices he simulates pathos. Tukā says, A man may wear the signs of devotion; alas! this avails not before Govinda.

### 1184

HE knows not what is right; he is dragged along by the organs of sense; he continues prating in the words which he has learned. Such an one goes to hell himself and would take forty-two families and the world besides with him. He shuts his eyes and utters things unfit for speech; he talks idle nonsense to gratify his pride. Tukā says, I have scrutinized him; I know him for one who dances in imitation of others.

### 1185

THEY grow long hair on their heads, and receive demons into their bodies; but they are not saints, there is no sign of the spirit about them. They assemble men and women and declare various omens. Tukā says, They are impostors; Govinda is not with them.

### 1186

IN this evil age men find their means of spiritual attainment in long hooka pipes; they accustom themselves to drink spirits and smoke bhāng. They make speeches about union with God, but they discover a fast attachment to vices; disciples follow them in abundance; they have fat bodies, staves, and mortars for bhāng. They love honour and wealth; they are full of high desires; they are filthy heaps of outward pretences. Tukā says, I have rated them well and leave them now.

### 1187

WHEN the preacher is fond of money, the listeners are alarmed. They say, he knows not what he sings, he opens his mouth to get something given him. He is as greedy as a cat; he goes begging from door to door. Tukā says, The measure and the sack are both empty.

### 1188

A SHOW of courtesy on the face, while the disposition within is very different—what is the use of such hypocrisy? It merely simulates sincerity in public. To prepare a banquet and to poison your guests would be to mislead them to their death. Tukā says, A Thug conceals his murderous trick; he acts courteously as though he were a respectable man.

### 1189

IF the preacher is fettered by desire of money and the listeners fearful of expense, the worship is all in vain; each party alike is greedy; they are both met together, but their attention is distracted,—such is the case. The sack is full of measures, but all are empty, says Tukā.

### 1190

HE turns to worship God when he meets with good fortune, while his mind is set on unrighteous deeds. Curse his affectation of virtue! He pollutes his mind before he acts. He loves wealth, he heartily desires gain; he has no particle of the devotee's spirit. Tukā says, He gains neither one nor the other; his life is wasted.

### 1191

IF you have any doubts when you utter his name, you do not know his nature. Listen while I tell you of him with absolute faith; eat joyfully what you have in your houses. One may carry the basket, the rosary and the marks of his sect, yet he is an impostor who deceives mankind. He extends his hand, for he has not renounced all; he shows people a stone and worships wealth himself. He soils his body with ashes and idly boasts himself the strongest man alive. He suffers desire to lay hands on his neck to bind him. It comes and swallows him up. What comfort is there in ashes, in lying face downwards with uplifted legs? Such an one brings pain and grief on himself; he falls into hell, yet in his folly he will not run away from it. He has learnt to vociferate loud cries, and collect a crowd of women and children. He fouls his body and demands small coins; but all his efforts are wasted. To show people that he is the strongest man alive he stands up and takes a plank and breaks it, he rubs his knees and elbows and pretends he has hurt himself. They wear themselves out by these worthless tricks; they shave their heads for a pretence; unholy deceit lurks in their hearts; they pollute their bodies and gain nothing by it. Do not play any tricks with this dust and noise; take the fragrant powder of civet and sandal. You will enjoy the sweet odour along with others; grandeur that is paid for is a worse disgrace. By tricks like these men have brought pain on themselves, without winning either wisdom or power. They are smitten on their backs; their faces are darkened by shame, yet their tongue waters for lustful pleasures. Listen to what I Tukā tell you: break away from these tricks; learn none of them. Come, let us eat first to fill our hungry stomachs; when we are satisfied, we will think of outward graces.

### 1192

YOU may treat me, O God, as you will, but I will not call these men saints; for they have set their hearts on rule and wealth. Their desires have made them the victims of hypocrisy. Though they be Brāhmaṇas, I shall hold them none such. They bear knowledge blindly as a burden. Tukā says, I shall not fear mankind in the person of such men, though I suffer for it.

### 1193

THE sacred marks, the cap, the garland, all the furniture of God he carries for his belly's sake—a vile burden. He wears in his ear the tulsi, the darbha grass in his hair; hypocritically he holds the end of his nose. As he sings the praises of God, he weeps and throws himself on the ground; tears flow from his eyes, though no true tears. Tukā says, Such is a deceitful impostor; Govinda is not with him.

### 1194

THOUGH you lay hands on them and seek to prevent them, they go violently down into hell. No persuasion will move these slaves of women. They have wasted their lives; they shall come to utter destruction. Tukā says, O Lord of Pāṇḍhari, they bring a stain on thy worship.

### 1195

THOSE who give or take money for singing God's praises go to dwell in the lowest pit of hell. They suffer the tortures of Rāva, Rāva and Kumbhpāka; Nārāyaṇa takes no pity on them. There they cut them up with swords and roll them on the hot ground. Tukā says, They shall not escape hell; they are caught in the grip of Yama.

### 1196

THEY practise worship according to their own ideas of pleasure and they say, "Nārāyaṇa has enjoyed it." They say, "God is present everywhere," and they break their heads over the meaning of the Vedas. They are ashamed to bear the ascetic's gourd and to wear his patched clothes. Their desires are set on shawls and pots and money; they assert in every speech that these things are perishable. Tukā says, God will never come to meet such people, though they be re-born time after time till the end of the world.

### 1197

THOSE who take and pay money for glorifying his name go both of them to hell. Make yourself fully into Brahma; remember the name of Rāma without ceasing. Do not be carried away by a sweet voice, or you will go to visit Yama. Tukā says, He counts the world too little for a present; he stretches out his hands for alms; fie upon him!

### 1198

CURSED be their shameless trade, that look to the alms pot for support; Nārāyaṇa pays no heed to such. They have no faith in the feet of God; their devotion is a vain outward show. They lead vicious lives; they have not offered their soul to God. They pretend to be weak and humble, and make mankind uneasy. In this, however, they are truly wretched—that they destroy all confidence in themselves. What will the Lord of the world not do for you, if you make truth your stay and support? Tukā says, The secret is, clasp his feet closely.

1199

THE belly with its disguises and its clamorous outcries sets us on praise and censure. Matted hair and ashes are a scandal when the mind has neither patience nor forbearance; they are like a decorated corpse, a dead and lifeless body. Tukā says, I speak of one who is passionate and goes on talking folly.

1200

HE keeps his wealth tied up, and goes about begging for pity; he entreats and harasses kindly people. This is the piety of a scoundrel, the persistence of a rogue; it ends in a sound thrashing. He conceals his god's house and pretends to have lost it; he howls and affects to be worshipping stones. Tukā says, These are the tricks of a monkey; the obscene motions of a whore.

1201

THE speech of a Thug is irreproachable; but his secret thought is how to ensnare you. How goodly he is outside! yet he is not sincere; he is a low scoundrel. He wears the mark of a saint, the head gear and the rosary on his neck, but he takes you aside in the darkness and strangles you. Tukā says, He is a rogue.

1202

IF a man talks of divine knowledge, while his heart is full of pride in wealth, what pleasure does it yield the soul to serve him? Many in this

Kali age have turned saints to fill their bellies. Rare indeed, says Tukā, is the man before whom I fall down.

1203

HE presents the buttermilk to his pupils; he declares that the butter is Nārāyaṇa, and therefore he swallows it. Such philosophers are as stupid as buffaloes, ruined by their desires; they preach purity to the world, but are no more holy themselves than Māngs. Victims to their lust and love of chatter, Tukā says, they are slaves of loquacity and lust; they wear an outer garb of ostentation.

1204

THE world is ruined for this piece of knowledge, which is worth no more than an onion; lust and age and evil passions break forth. He demands money for worship; what does he say to his pupil? Tukā says, Where is Brahma in his doings? They are a carnival of lust.

1205

OUR Gosāvis profess that they beg no alms; they set their disciples to preach. A stone boat is naturally heavy; how can it bear a freight of stones? Tukā says, They bring disgrace on their garb, though they try to play the part.

1206

WHOSO has not found his own true gain seeks to ruin those who sit before him. This mischievous trick of his will swell his heap of guilt; his purposes will hasten on his fall. When a man has to pass through what he has stored up for himself, what can God do for him? Tukā says, You should ask your way from one who is already going to the same village.

## 1207

SOME proclaim themselves teachers and collect a crowd of followers, who are not men but dogs, though they have neither a tail nor four legs. Adulterous and drunken brutes, they fatten their bodies. Tukā says, They are fully prepared to go down to the pit.

## 1208

THERE is no one who will save others; there are plenty who will destroy what is sound. We had a store of pure gold in the house; the goldsmith has destroyed it and made it into ornaments. Where there is moist, dark soil, and black seed sown within it, how could you get hold of the actual seed again? Wheat is all the same by nature, but it is made into many viands, cakes, porridge and boiled grain. Tukā says, Some people can make even poison taste sweet, while a bad cook will spoil butter.

## XXVII

# Krishna

## I.—His Birth

### 1209

KRISHNA is born in Gokula; the evil have begun to tremble. When Kṛishṇa became incarnate, from house to house there was great rejoicing. With great affection all sing his name; they dance for joy continually. Tukā says, Sin vanishes away; they call on his name joyfully.

### 1210

HE who has all the worlds within him, Hari, becomes a child in Nanda's house. How great a marvel! We cannot understand Kānhobā's character. He who satisfies the thirst of the world is fed by Yasodā. He who fills the world, the husband of Kamalā, the Gopīs carry him on their hips. Tukā says, He enjoys the love of women and still he is chaste.

---

## II.—His Childhood, his Tricks, the Complaints of the Neighbours and his Mother's Scoldings

### 1211

AS Brahmā sports among the cowherds, the girls fasten his throat to the churning staff. He runs up to Yaśodā and asks for a meal; he runs after the cows through the wood. Tukā says, He is a cunning fellow; he feigns simplicity and comes begging to you!

## 1212

THE infant Hari is playing in Mathurā, with anklets on his feet, necklace, girdle, and armlets. His mother looks on his face; her spirit cannot contain her joy, "Blessed are mankind to-day; Brahma has been embodied in their store of merit! Sweet child! Yet I waste my time in speaking so,—child dearer to me than life itself!" Men and women of all classes gather in crowds; they forget who they are; mothers and daughters have forgotten their homes. They lay aside fear and all that belongs to it; hunger and thirst are vanished; even though they stay at home, their spirits are with him; eagerly each seeks to find a time to meet him. All delicacy, all care of their persons they have forgotten; there is no place for shame here; each forsakes her pleasant bed and runs towards him. Girls, men and women, all are fascinated; women playing with their children have forgotten even them. Young men and maidens have lost all sense of themselves; when once they see him, they cannot remove their eyes from him. Enmity ceases among them; none distinguishes himself from others. Grief, longing for home, and sorrow are crushed and forgotten. Tukā says, He has filled them with joy like his own; my lord plays with affectionate joy in the image of a child.

## 1213

HIS mother sees him eating dirt; she ties him with a tether. He takes his net and blanket and stick; he strings his horn behind his back and tends the cows. Great is the might of faithful devotion; God has become their child. Tukā says, As a reward for our devotion God comes running after us.

## 1214

THE Gopīs look and find the milk-pail upset; they say, "Nanda's boy has been thievish today; no one but he can have made this waste." Tukā says, I keep company with him; he has blotted from my mind the distinction of good and bad.

## 1215

WHEN the feast is set, Kṛishṇa begins his frowardness; the garlanded god mixes all the food together. "Give me each kind separately!" he says to his mother, and he claps his hands together and throws himself on the ground. "What a froward child you are! You mischievous boy, take something else!" Kṛishṇa says, "I don't want it!" "Now what am I to do? I must not beat him; he won't be pacified, if I try to reason with him; I don't know what to do. You have mixed them up; now separate them! Why do you torment me?" says his mother to Hari. So she makes him undo his work and puts an end to the confusion; he was pacified and sat up. O mother, you have brought him well to his senses, laying aside your own pride. How one word put the trouble right! He covered the dish with his skirt, and restored all as it was before, separating each kind of food. His mother was amazed; when she grasped his intention in her mind, she says, "There is no one like you!" She rejoiced with overflowing gladness; she folded him in her arms and embraced him. A stream of joy was let loose at that feast. Tukā says, O leave some remnant for me!

## 1216

WHAT do you need? Why do you go stealing? How often must I speak to you Hari, and you heed me not! You keep running away from me further and further, you unnatural, unmanageable child! I love you with a mother's fond devotion; how long shall I suffer the blame that people give me. Time is ever passing on; you must learn to keep still, and set me free from blame. I am occupied with many tasks in the house; you run away, Hari, and escape my sight. I follow you up and leave no pains untried, but I cannot keep sight of you for a moment. O infinite one, I cannot love you too dearly; when I say so, do not vanish from my eyes I want no one with me, none but you, O Kānhobā, lord of Tukā, possessed of every attribute!

## 1217

FIVE or six cowherd damsels meet and complain to Yaśodā. "Why have you borne such a thievish child, such a strange and impudent creature? There is neither milk nor curds nor butter hanging from the peg; the pantry is empty. He has taught his mischievous tricks to our children, and infatuated our son's wives. Make haste and teach him better, or we shall lose our own souls and have nothing left. All of us women will meet and plague him; you and I will cease to be friends. He pays no attention to other people's rights, or public opinion; he acts anyhow and goes anywhere. When we are not at home, he looks at and enters our houses; he kisses our clothes and rolls upon the beds. He breaks the hanging pots and the vessels of milk; we cannot catch hold of him. Now we neither love nor fear him; he pays no attention to us; if we can seize him, we will do as we like with him. We have put up with him for a long time; we never formed any plans against him, because he is your only son." "I will heartily bind his feet to a pillar so that he cannot stir; though you offer me gold or life, I will never let him go; I do not care what happens to me." Kṛishṇa's mother takes him and hands him many a time to the cowherd damsels. "If you speak harshly to him, my child will grow passionate. Where he lays his hand, butter is formed and waves of nectar." When they saw Tukā's lord, all the women forgot their cruelty and themselves.

## 1218

THE cowherd damsels meet and complain to Yaśodā, "There is neither milk nor curds nor ghee left hanging from the peg; he collects the lads and comes in to steal it. He carries it off smartly and eats it before our eyes. This is a trick of Hari's, a trick of his; keep him away—even if you are not ashamed of him! If we catch him, you and I will have nothing to do with each other; you think it amusing and he enjoys himself. What are you laughing for? Have you gone mad? Shall we follow your example? The lad has misled our girls. How can we tell his naughtiness? We feel ashamed to mention it. He soils his face with dirt and stands with his head covered." Then says Daśavantī, "Bring him here and we will teach him! He torments everyone at home and abroad; even the watchmen themselves. He gets into the big pot of foaming milk and eats the butter there." The milkmaids have met together and tied a halter round his neck; they fasten him to the stone mortar and tell him to be still there. "Ha! we have caught you, Hari! you won't go stealing from to-day." They look at each other and laugh. They all went their ways; then Hari lifted up the mortar, and with it he broke the two white arjuna trees; a loud crash arose; Daśavantī was alarmed; she ran speedily to Tukā's generous lord and embraced him.

## 1219

"NOW," say the Gopīs, "we will catch them both and beat them, or they will never give up their mischievous habits, now they have found how sweet the milk is; we will shut them up in the house; we will look out for them without speaking." Still, says Tukā, a great band of Kṛishṇa's companions call out to him.

## 1220

ARE his tricks few? No indeed, they are many and passing false. The cows are continually let loose and the little cowherds get into disgrace. They are always shouting after them; nobody can keep them in order. Tukā says, His mother often beats him at home.

## 1221

I HAVE often got into disgrace by joining his tribe of comrades. The son of Nanda has thoroughly shamed his parents' faces. They proclaim a bad name for me; they hide their faces when people complain of me. Tukā says, How many such fathers and mothers I have had in ages past!

1222

I WILL sing the tale of his frolics; he guarded his comrades and the cows; he stole the butter; he got himself tied by the neck; O Gopāla, this is how you amused yourself! He enchanted the cowherd damsels with the strains of his flute; let us sing of his merry exploits! His fond and coaxing tricks with his parents—let us recall and enjoy them in our minds. He crushes the wicked, he protects the faithful; thus, let us say, our master shows his might. Tukā says, Let us exalt him by proclaiming all this; let us dwell with him continually for evermore.

---

## III.—His Amusements with the Cowherds

1223

THE father of the world calls Yaśodā "Mother"; he gives to his worshipper such portion of this love as he can accept. He remained apart and free from desire; he set the damsels longing. Tukā says, The infinite has assumed a handsome form.

1224

HE tends the cows; he comes to our houses, time after time. If you utter his name, he is at your side; our mighty Kṛishṇa is very gentle. He leaves no want unsupplied; he says, all is acceptable. Tukā says, We desire him not to leave us.

## 1225

THEY have compassed the mystery which Brahmā and the rest cannot comprehend. He plays on the flute and the fife, he runs after the cows. The leavings of his food, which god cannot obtain, fall to the happy cowherds. Tukā says, Great is my gain; I have found my mother.

## 1226

THE cowherds say, "Let us go to Kṛishṇa, and ask him for something; let us tell him our heart's desire." Some say, "We will just be content to follow him; let no one stay sleeping at home; wake up, all of you!" Hari knows, but pretends not to know, and sits quietly in their midst; without hearing any words of theirs, he understands their wishes; he brings their secret desires to their lips and gives to each accordingly. Some say, "We are harassed by earthly desires, yet the world gives us neither rice nor curds, but only whey to drink; we are wearied with tending our cattle, we want water and shade; let us fall at his feet and ask him to fill our stomachs." Others say, "It is a small thing to ask for a bellyful; let us ask for buffaloes and cows and horses, for wealth and treasure and elephants; if we have Kānho for our friend, we shall lack nothing; we shall be rich enough to give all our servants bedsteads to sleep on." Others say, "O children, who cares for these things? A horse is no better than a donkey; you are sick of the disease of the world, which will not leave you even on your bier. We will take staves in our hands and with shaven heads we will wander at large through the forest." Others say, "In the forest are many fierce animals; they will devour your eyes and tear you limb from limb; where is any one strong enough to protect himself and others? Yours is a foolish choice; we will stay quietly at home." "When we stay at home, people will set us plenty of work to do; no one will like to see us idle, as well we know; we shall have to choose some occupation that pleases the public, and slyly amuse ourselves and our companions with pleasant games." Others say, "Will those good friends agree? Men try to put down each other and get their own way; then mischievous games are set on foot and end in kicking; someone gets annoyed, then follows an uproar and kicks." Others say, "It is only children that spend their time playing. Is that possible here, where some are young and others old? They all take offence when they hear another praised. Since dissension arises in company, we ought to avoid it by solitude." Others say, "Where will you find solitude? Everyone is busy making and giving up places; your proposals are waste of words. Stay where you are, do not weary yourself with travelling; you have a load of actions in your bag that you cannot lay down." Tukā says, What is the use of all your tales? Shall we lick up your words to satisfy our hunger? Let us wake up Kānho and ask him for a morsel in our dish; then our friends are pacified and Tukā is satisfied, because he has Viṭṭhala's name in his throat.

## 1227

WE accompany you Hari, because we have no shame to keep us in our due place. You lifted up a mountain, a splendid feat, and saved us! Now let us play no more; our cows have wandered away; it has grown late. Keep back those stragglers, lest they go too far! When you jumped into the Yamunā, you saved us gloriously; verily we are shameless creatures, that we are not utterly afraid of this infinite one! When you were a child, you played with us, you ate fire and dirt like a child, but we want your company no more in this guise. We desire now that he should surround and protect us. Tukā says, In your company no wish remains unfulfilled; you withdraw farther and farther from the wise and consort with the simple.

### 1228

THEY run a race with the river; he satisfies them. He is so fond of the cowherds that he runs wherever they go. He commands the river to stand still; he says, "The current is weary; take rest." This is why, says Tukā, he carries the horn, the flute and the staff.

### 1229

THEY beckon to Kṛishṇa, "Come, let us play at a dinner-game." The children are assembled in a fond and gleeful mood. He conceals the illusion from them; he knows his own secret; he pretends to be playing; he does not open his lips; he gives his attention where theirs is given. They have filled Kṛishṇa with unnumbered fancies; he pretends to approve whatever plans they make. Body, speech and desire, they are all entered into his form. They enjoy a solitary bliss with their masters. Know this, they all attended on Hari; he took them with him on his secret expeditions. He does not let their families know; he involves them in his thieveries; they pass the plunder from hand to hand and carry it away. The children play together full of deep delight; they have left strangers behind them. There indeed is one in one; no difference of nature persists. Tukā says, There is Nārāyana alone.

### 1230

A FIRE broke out round them. "O Kanho, what shall we do? How shall we save our lives? Run, Hari, we are in a fire! We do not know what to do in this fire: on a sudden we saw the flame overhead; when we turned round, we saw it, for we had been looking the other way; we are surrounded; we cannot run away." Tukā says, You know what to do; do it, O infinite one!

### 1231

"FEAR not; cover up your eyes. If God undertakes the task, there is no fear." "We know our father is God of gods; he hides from us the miracle that he works or sets to work." He, the pervading one, opens his mouth and eats up the flame. At the appointed time the cowherds look forth. Tukā says, Before now we feared without cause; now we have learnt that there is no distress by his side.

### 1232

HARI teaches true devotion to the ignorant; he puts aside shame; he dances and plays the flute and fife. "Come now, let us fall at his feet. He saved us amid the great fire; O Kānho, how did you swallow that vast flame? We see no scar upon your face." Tukā says, Why do you wonder? He eats our offerings and that makes him strong.

### 1233

THEY have arranged a game on the banks of the Yamunā; the cowherd says to his companions, "Let us have a game at hāla, stop wandering idly about! Pick up your sides—then nobody need complain." Tukā says, Then Kṛishṇa makes his companion of him who can forget sesamum seeds and rice.

### 1234

KṚISHṆA does not force any one into the game; he sharpens the powers of the mind. O God, let us play together freely, to find you out by mutual faith. He comes and goes from time to time; they find their parts unconsciously. Tukā says, Clasp him to your heart, embrace his feet heartily.

### 1235

WHEN he climbed up the kalamba tree and leaped into the Yamunā, they cried, "Hari is drowned; shout for help!" His own household did not know the truth. We cannot see beyond the sea of the world, within it dwells the great poisonous snake Kali. Tukā says, What avail your cries? You have lost what you possessed; you may wail for it now!

### 1236

THEY all came together and lamented, "He was with us but now, and he is gone!" They all lament with diverse notes, each according to his own idea of the case. "We offended him while we were playing together; that is why he has left us." Tukā says, They all run to the bank, but no one ventures to jump in.

## 1237

THEY are frightened, because they have lost God; they do not know that he is near them; they utter loud cries and beat their limbs and faces. We do not learn that God is near us till we have reached the uttermost limit of grief. Tukā says, He is keen to discern; he can tell true from false devotion.

## 1238

HE chased away Kali and emerged; they point him out far away from them. While they thought him a stranger, they could not recognize him; they doubted whether it were he or not. There was a change in his aspect; dark as he was, he appeared bright. Tukā pats the cowherds on the back and confesses "Truly he is God."

## 1239

BLESSED were those cows, blessed were the blanket and stick, the flute, the fife and the armlet that were his true symbols. Blessed was Gokula with the cowherds and all the men and women therein. Blessed were Devakī and Jesavanti; the good fortune of Vasudeva rested on both of them. Blessed were the sixteen thousand young wives of the cowherds; all the race of the Yādavas was blessed. Tukā says, They were blessed from their birth; they enjoyed with full devotion the joys of Kṛishṇa's company.

## IV.—How they made a Meal together

### 1240

THE cowherds say, "Come, let us mix our provisions together!" Let me see what victuals each one has got. Speak the truth; do not keep anything back. The cheat shall find himself cheated; drive him away! God gives nothing of his own without examining what you have got. All keep their eyes on each other; nobody is let off; one brings butter-milk, another rice, another bread; God sits in the middle and takes what is brought, though he does not force an offering from any one. Here is an impatient one; hurriedly he empties out his bag; some will be untying their knots, others are still coming up. One stands still with his load, an idle insincere fellow; some bring up their boiled grain and look pleased as though they were ready; some have halted their cows; some turn them away; there are others whose cows are intractable, they wheel round and scatter themselves. Some cowherds fasten on the broken victuals; they are not intent on real satisfaction. Some say to each other, "Come along," some go on dancing round. Some have sent astray the simple and ignorant children among them; some are sunk in worldly affairs and have left the flowers on their garlands to wither. Some will not open their bundles; they eat what others have brought; they are like pressed men carrying a load, who die under the burden. Some are immersed in family affection; they are deeply engaged; they know nothing of this occasion, for they know nothing of anything. They were doomed to eat what stale food they had; when they had finished it, then their eyes were opened. Some put streaks on their arms and legs; some covered themselves with ashes. Some have shaved their heads clean; some have removed their tuft entirely; some are idlers at heart, but make a pretence of penance with uplifted arms. Those who employed their intellects without any offering to God have all been made miserable. Tukā says, Now let Kānhobā give us each our share; thou knowest we have kept nothing to ourselves. If thou leavest us, whom shall we go to? The merciful one has shown mercy to us; let us eat our fill.

### 1241

"SEE here is a mouthful which I got from him; it belongs to me; God gave it me; you may go and meet him too, if you like. It has filled my stomach like this!" So says he, describing it with his finger. Tukā says, When were we fed like this at our own homes?

### 1242

WE are rustic cowherds, not the impudent among worldly men; let us bring our victuals together and divide them with each other. Let us play together; we have our own resources in ourselves. Tukā says, Without knowing it, we have united ourselves to Kānhobā.

### 1243

THEY had their fill of Hari's company. They would give him their own food, and eat what he gave them. He does not leave the debt of gratitude unpaid; he hungers for their love. He is resolved to live along with them. "Kanho, eat many a morsel with us," they say. The simple cowherds love God dearly. Tukā says, Now we will go home; we will say, "You have saved us, O generous one!"

## 1244

ON the bank of the Yamunā, the garlanded god says to his companions, "Bring all your victuals, let us make a joint feast; let us bring all together and then taste it; I give you what I have." The cowherds say, "Excellent"; they overflow with joy; they make it known on the flute. They have opened their bags on the rock; they have put all together; Hari presides over the mixture and gives a share to each. One after another stretches forth his hand and opens his mouth; each who gets a ball feels an increase of joy. They say, "Delightful! Give me another! I am not satisfied.' Kṛishṇa moves his hand towards the face of one, he opens his mouth with desire; lo! he eats the morsel himself and makes faces at him! He embraces them and runs away; they run after him; they kiss his face and eat morsels from his lips. They say, "O Kṛishṇa, you are a cheat!" He sets one running for a morsel and runs into the jungle himself; he is a wise man who follows close on his heels. He eats the food offered by all; 'tis a wonder Kṛishṇa can hold it! The best of gods exclaim, "Alas! we have missed real joy!" Kṛishṇa throws a ball at the back or face of one; he cries "Enough, Hari! I can bear no more!" He cries to him entreating, "Dear father, I cannot bear the ball!" He says. "Let us play fairly now," expressly he made this request. Setting Hari in the midst of a circle of joy, they wheel round him in circles, blowing horns and flutes. Crooked men and stammering, mis-shapen in hand and foot and lame, Kṛishṇa rejoices to see them before him, for their hearts are faithful. He delights to look upon their faces; he rejoices and laughs out loud. They are not ashamed to eat the food left by each other; their timid hearts were made bold by his presence. If any one still is hungry, he opens his mouth. Hari gives to all the same pleasure. They say, "Hari is good indeed; excellent is thy company; now though thou shouldst send us away, we shall worship none but thee." The cows have forgotten their food, the birds and beasts their prey; the Yamunā stands still, its waters stay their course; they all gaze upon the god; their mouths water at the sight of him. They say, "Blessed are the cowherds, wretched are we! What are we to do! Let us become fish in the water, to taste the food he has thrown away." The gods come in a crowd; they fill the banks of the Yamunā; quick and eager is the loud sound from their lips. Joyfully Gopinātha sports with them; he says, "Do not wash your hands in the Yamunā." They say, "He knows the secret, he knows it." He who is ashamed to meet God, what does it profit him to be here? The remains which Kṛishṇa leaves are the chiefest blessing. Happy is the time; to-day we have found Gopāla; they say, "You have comforted us with your hand." His companions feel gratified by each other's pleasure. To-day they sit in a row and feed on curds to their hearts' content. "Excellent is your society; bestow it on us for ever; do this, O God, and guide our souls for ever." Then says Vanavali, "Take your sticks and blankets; now let us go off all together to pasture the cows." Tukā says, They were delighted by his love, hence they could bear no further journey. He has made the cows and cowherds like himself. "To-day we have gotten joy; the fountain of joy has come into our midst."

## 1245

THE cowherds have all put away their desires; they say, "The time has come; bring the victuals together." They give all they have got; they make the cows keep in their own sheds. When the company is met, Hari belongs to all, to the pot bellied, the stuttering and the stammering. The devotees make excellent dishes after their own taste; Hari chooses out a sweet dish for himself. All have brought their burdens on their shoulders, till the assembly is met together. In the presence of all every load is set down. If any one is in a hurry for his share, his friends grow angry with him—"What brings you with a false deceitful desire?" Then, as they talked to each other, how they were filled with the joy of Brahma. Tukā says, Come let us worship the feet of Hari.

## 1246

TO-DAY Ămarāvatī is deserted; the gods come to see the meat; they forget their own nature. The cows and ravenous beasts alike are lost in wonder at the sight. The earth cannot contain their joy; they have forgotten food and drink. The God of gods stands here enjoying himself; Kānhobā is playing with the cowherd. To enjoy that pleasure he has set foot on the earth. Tukā says, The sages searched for it in vain.

## 1247

IN the hope of sharing the food the gods entered the water and became fish; he laughed as he wiped his hands on his thighs. "If any one is ashamed to take my favours, give him no portion"; he knows the heart. The humble he takes to himself; if one tries to choose means of access to him, they turn out false and misleading, but if a man comes before him with uplifted hands, he will not neglect him. Take therefore his gift with a quiet spirit; let each take what he shall receive. Tukā says, I taste the joy of love.

### 1248

"TAKE bread and juicy berries and curds and rice for a meal on the road; if any has brought whey, let him throw it away. Take in proportion as you give; if it be little, let it be pure. Aim at a share of what I offer; or else go away home. Deceive your mother then and bring back butter with you." Tukā says, O Hari, I have nothing at home; do not send me away from your feet.

---

## V.—How they stole the Butter

### 1249

THE wives of the cowherds have met and form a futile plan; they say, "Come! we will catch him to-day and imprison him in the house." They open the door and stand in the shadow behind it; five or six of them wait in a silent group. "He has formed this bad habit, and he never gives us a chance to tell him our mind. Now if we catch him, who will let him go as long as she is active?" Hari knew all about it and came stealthily into the same house ; he left his friends outside and entered by the eastern door. He is on his guard against the women, and goes along arching his neck as he looks round him. He catches sight of the butter in front of him ; he takes the pots down from the chair, and tastes them to find which is exactly right. What is sweet he gives his friends to pass away from hand to hand. He knows they are watching and therefore he does more mischief than usual ; he wipes his hands and conceals the traces to let them know he is stealing. One woman perceives him and closes the main door ; they shut him up inside and imprison him in the house. "Why do you ruin us? You have set about our chief store. I'll make you pay for all you have eaten up to now." They seize him by his two shoulders and arms and take him to his mother. "See, what mischief he has done in the house!" Tukā says, His countenance never suffers grief to swell ; Daśavanti amused them all by admiring his trick.

## 1250

"HE has given a sweetmeat to everyone, but he won't look at me!" So some cowherd cries sobbing, while he rubs his eyes, and beats his thighs and smites his face. "He prefers the high and mighty ; I am a poor wretched boy!" Tukā says, God looks to the inner faith, when he distributes happiness.

## 1251

"THE pot hangs up aloft in the rope ; I will rise to the height of three men. You stand on each side, and open your mouths ; as the streams flow out, let them run down your elbows." Tukā says, Judge of the weight by your arms; he gives neither more nor less to any one.

### 1252

"YOU must look on; you are not wanted here; I will bring your fair share outside to you. Cowherds, keep a look-out; if there is any sign of the master coming, run far away from me. I am a practised thief and can make my way where there is no way at all; you will be frightened and waste your labour groping about." Tukā says, You will win the prize when you give your own soul for it; in the end, when he gives it, you will find it sweet and smack your lips over it.

---

## VI.—The Condescension implied in his Conduct

### 1253

TO look at, they were mere cowherds, yet he eats the morsels left by them. The companions of Kṛishṇa contemplate his name. When the time comes, he will give them a triumph; now he runs after the cowherds. Tukā says, In one spot food was prepared for the faithful.

### 1254

BLACK as we are, we are God's cowherds. He will not let the food be spoiled; he sets us down to eat with him. Black as it is, he wears my blanket. Tukā says, There is no difference between me and him.

## 1255

HE watches greedily for the unhusked grain of one; he accepts the feeble compliments of another. Such were the manners of the cowherds, but he delighted in their faith He eats the food left by one; he goes and cheats another. Tukā says, He is easy to approach, for the infinite one has many forms.

## 1256

WE have made Hari sit down in the midst of our company; he comforts all of us in like measure. Every one who looks sees him face to face, and enjoys all his doings. He catches from their hands the morsels they offer to place in his mouth. As they speak to him, he answers them; they take whatever he gives them. It is a secret between the giver and the taker, a third cannot perceive it. Tukā says, O God, your delight is to show love to others; you drop no poison into the heart of any man.

## 1257

WHEN they were satisfied, their companions raised a clamour. They cried, "Come, Nārāyaṇa, we will whisper some secrets to you." They carried him on their shoulders till they were tired out; Tukā's generous master then made the children happy.

## 1258

THE eternal Brahma became a cowherd to taste a mouthful; with joined hands he puts the food to his mouth, in the chinks between his fingers he holds the spices! How great a privilege was that!—beyond the reach of Brahma and the other gods. He plays at *hamāma* and *humbari*; he blows on the flute and the horn with rhythmic music; among the encircling cowherds Hari dances with delight. If they had no food in their house, he went and stole butter. Tukā says, In his company we have learned the trick ourselves.

### 1259

WHEN the cows low, he listens to them; he, the treasure of salvation, stands listening to them. He who wears the garland of wild flowers took pleasure in the cowherds' worship and the morsels of food they left him. He stole the milk and the butter and ate it; by faith the wheel-handed one was caught and bound. He who is void of desire became greedy and desirous; he sits waiting for the cowherd damsels. The lord of the world desires one leaf of tulsi; he can, all of him, be purchased by faith. Tukā says, The purple spirit of life pervades all, yet remains separate.

### 1260

"RUN, Kānhobā, our cows have strayed!" He does not say, "Who am I? What is this?" God loves to hear the voice of his own and he serves them. If they ask for his aid, he gives them the victory; he does not think, "I am high and mighty." Tukā says, So he behaves to us; we ought to follow him with all our heart.

### 1261

HARI meets all the cowherds, mingles with them and embraces them. He loves the devout and opens his heart to them. He whom the yogis cannot attain to rewards their contemplation; he asks them for a piece of bread to eat. Tukā says, He withdraws himself from the wise; like a slave of the simple he beckons to them.

1262

WHATEVER actions are performed, their merit or demerit is brought to light by time; he plays along with the cowherds; whatever they do he puts up with it. He cares not for spells and rites, or oblations in the sacrificial fire. Tukā says, Along with his devotees he even acts like a thief.

---

## VII.—Various Reflections and Comments

1263

"COME, let us collect our cows; why are you asleep? If we make an uproar, our mother will beat us when we go home. Cry out the proper cry to your cows; each cow will turn round at her master's call; that will be enough to rouse her attention. If you do not understand the game or the opportunities when they come, you will find yourselves all unhappy together." Tukā says, If you won't learn, you will be brought to beggary; run all of you in turns and catch the cow of the mind.

1264

A WORD is enough to the wise, to him it serves as a hint; advice is for the many, but they must be able to receive it. Even though a man be not caught beyond hope, still distress will get hold of him, and his soul will be troubled. Tukā says,

You who are hearing, do not grow angry; you will come to grief, if you do not open your eyes.

## 1265

"COME, let us drive the cows about, let us not leave them to pasture in one place. We have travelled far through the jungle; we have worn ourselves out with wandering. Laden and hungry as we are, what pleasure can there be in playing?" Tukā says, Run, run! and all will be well.

## 1266

NOW, Kānhobā, you and I are cronies; I shall not let you go to another. I will carry your food on my own head, it shall not be carried in turns. We will milk the white cow of Vedic truth; we will wrestle with the Vedas ourselves. Tukā says, We will have those punished who do not listen to your words.

## 1267

WHY have you lost your cows? Your turn has come to bring them in; so go. There is something that pursues one: do you not know what it is? You have been put to shame altogether: are you not continually punished and disgraced? The clog is strong, and the nail is stout, who can release you? If you try to run away, your clog will pull you down. Run as you will, says Tukā, till your intellect has reached the true goal, you will not put off the sense of self.

## 1268

"O GOPĀLA! Leave us alone; the cows you have given us are restless creatures; who can keep up with them? We lose ground in endless mazes. They never stay still, they run in every direction." Tukā says, Do you restrain the cow of the mind; we will look after the rest.

### 1269

KĀNHO has bid me milk the cow whose udders are filled:—"Take that milk and divide it carefully amid your friends." I have done as he bade me; this is no religion founded on sacred rule. Tukā says, I do not distinguish old rules from new; who could endure to be drawing this distinction?

### 1270

THEY say, "Now we are well satisfied, we need no more food; now let us not forget him for one instant. Come, Kānhobā, come; let us start a game in the forest. Let us bring our cows together and fasten them up in the shed. We do not want to go home, if we can avoid perpetual going and returning. You are our father and mother and our bosom friend." Tukā says, Our stomachs are filled; now what crying want can there be? Behold, there is no further path before or behind us.

### 1271

IN company with thee we have lost all care. We have obtained an invisible boon, the solemn enjoyment of real happiness. At home we have a sea of buttermilk, but here we have abundance of true butter. Tukā says, Now we shall not go, though you threaten us.

## 1272

"KRISHNA, you are a silly child, shameless and impudent; I have tried scolding you, but you won't leave off your tricks. You go on hour after hour, you cut off our affection from you. You are a regular cow-boy, thoughtless and unruly, thievish and vicious; I'll have a proclamation made of it." If we make your mother a common strumpet, says Tukā, you will think it a credit to you.

## 1273

"YOU Gopīs and boys, what do you know about me? I created Indra, the chief of gods; Indra, the sun and moon, Brahmā, the three worlds and Yama-Dharma, all are mine. From me are the soul of man and Śiva alike; I am Kṛishṇa, God of gods." Tukā says, Kṛishṇa speaks to the cowherds; I am no better than a stone.

## 1274

O COWHERDS, while I stay with you, I loathe the proud; you are endowed with all gifts. O avoid the burden of daily toil, by securing the true essence of all things. Tukā says, Let Nārāyaṇa keep my life free from anxious uncertainty.

## 1275

I KNOW nothing of time; I have been comforted by thee! O Kānhobā, there is no fear left in me. Do you tend the cattle and leave us enough for our stomachs. Fear at thy side! I will not mention such a thing! Tukā says, I have found by experience that words are waste of breath.

## 1276

THOSE that run away are cowards; they find many difficulties in the world; as for those who take courage, Hari brings them down abundance from the pot on high. Those who trust to their own intellect remain unsatisfied. Tukā says, Take it when you can get it; you will never reach the spot yourselves.

## 1277

BY dwelling close to him we have somehow learned that there is no division within Kānhobā. It is our own feelings that oppress us, following on our own desires. God witnesses our actions and watches our diversions and our curiosity. He enters into our game of life, but cares nothing for victory; he bears the burden of every man. Some fall into the snares of the world; others try to read the great riddles. Tukā says, If any cowherd takes a morsel in hand and gives it him, his recompense is equal to his devotion.

## 1278

GOD has created ignorant children and set them to play games, while he makes their cattle stray. As they play, they begin to fight, while he keeps far from them; they slay each other without pity, by fraud and by injustice. Tukā says, I follow Kānhobā, so this revelation has dawned within me.

## 1279

THIS shall be my theme for ever, as I keep the festival of Kṛishṇa's birth. Our generous milch cow overflows; we have all things freely given us, enough to fill the sky. Sanaka and the sages form rows of lovely guests; to each man is given according to his taste. Tukā says, We will set Nārāyaṇa in the midst, then we shall never be distressed.

1280

WHO is my comrade, who? Choose him from among these many natures. We will meet each other and play together. Keep far from unquiet spirits; send the timid to herd the cows. Tukā says, Let no unclean persons approach God.

---

## VIII.—The Passion he inspired in the Cowherd Damsels

1281

COME, women, let us behold Pāṇḍuranga on the sandy shore; the crowd of cowherds have made a feast and set him in the midst. Joyfully they feed each other; they do not call each other either great or small. They play at hamāmā and humbari; they blow the flute and fife; they set Hari in the midst and dance round him; men, women and all creatures are filled with desire for him. They forget their own nature; there is no doubt left in their minds. They bury him in flowers and wave about him lamps innumerable; they weave garlands of tulsi and put them on his neck. Kānho, king of the Yādavas, the joy of the Gopīs,—Tukā says, They rejoice to see him.

1282

"I WENT into the wood with Govinda alone,—such experience was mine. Call me not a lascivious woman; for I did not approach a vicious man. I had seen no other path; therefore I made this bold approach to him. With reverence I embraced him and couched by his bed; with familiar gesture he clasped my breast, and I endured it. I conceived a child and thereby I am a lawful wife; why need I tell you it?" Tukā says, She ended her speech; thus she protected herself and Govinda; this was what she had long desired; now the vow of vows was fulfilled.

## 1283

I HAVE met Govinda as I desired; now I will serve him without fear. Give me, O give me repose by your fellowship! I am weary with the revolutions of many a re-birth. When I am with him, I cannot bear the wind to come between us; shut the doors and keep everything else from us. The primal power we can restore by deep effort; then he will not leave us for a moment. Through love of him I have forgotten the world; now let him come and follow me; I am mad with passion. I have secured the very height of good fortune: I have entered smoothly into perfect peace. I have secured a sweetness of perfect savour. Tukā says, This day will never return!

## 1284

THEY have learned what the pleasure of the self is; they will tell their experiences to each other. They are all wrapped in complete wonder; each testifies her wonder to herself. Each tells her wondrous tale to the rest; be the theme fit for speech or not, they dwell on it. As clouds drink their moisture from one dark cloud, so from the depths of their hearts they long for his sweetness. Hari is the only object of their desires; all else pleases through pleasure in him alone. To the world around them they were blind and deaf and dead; yet their fame was sung in the Purāṇas. Honour is sweet from the lips of others; we esteem the praise of those we love. There is mutual feeling where respect is returned; when good men meet together, there is endless delight. Throughout the universe God does not break the union of lover and beloved; he has left the distinction of sought and attained. He keeps his worshippers near or far from him according to their stock of merit; Hari has to change according to the line of his worshipper's piety. Tukā has secured a meal of leavings; he has spoken out through overflowing love. The efforts of that spirit have fallen on his ears; with complete faith he has grasped the feet of Hari.

## 1285

A MARVELLOUS thing has happened to-day: I came into this wood, and Nanda's son Kānho suddenly met me; people tell me I am caught in a snare, but I say it was my store of merit which brought him. It came to this, that I could not help myself; he signalled to me, when there was nobody near. He held me fast, and what could I do? A fine thing, O women, it would have been, to keep one's honour! Before this I had much work to do and no repose; when I had finished one task, there was another waiting for me. To-day I have laid them all aside; to-day I have managed to find another and greater delight. In the midst of my cares I was reft away by Nārāyaṇa; we met and embraced each other. Through his virtue I am saturated with delight. Tukā says, There is no more coming and going for me now!

## 1286

SOME damsel has upset and emptied a pot of water; she wants the excuse of fetching water to visit her loved Govinda. She skips away from the path, and looks slyly round her; she sees him standing ready for her. The lord of the cowherd lads and damsels has created their passion; he perceives the form he loves everywhere. He displays his passion in many a style and garb; the being void of qualities has sought his diversion in the drama of the world. The damsel answers him as she pleases, taking advantage of some pretext. "Stop; why did you throw a stone at me? why do you keep me talking and answering your questions? Give up this habit you have formed; these jokes of yours will not pass with me. I shall give up this life at last and embrace you; I cannot see through your disguises. I am rough outside, but I feel an inner joy; why do you make a jest of this disguise? How can you bind us two in bonds of love and still pride yourself that you are Nanda's son?" He assumes a visible form to bring about an inner pleasure, but he keeps the truth from every one, be sure. Spirit is united with spirit, says Tukā; this inward pleasure leads to Nārāyaṇa.

## 1287

"WHY are you sad to-day? Why are you ill-disposed to work? You forget what you were given to do: I wonder whether Hari is seated in your mind. Away, away, you have turned into a vagabond; how dare you show your face to the world? You hussy, you have disgraced your mother; you cannot rest either at your father's or your husband's house; you have broken with both. Your hidden nature has come to light; you made a fine show and concealed what lay beneath it. Unbridled in your boundless passion, your mind is set on Govinda, while your body goes about your work. You answer nobody; you let others treat you as they please; you eat whatever is given to you. You do not notice when your dress is undone; we see you are indifferent to the experiences of the body. I do not know you formed this unheard of passion; this idle chattering goes on everywhere; you meet together to talk; you put your hand in his unashamed." Kānho is at his tricks, he shows his skill and subtlety; he sets the mother and the daughter-in-law quarrelling. But know that this devotion is pure, says Tukā; let all men learn this.

## 1288

ONE damsel has become oblivious; as she sells milks and curds, she cries "Buy Hari!" Since her eyes have beheld him and he dwells in her heart, his name rises to her lips. In her simplicity she forgets her own belongings, through the miraculous desire of Govinda. Tukā says, People laugh at her, but she has no ears for them.

## 1289

HOW did I come to keep company with you? The world pursues me with rebukes. Begone, you mass of uncleanly faults; do not teach us your deceitful tricks! The beauty of your form has diverted every impulse of my soul; I can see no such distinctions as "I" and "mine". Tukā's lord has come to dwell in my soul; he has taken away speech and left me speechless.

## 1290

THE cowherds and their cows came to water at the bank of the Yamunā, bringing the lord of the world with them. They start a game of *chendu* in the pebbly bed; the girls cry, "Come, let us behold him with our eyes!" The cowherd damsels were so fired with passion that they panted to behold Hari. They pretend at home that they want to fetch water; twelve or sixteen of them at a time assemble; while they are washing their robes and bodices, they fall into a trance; their thoughts are uplifted to Kṛishṇa's form; not one remembers her lineage or family; they stand gazing without a quiver of the eyes. She stands with her finger in her mouth cleansing her teeth; drums are sounding and people talking, but she heeds them not. If any one listens to the music of Kṛishṇa's flute, Tukā's lord will fulfil all his wishes.

## 1291

"NANDA'S son Kānho has caught the end of my dress and will not let it go whatever I do. If I had expected this, I would not have come alone; why did I plunge into this thicket? Loose your hold of my dress; let me go; it is getting late; they will be angry at home. My husband's mother is cruel, his father is harsh. If I tell you more, you and I will both be nowhere. I had friends with me and maids, but I lost them and you got your chance; if I had not come near you, how could you have caught me? You came and surprised me." How faint she was with these appeals; she kept pushing away his hands till she was worn out. Tukā's lord is cunning in taking his pleasure; where he takes his pleasure, he saves the good name of his companion.

## 1292

THE damsels have gone to take their milk to the market; how did Kṛishṇa behave himself? He stood in the way and caught one by the dress, "Give me my dues first and then you may go!" "Off with you! let me go! This is the first time you have met me! You have ruined all my stock; I can never go to market again!" She snatched away her dress, but he caught it by the other end; the rest seize his hand, "What! are you mad? We've come and gone this way many a time; we don't know whether you are black or white; off with you, lad! What are you talking about?" "I am in authority here; you've cheated me up till now. Now I found you out, I want to know the price of what you have sold." They replied laughing, "We live with our husbands' mothers; don't come so close; stand further off and speak to us! We belong to other men; you gain nothing by clutching our dress; if our people find it out, you and I will both be nowhere." Still he clung to the women's hearts, he would not let them disperse; if any one tried to go, he held her by her secret part. They were all caught; they were set free from toil at home or in the market place; those who have joined Kṛishṇa do not turn back again. Tukā says, Lay aside idle grief, the fruit of your past has overtaken you to-day.

## 1293

ONE fond damsel, as she leaves him, sobs at parting. "Here he is! there he is!" Now she wakes up, now she sinks dejected. In a reckless mood she flings herself down and stares round her; she tries to run away from her family. Now they have all exhausted their efforts; she cannot tell her own people from strangers; instead of their names she cries," O Lord of Lakshmī!" The other damsels find it a wondrous sight and laugh. She runs out into the wood; she will not stay at home; she feels no ties, for Kṛishṇa has entered into her. She has forgotten her husband's house and her mother's; gazing on one, she has forgotten the other spirit that is hers. Tukā says, Be still, all of you; this is no place to show yourselves perverse. Every man's state cannot be learned from his own lips alone; where many opinions are offered, all conjecture will be wide of the mark.

## 1294

"HARI, your complexion is blue, but I am white like a champak flower. The sight of you will turn me black, and people will put me out of caste. Be quiet and tease me no more; how often must I tell you, lad? Your blanket is tattered and dirty, O son of Nanda; your person stinks; you eat up greedily milk and curds and butter; you are a thief at home and abroad; I am fair and delicate as a star. People will laugh me to scorn, when they see me; they will spurn me, when they see your marks upon me. You are void of fear and shame; but I have shrewd and virtuous relatives. I will speak no more to you; why don't you respect me?" She breaks off and refuses to give him her hand; he sees she cannot bear a word from him. Tukā's master, the lord of the yogis, throws her into a trance and enjoys her.

### 1295

"I AM fallen into a trance; I run wildly to and fro; deeply I love Govinda; I delight in his coming. Now I have given up all clamorous cries; I lay my forehead in worship at his lotus-feet. Tell me, some one, news of Govinda; he sat me on his shoulder, but now he has vanished; when did this pride of beauty enter my head? O merciful one, O sea of compassion, I beseech thee to pity me! Through pride many lost thee of old; through the self-same cause that has now lost thee to me. Looking on thee, I have renounced the body that I clung to at first; the journey is ended; the world has vanished." If we lament the loss of all when we renounce it and then seek thee, this is a transgression. Thus I pronounce, when you condemn yourself; there is a clear vision of Tukā's lord.

### 1296

"MY fever is high; lay nothing on my body, I cannot bear it I am pierced with sharp mental pain; bring me speedily to Nanda's son. To you dearest and closest friends, I speak in confidence; I am tortured by this passion. His purple radiance has penetrated me; I know this well, for my passion tells it me. Let me keep it to myself and tell no one the secret; let my passion find him out in a solitary place. With a swift impulse my mind tells me the truth; yet I know not when the happy hour shall arise. I have tasted misery and sleepless wakeful nights; I have looked upon him with fully opened eyes of love." Now all has vanished but his feet alone. Tukā says, The sight of these has brought the real awakening of my soul!

### 1297

I TASTE a sweetness that I cannot describe; O friend, it has fastened on my tongue. I am frenzied by the lustre of this loveliness; "I" and "mine" and my own limbs have vanished from me. My eyes are fixed upon that spot; my spirit has sunk to rest at his feet. Now that I have met Tukā's lord, I have broken with all I have left behind.

### 1298

NOW I will come back no more; I have fallen in love with him. How can the anger of the world harm me? Why do you make such an uproar? You are strangers to me everyone of you. You may say what you choose to say; it will be false when you have said it. My mind is full of the thoughts of meeting him; my eyes are riveted to his primal form. I cannot bear to leave him for a moment. I want neither acts nor deeds. I have no pleasure in any speech but speech of him. He has pierced my heart with a shaft of love; perish my life apart from him! I have admitted him to my thoughts; I will not turn back now. Now for ages to come you need form no affection for me; Tukā's generous master and I have lain down together.

### 1299

"O KĀNHO! I have offended you and here I am left alone; I am but a weak woman, I tremble in the wood. When I want to go abroad, my mother and father keep me at home; O Hari, how have I come to be with you? As I came, people told me you were false, but I had formed a passion for you. I turned to the jujube tree because it was ripe;. where has Hari disappeared to? There stood a thicket in my way; Hari is up to some mischief." Tukā says, We will keep to the road we started on; we shall see Hari; there will be no thorns to wound our feet.

### 1300

WHY do you keep me at home? Nanda's son and I want to play together. I met him long ago; I feel I can never part from him. He charms me with his gentle speech; I cannot close my eyes. To-day I have cheated them all and run away; why do you chase me in vain? What business of yours have I interfered with? Is it kind of you to imprison me at home? In the name of Tukā's lord, master of Gokula, I say my last word to you, "Begone!"

### 1301

"HARI has caught away my spirit; I have forgotten my wealth and other burdens. How shall I go home again now? I have lost my reputation. If I tell my tale to strangers, my family will thrash me." Tukā says, Keep still; gaze on what you have seen till you are satisfied.

### 1302

"WE women followed you closely; let no stigma fall upon us now. We tremble before our father-in-laws' kindred; our souls are drawn towards you; save us now from shame between the two! We learned to follow you as playmates, before we knew what we were doing; later on anxiety dawned on our minds." Tukā says, It was best for them to be as they were; holding this, I have put the tale into words, and made it into an ornament for myself.

## 1303

UNSTEADY by nature, the women cling with steady passion to Hari; they wait their chance to enter into him. The delighted spirit enjoys with all its powers that highest object of delight. Speech fails in utterance; knowledge fails to point out where to go or what to do. Tukā says, Like God himself they were exalted and frenzied after God.

## 1304

WHEN we look upon the sky, we perceive its excellent beauty. He has come to dwell in my spirit; you need not try to make me look foolish. He is dearer to my soul than my soul itself; I will not leave him for a moment. I, the servant of Tukā's master, am become like the lord of the world.

## 1305

I HAVE come running to meet him; now it is late and I am left weary. What shall I do? Tell me how to find him. My spirit is broken for Hari's sake; I had great hopes to meet him; but many delayed me and many drew me away. Body and mind I have laboured to find an opportunity, I have suffered pain and grief. Cursed be this mortal life; how can I bring it to a close? My life is drooping for Tukā's lord Gopāla.

### 1306

"COME all of you and join in the rites of Vṛindāvana; Gopāla blows the flute; we hear the sounds and our spirits are stirred and fluttered. Leave your work that is still undone; escape from the world; this, I know, is the time to meet Gopāla. The sight of his holy face will soothe my eyes." They say, "Now we will endure the troubles of our homes. We care for nothing compared with meeting Kṛishṇa; if people cry shame on us, we will not heed them." Tukā says, The Gopīs have started off beckoning to each other; God has filled them with his own form.

### 1307

HAPPY were those Gopīs! The food prepared for the worship of Indra, Hari takes and eats. O Kṛishṇa, the gods look for help to Indra; who will assist them now? Tukā says, God shows a device of his own; he eats the offering and begins to laugh.

---

## IX.—How he stole their Clothes while they were bathing

### 1308

MURĀRI went in a sportive mood to the bank of the lake; there he saw the damsels naked. He invented a crafty trick, a piece of merry guile; he hid himself and went along arching his neck. Ah! he has set his wits to work! You may fall at his feet, but you won't get them back, he won't restore your silken dresses. Robes, silks, muslins, tassels, laces and bodices—he bundles them up, carries them all off and runs to the Kalamba tree. Grasping a bough, he looks out, and sits up aloft and draws the leaves round him; he laughs a boisterous laugh. All the damsels go on playing with waves of merriment; they leap nimbly about; with emulous noise they scream and counterfeit buffaloes and oxen; some are trying postures; with eager spirits they start every kind of game. At last one damsel leaves the water and looks for her dress; she cries, "It is gone; some one has stolen it! How can I tell when?" All the rest raised a shout; they left the water. "Now," they say, "how are we to get home?" Then he who wears the wild garland laughed up aloft as he saw them all. They felt ashamed and went into the water, covering themselves with their hands. "O Gopāla," they cried, "save us all from shame! This time we will give you any sweetmeats you like!" "Join your hands and come all of you before me; make no idle uproar; I want neither dainties nor jewels nor wealth; concentrate your thoughts on me and approach me." They look on each other and forget their shame. "Come," they say, "let us approach him!" With their hands joined before them how still they stood! Tukā says, Then he closed the scene and saved them from shame.

## XXVIII

# In Praise of Rama

### 1309

RĀMA has gone to dwell in the forest; thereby the land is filled with inhabitants. If we lay to heart his name, we style him the almighty and no other. Rāma sits weeping in the forest, so the Purāṇas tell us. Tukā says, This the ṛishis predicted; if we know this, why are we confounded?

### 1310

WHOSO utters the name of Rāma, at every morsel he eats, though he has eaten, yet he is fasting; blessed is his body, it is the natural home of all holy places. Whoso utters the name of Rāma, as he goes about his business, he enjoys for ever divine bliss and peace. He who utters the name, as he walks along, makes every step a sacrifice. If a man utters the name, whether he tolerates the world of sense or renounces it, the course of actions cannot cleave to him. He who utters the name continually, Tukā says, he has attained liberation while living.

### 1311

HE who made heavy stones swim in water, what cannot he do for you? Why are you not humble at his feet? By the tread of his feet he caused a stone to become a woman. Tukā says, He brought about the capture of Lankā at the hands of the monkeys.

### 1312

UTTERING the name of Rāma, you become Rāma; sitting at his feet, you attain to his degree. Such joy arises from these words; with full confidence seek this experience. There is no juice that compares in flavour with the juice of this name. Tukā says, I smack my lips as I tell you, for I have tried it myself.

### 1313

"RĀMA" contains the best of all syllables; Śaṅkara himself takes them in his mouth. How far the best are they of all means of salvation in three worlds! See, these cooled the poison of Śiva. This was the charm and the resource that saved Bhavānī from re-birth. Tukā says, This name is old and ever new, full of pleasure; I have made it my own with full confidence.

### 1314

UTTERING Rāma, wise and ignorant alike are saved, men of high and men of low degree. You need put forth no other exertion; though you have committed grievous faults, they are all burned up. If you utter "Rāma," no evil spirit can draw near you; the servants of Yama vanish. He who utters "Rāma" passes over the stream of the world and comes back to birth no more. Tukā says, Drink with absolute faith this stream of nectar, this means of attaining bliss.

## 1315

"RAMA has crossed over," they say, to Rāvaṇa. "O Lord of the world, why are you sleeping? Lankā is full of Rāma's servants; they have occupied the whole land. All your friends and warriors are slain; you must sue to him or make yourself ready for battle." Tukā says, Go to meet Rāma with perfect faith; break off from your old associates.

## 1316

RĀMA has come to the battle-field; he has caught sight of Rāvaṇa. How they struggle both of them, sweeping away each other's name in fight! Their meeting was in joy and love; each with his own arrow kept aloof the arrows. Tukā's master is Raghunātha; hence he knows the story and has told it.

## 1317

HE slew Rāvaṇa and scattered all his band; he established for ever Vibhīshaṇa in Lankā. How can we set any limits to his generosity? Tukā says, My generous master Rāma set Sītā free.

## 1318

RĀMA bestowed on his mother Kausalyā the form of Rāma, for Rāma dwelt in her mind, her contemplation, and her thoughts; whoso accepts this without doubt, he is turned into Rāma himself. All the people of Ayodhya became Rāma; the monkeys remembering Jānakī assumed the form of Rāma. Lo! to Rāvaṇa Lankā became as Rāma himself. Whoso contemplates Rāma continually, Tukā bows down on his feet.

## 1319

ALL the world rejoiced; men and women and servants all rejoiced with sound of shells and drums and pipes. There was great joy in Ayodhya, when Raghunātha was come; shouts of victory were raised as he embraced his brother. They kindle lamps and wave them around the hero Raghu. With Lakshmī comes Lakshmaṇa; the kingdom of Rāma is established. All rejoice, says Tukā, men, women and children, cows and calves together.

## 1320

THE kingdom of Rāma is established; what do we lack? The earth yields her harvest, the cows and buffaloes their milk. From hour to hour, women, let us sing strains in praise of Rāma, while we grind or pound or take our meals. No one now ever sees or dreams of sorrow; as his name resounds, destruction trembles. Tukā says, Rāma has given us his own bliss; we shall return again to the womb no more.

## 1321

AHALYĀ was saved by Rāma; Ganikā was taken by his name to the other world—O Rāma! O Raghu! O mighty prince! Calling on thee, he who bears the trident found repose! Bhavānī became immortal. Thy name is the spell of salvation at Benāres; it made of Vālmīki a sage. Nala found the master secret in his name, whose might caused stones to float upon the sea. O Raghunandana, Tukā's lord, the sages of old found life in thy name.

## 1322

I AM weak and feeble-minded, how can I describe thy nature? Thou didst make stones swim in water, such was the glory of thy name. Let thy excellent name continue in my throat! Thou didst save the monkeys; thou didst set the demons free. The consort of Sītā set the monkeys to bring the mountain. He exalted his reputation when he met his brother; he made a woman of a stone; illustrious is his glory. How was it Hanumanta burnt Lankā? Rāma is the life of Jānakī, the centre of the yogis' contemplation. Tukā adores the feet of Rāma, the lotus-eyed.

# XXIX

# Abhangas Employing Various Stories from Mythology

## I.—Ganesha

### 1323

FIRST, I bow to thee of one tusk; the story of thy life takes us into a region of delight. Thy strength fills my intellect with joy, that forthwith all darkness is dispelled. Where the flood of thy mercy swells, what is there left to wish for? This is a path that leads to all attainment; thou alone canst bring one to the end thereof. Before beginning aught I adore thee; so do all gods and sages and all that have written sacred legends or tales. How could I describe thy powers? I have no gift for such a task. They call thee Lord of the lowly; O vindicate this title of thine! When I am swept away by the stream of illusion, and sunk deep in the sea of life, who can save me but thee? O bless me speedily, says Tukā.

### 1324

FIRST of all, the big-bellied one, the giver of all success, he of the four arms who wields the axe, the limit of whose nature none can tell; a handsome god is he, the son of Gaurī, with the loud anklets clasping his feet. Narvada and Tumbara attend upon him; all impediments flee before him. The stage is prepared for the dance; he waves his arms and sways his body. He is beautiful with vermilion paint; on his crown is a graceful serpent. Gods and sages adore him. I cannot take my fill of his sight; the demons lie at his feet; he is supreme from first to last. He is the giver of all success; there is no limit to his form. Tukā says, Our generous lord will convey us over the sea of the world.

---

## II.—Hanumana

### 1325

O LORD Hanumanta, O messenger of Rāma, I have come to seek thy protection; show to me the glorious paths of devotion. You are stout and enduring, ever active in your master's service, Tukā says, O Rudra, son of Anjanī.

### 1326

YOU found a clue to Sītā, and set in motion the invasion of Rāma, so great was your glory; such a hero you were amongst gods; such an ornament to the pious. You went down into hell and disgraced the goddess of the Asuras; you stole back Rāma and Lakshmaṇa. With folded hands you stand upright before us. Tukā says, O son of Vāyu, in calling on your name we put off sin.

### 1327

HE put fetters on the god of love; he brought death down to misery; therefore I make my bow low before him, Hanumanta of monkey race.

His frame is like adamant; with his tail he can encircle the universe. Tukā says, I have come for protection to the servant of Rāma.

1328

HANUMANTA is mighty indeed; he burned the beard of Rāvaṇa; I make my bow to him many a time, never ceasing. He leaped into the air and conquered Lankā, truly he searched out Lankā; blessed, blessed is he, says Tukā.

---

## III.—A Complaint of Radha

1329

"SHUT the door; the long night has passed; I am filled with loving passion,—why has sorrow overtaken me? Some happy one has seized him; to-day I am desolate, I do not see my husband on my bed." Thus Rādhā speaks to her maid, "Nārāyaṇa treats me lightly. You may call him gentle, but he has no virtuous heart; I will speak to him no more, I know him thoroughly now. He once sent away Garuḍa and brought Hanumanta; he sent for Satyabhāmā to come in the form of Sītā. He made her ashamed, for she could not change her form. He became Rāma, and Bhimakī took Sitā's form. Satyabhāmā gave him to Nārada; now I have learned his real nature. He could not be weighed against heaps of gold, but one leaf of tulsi balanced him; why then do I imagine him to be my spouse? He enjoys us women and yet calls himself celibate. Had this been false, would the Yamunā have made way for him? You and I do not know him yet." Nārāyaṇa knows the hearts of men; he pervades the world, yet he hides himself from our eyes. When Rādhā comprehended this he came to embrace her. Tukā says, With him faith is the condition on which he gives.

---

## IV.—A Complaint of Satyabhama

### 1330

SATYABHĀMĀ has made her preparations and sits at home waiting; the night has flown by. God comes not; the flood of her passion swells; she falls into a sadness, then she hears a knocking at the door. "Begone! I know what your fidelity is worth; this subtlety is meant to gain your own ends; what you say is all pretence; you have waited till daybreak on purpose. I am a silly creature, forsooth, and you are not to be blamed! How you brought scorn on me when I gave you to Nārada! Another time too, when you made me meet Hanumanta! And after all I have trusted your words till now. I know now what an illusion it was; I believed in your goodness. Your actions are vile and do not answer to your words; you lord of Tukā's brother, you are a fraudulent schemer."

### 1331

THEN says Hari, "My dearest! Why do you aim these love taunts at me? God knows why you are so angry. Why do you utter these idle words. Think before you speak; give up your folly and be calm. To publish all this would bring a stain on both of us; open your eyes, now, at any rate, and be sensible. Was anything like your conduct ever known? Did any other woman ever give her husband away? How can you say I am not good when I put up with that? You feel angry, but for my part I am astonished at you; tell me how I made you ridiculous. It was your own pride that bade me send for Hanumanta; you gave pain to me and Garuḍa and Bhimakī." Tukā's brother says, Neither truth nor falsehood can touch him.

## 1332

THEN she replies to the lord of the senses, "Granted you have extolled yourself, why did you defraud me over the flowers? You are a good actor and know well how to play your part. Begone Hari!" Says the daughter of Satrajita, "I know well your skill in speech; you have deceived me in the same way up till now. I was carried away by love, I did not want to lose you, and I formed a plan to keep you as my consort in the next birth; then you made every one turn their backs on me—how could I see through your subtlety? What can I do? My passion has turned me crazy and brought all this suffering upon me. If it had not been for that I should have seen your faults—why, every title of yours proclaims you an adulterer. Your qualities pass all description; no voice exists that can tell how cruel you are. You do not distinguish your own and other people's mother and sister; you delight to set mother and son's wife quarrelling." To all this the King of Vaikuṇṭha replies, "Do not bring up the past; I will do so no more; I swear and vow it." Tukā's brother says, Kanho loves his worshippers.

# V.—A Complaint of Sita

## 1333

SĪTĀ is lamenting in the Aśoka wood, "Why is Raghunātha parted from me? The evil one entered the cave and stole me away; why has he brought me to this fastness of Lankā? Tell me, O Trijaṭā my friend, will Raghunātha come to me or not? My spirit is impatient; the way is long; my soul refuses to dwell within me. What evil had I done? What sacred place had I polluted? What vow had I broken? Had I separated cow from calf or husband from wife? I cannot understand the fruit of my past; I am parted from his feet. By the hope of the golden deer I was ruined; he drew Raghunātha after him. I disobeyed his command; how was I to perceive the treachery? Through looking on an idle prize I am become an idle thing; now I see no trace of a path nor opportunity nor convenient means; I hear nothing save the name of Rāma." He spurned the bird with his foot; now here she is in her island prison; what help is there? The daughter of Janaka is worn out by sorrow; she is like a doe that has strayed from the herd. Trijaṭā comes and pacifies her, "Rāma will capture the city of Lankā."

XXX

# Abhangas Employing Images from Games

## I.—Sututu

### 1334

HE sets the two sides opposite each other, Jīva and Śiva, Diversity and Unity; so they meet on common ground. One player cries "Sututu"; he looks back to his friends for help; see if there is a strong fellow behind you; break away from those before you. A good player looks out for the line; a rash player is tossed down to hell. A strong stout boy plays well; he goes on while his breath lasts; a drone gets caught; one whose breath lasts well is a good player. He wins who keeps looking round him; one who trusts to weak support gets caught. Play on, brother, in your own strength, never heeding the help of others. Tukā says, I am no player; wherever I go, I put up with what I meet.

---

## II.—Cipari

### 1335

THEY have started a game by the river; the devotees of Kṛishṇa are dancing, O brothers! Pride and wrath they have made into a footstool;

they will embrace each other's feet. They dance with floods of joy; they sing strings of holy names. They have wrestled with the evil age; they surpass all others in faith. They have marked their foreheads with clay; they have adorned their necks with garlands of tulsi; they carry cymbals and tabors and streams of flowers; this is a solemn rite of incomparable joy. Through the sound of these charms the unlearned men and women have fallen into a trance, together with the wise and learned, those versed in mystic experience and possessed of mystic powers. Pride of caste, caste itself they have forgotten, they fall prostrate before each other. Their minds are purified by the butter of faith; the stones begin to melt. The sky resounds with cries of victory; the stout devotees of Vishṇu are frenzied. Tukā says, Thou hast made an easy path to cross the ocean of the world.

## 1336

IF you play with one earnest impulse, you will not fall into the snare; if you attend to two things at once, you will be taken in, my brother! You will be wearied out by the whirl of the three qualities, so attach yourself to these four! Finish the play and stand aloof, for you must give up the passion for pleasures. This is how to be leader in the game, be assured, my brother! There was a tailor's boy, Nama, who played in it; Viṭṭhala made him a leader. He taught his playmates how to play well together, so he kept his side unconquered; a side that plays well together never loses; the saints honour it. Dnyāneshwar, Muktabai, Wateshwar, Wasāngādeva, Sopāna, these all play rejoicing. The cowherds made Kanho a leader; they dance around him joyfully. Those who play well together, Brahmā and the other gods fall at their feet! Rāma was a leader, Kabīr a player, a stout pair they were! His five companions formed one group; in that company an excellent music was devised; Brahmā and the other gods, in agreement with each other, chose this game. Ekā, the Brāhmaṇa's boy, was a devout player; he made the people fond of the game; he made Janārdana his leader; so he brought together a band of Vaishṇavas. He plays with one steady impulse, so men have made him their leader. Other players have passed away; I have no speech to describe them. Tukā says, O comrades, play skilfully, thinking of service to those who will follow you; he who fails to play this game well will fall into the gambling games of the world.

## 1337

INWARDLY there is a group of twelve or sixteen players, the seventeenth player, the leader, is the self. Our feet shall keep time to the measure, so we shall attend thoughtfully to our sticks; our cymbals will ring to the heart's tune. We will go dancing to play at Pāṇḍhari; we will see Viṭṭhala and Rakhumai; he is beyond the six Śāstras and the four Vedas and the eighteen Purāṇas; we will sing to him and beat time together. The birds forget to take food and water; the young women forget their youth and beauty. The joy of this game gives speech to the dumb and hearing to the deaf, eyes to the blind and feet to the lame. Tukā says, It makes the old young again.

## 1338

THE two sticks yield one sound; even so there is no distinction of the qualified and the unqualified. Skilfully the players sway their bodies; they bring their limbs together in time to the music. Not a motion of theirs is lost, for they all obey one leader, making them conscious of himself; the transcendent one, he allows no emulation to creep in. Saints and sages will play with one impulse; watch them, O my brother! Carefully they strike their sticks together; when the two sticks meet together the player feels comfortable. If the rules of religion are broken, all is lost; what avails it then to have adorned your person? He who will not join the enthusiasm of the saints, they shall separate him and cast him out. You need no prescribed forms; cease to be ashamed; cease to doubt and join the game. Those that were ignorant have attained to honour, through the strength of Viṭṭhala's name. They hoist the flag of streaming hair on their bodies; through the strength of faith they employ their bodies in the game. Tukā says, My throat is choked with half-uttered sounds, because I feel the presence of Viṭṭhala.

## 1339

COME, my comrades, let us play together, wise and simple alike; let us sing the name and beat the cymbals for our own profit. Take what you have gained; Pāṇḍuranga is generous in love. To-day is a golden day; we have set marks on our persons. There be some that wander through the thorny jungle, through the haunts of snakes, but we in singing and dancing find a joy greater than theirs. Tukā says, Brahmā and the rest find it hard to attain the joy of Kṛishṇa's presence, but we have attained it freely by uttering his name.

## III.—Chenduphal

### 1340

CATCH the ball while it is in the air! One who misses will have it thrown at his back. The ball with us is the three qualities; catch it and throw it from you; with uplifted face fix your mind and your eyes upon it. One who springs up and catches it aloft,—he is an active fellow; a duffer gets confused in turning about. If any one is caught idling, he is not allowed to sit down; he has to bend over and take his companions on his back. With his head bent down he has to suffer mountains of pain; he carries his burden, and the rest stand round in a circle to compel him. Tukā says, He alone has excellent fun who wins; some one else loses and has his face blackened.

### 1341

YOU stupid child, why did you not cry "Enough"? Because you feel ashamed, you put up with it and you have been sadly plagued. You were quite free; why did you join in the game? Now you cannot shake off the rider who is mounted on you. Suddenly you joined the company and embraced the game; you chose one side and took many riders on your back. Time sets the humble on high and brings the high down; you cannot escape while you are engaged in the game. You have given up your old shelter; now you are grasping at straws; but he who leaps up will fall down: remember my words. Tukā says, As long as you kept your hands and feet from the game you suffered no misfortunes.

## IV.—Atyapatya

### 1342

LOOK before you and behind! Take care of the squares on each side! Some one will get past; each must look after the man opposite him. O captain, run along the central line; wake up your men on each side, as each one meets you, say, "We depend on you!" Set each of your men to mark his man; where the strength is fairly balanced, leave your men alone. Say to them, "The strongest player is powerless if you stand up to him!" Pass on to new squares, and catch your enemy where you can. Win the game, O Captain, raise a shout and keep your men well in hand; you have been playing the game for a long time and you are tired. Some strong opponent will break through your side, if you don't catch him; any one who finds an opportunity to escape will reach the goal. Tukā says, Why do you go on playing so long?

---

## V.—Witudandu

### 1343

FINISH your Witudandu, and let us begin another game. In this we suffer many a hostile blow; we can never be still anywhere, one strikes the witi in the hole; another catches it and puts him out. The captain summons his side together, and takes up the net; the names of the players are called in turn; you can't avoid your turn, so off you run! There is a boundary line drawn in front of you; when you start you take your partner with you and plague him. One stands eager to run; another claps his hands and runs. Tukā says, Let us wind up this game.

---

## VI.—Phugdi

### 1344

SHE stands up to play at Phugdi; they look on each other's faces without shame. "Phugdi ho! Leave the world, leave the world behind you; then you will know what sweetness is. Speak out the lesson you learnt of old; as you bind up your scattered locks and knot them on your back, so bind up the three motions of sense and control them within the base of your spine. Govern your feet that press forward; you will win for yourself honour and the approval of the three worlds." Tukā says, There is one spirit between us; let us take the weight with an even balance; we will reach the highest spot.

### 1345

PHUGDI PHU, my rival you! You have soiled yourself. People will spit on your face and back. You are tired out with whirling round; begone, you slave of the world. Foot and hand are wearied; you are tired out with whirling round and round. Unless you bring under control the seven and the five, how can you last out, child? You have lost your breath; your feet are weary, yet you go on spinning round! Tukā says, Silly one! Now do what you have been told to!

## VII.—Humbari

### 1346

O GOD, who can keep up the whirl of the game with you? The six Śāstras, the eighteen Purāṇas, the four Vedas faint away in your praise. In spite of his thousand mouths, the serpent is fatigued in reciting it. With your *chendu* you leaped into the Jumna; you mastered and overwhelmed Kali. You drank the impure milk in Pūtanā's breast and showed no mercy; you destroyed your mother's feigned sister. You destroyed the household of Rāvaṇa, with his wife and children. You are known to us as he who killed his uncle. To play with him is utter destruction; Tukā's lord is a master of the bow.

---

## VIII.—Hamama

### 1347

COME, boy, take your turn with me; I will prevent you from passing down. Hamāma, boy, hamāma! Play hamāma with me, but mind how you pass down! If you have the essence of true love, then talk to me, I will destroy your worldly isolation. Be true to me; but I shall not let you go home! Amid this jubilation no alien can stay in the company. If you promise to play with Tukā, Hari will destroy your individual soul.

## 1348

HAMAMA, ho! Hamāma; the child is tired of playing it; he pursues the eighty-four lakhs of re-births. In the first period of life a man comes to blossom; he takes his turn in the delusion of individuality. When he sees the company of mankind, he forgets all, he is enchanted with his own self. In the second period he gladly takes his own way, in one profession or another; as the days go by he enjoys himself, but he knows not what lies before him, he is a mere child. In the third period there is still the burden; his private interests keep him restless. Allowing fondness to creep over you, you fall into the snare. This is my true conclusion. In the fourth period you have still your privy desires; you find your hands and feet trembling. You will fall into the snares of Sūrya's son. Tukā shrinks from this game of hamāma; he has left the company of his friends; he feeds his kine along with Viṭṭhobā, the son of the Yādavas.

---

# IX.—Riddles

## 1349

A RIDDLE, a riddle, listen to a riddle! Unravel it thoroughly and set yourself free! I ask you; you must tell me, what is "I" and "mine"? Do not be angry! If you cannot make it out, you will commit incest with your mother! I tell you the truth that lies at the root of all; do not feel disappointed; what is born, let it be; what is dead, let it be dead; all is determined by our past. Tukā says, Let all abandon pride; let them keep illusion far from them.

## 1350

I HAVE unravelled the mystery and told it you, O brothers! Verify it for yourselves; keep your spirits pure and eager. There is no mystery left now; I myself have beheld myself. Your skill will be valued in this world; do not be offended at my advice; I cannot choose any one whom I should praise here. Tukā says, Kṛishṇa who wears the wreath assumes more and more glory as the last resort of all.

## XXXI

# Various Village Characters

## I.—Johara

### 1351

I SALUTE you all! I am come to collect the revenue from house to house. Get together arrears and current dues, or I shall put you in the pillory. You must not disperse without being presented to me; whoever is at home, tell me who is the head of the family. To-day, good man, you must get change ready to pay me; there will be no time to-morrow. Tukā says, You will gain nothing by your excuses; at the end of the year they will sift everything.

### 1352

COME, give something to the gate-keeper! Bring out some well-kept morsel. Whenever I come, my hands are empty and you say "No"; sometime or other you must give me something. Tukā says, To-morrow I shall come dunning you, and you will have to go begging from door to door.

### 1353

TAKING and giving, they have gone away to prison, leaving their homes unoccupied. They fall not into the pursuer's hand; they have passed through the night of dense ignorance. All merit and demerit of theirs is put away; there is none left. While they acted their part in the world they showed their faith; the false illusions that surrounded them once have vanished. They have taught themselves to look on their home no more; all their treasure there they have surrendered to the king's court. Now Tukā is safe from any man's grasp; he enjoys perfect peace, indescribable.

## II.—Lakhota

### 1354

ROLL up the letter; tuck your cloth up behind your back. I have taken faith for my escort;. now see where I am! If you entangle yourself with the world, you will lose true life. My confidence is unfeigned; I have given up idle words. O embrace Hari, escape the cycles of re-birth! O fool, be ashamed! madman, trample on the world! Let faith dwell within you; listen to my words. Give up the object you have fondly chosen; fix your desires here; turn your back on the world; rock yourself to and fro delightedly; put away those weary speeches. You are weary. O child, feebleness lies before you. Now stand still, stand upright and observe; be a pig, an ass, and a dog no more. If any has won for himself a good name, I have. Tukā says, Other girls have been worn out.

## III.—Gondhala

### 1355

THE fair and royal young goddesses have come to attend my song! My mistress, my transcendent joy, stands piercing the spirit with her lustre; she emits the splendour of a million suns and moons. Viṭṭhā, my royal mistress, I gaze upon thy feet. I have renounced the four Vedas, O take me to bliss with thee. How full of beauty are her delicate feet! She wears a garland of tulsi about her throat, as she stands on the bank of the Bhīmā. Her teeth shine like diamonds. The wheel and the shell grace her hands. She is beyond all form and shape; her form is unknown to the Vedas; The Śrutis cannot find the limit of her nature; Śesha and the rest are exhausted in the search. She uplifts and lays on her worshippers the hand that calms all fear. She has visited Pāṇḍharpura and displayed herself in the form of the Bowman; where she sees faith and love, she descends in a shower of nectar; Tukā's mistress offers her servant her loving overflowing breast.

## 1356

THE happy day has come, the happy hour; we have marshalled a procession for thee; we have the five vital elements for torch bearers, the two eyes for lights. O dweller in Pāṇḍharpur, I dance on the stage prepared for thee; thou knowest my heart's desire, fulfil my vows! We have established a temple for thee amid the three worlds. We have prepared the platform and set the pot of water in the centre on it. The goddess is seated; before her the Vaishṇavas sing with wreaths of tulsi round their necks; they cry to her aloud. We have a vessel of inner joy wherein are lights and incense! We have kindled the five elements of our nature to wave round our mistress Viṭṭhā. Thou hast thine own portion; now fulfil our desires. Tukā says, Protect thy suppliant.

## 1357

FAIR is her lovely face; graceful and charming her ear-rings. The hooded cobra is coiled in the braids of her hair; saffron and musk are smeared on her forehead. Large and massy are her eyes; the wreath of wild flowers glistens on her throat. Her waist cloth is of silk; sandal powder has been rubbed upon her comely form. Very fair is the young goddess; with all her graces displayed she has come to my song. Bright with royal splendour comes my beloved mistress, wearing her illustrious jewel! Before her fade away the splendour of a million suns and moons. Brahmā and the rest cannot fathom her incomparable diversions. Purple is the hue of her delicate face. White are her four lovely arms. Deep is her bosom, and there shines a handsome brooch; about her waist are set little bells that send forth a pleasant note; anklets twinkle on her feet; she performs music and a dance that are new to us. She is lovely in her eight limbs; let us praise her shapely form. It is a mine of beauty and fragrance. She possesses all accomplishments; she speaks in gentle tones with smiling lips. She takes upon her many forms! She is the primal goddess Nārāyaṇa. Her inaugural rites have been performed in the great city of Pāṇḍharpura. Her canopy is prepared in the sky, raised upon three stories. She has begun her song on the bank of the Chandrabhāga. She has come to repay our devotion, our mistress, Kṛishṇa, queen of the yogis. With her are thirty-three million gods, Chāmunda and eight million Bhairavas. Lamps are waved round here; they shower down flowers upon her. Those that bear the vīṇā and the drum make music ; Gandharvas show forth the joys of Brahmā. Tukā's brother honours the dust of her feet.

---

## IV.—Vasudeva

### 1358

LISTEN, I am the Vasudeva singing to you; attend and listen in a spirit of faith. Do not shut your eyes and create night; death sits numbering your days. Remember Rāma early; secure this gain; prevail over the old fetters. Cast off idle distractions; let your thoughts dwell on Govinda. Consider how transient this body is; a hundred years are appointed for it, but night eats up half of them. Before us lie, in fancy, vexation, disease, and decay; consider what is left for devotion! We have no ground of assurance that lasts a moment; O awake! Renounce affection and hope! Strength avails not; the net will fall upon you; when you awake, you will find yourself caught in the long revolution. Attempt to follow him, much or little; be devout, be strenuous in faith, if you mean to secure happiness in the end. I fold my hands and entreat all men, great and small; give this little gift to my piteous prayer. Tukā's brother says, Cry to Rāma!

### 1359

THREE watches of the night have passed; why are you asleep? Awake and bestow some alms upon me; as you hear my words, do not close your eyes. O people, bethink you of Hari-Rāma-Kṛishṇa-Vasudeva. Take the wooden clappers in your hands, and repeat with your lips the name of Nārāyaṇa. Whatever any can give up, be it fruit, flower or water, give it, O brothers; do not pretend you are asleep; it will not be well with you if I have to turn away. For God faith is enough, you need not offer him wealth. It is much if you fix your thoughts on him; to save such a little pain do not destroy yourselves. I have travelled thus far with great toil, to beg for this boon. Do not think it a burden; do not leave me hopeless; charity is the true fruit of mortal life; he will come back no more to visit this city. Tukā's brother says, If you refuse to know him, you will go down into the terrible pit.

## 1360

"RĀMA RĀMA!"—But two syllables easy to learn and easy to utter! Awake in this last watch; truly it will be a sweet savour in the latter end. I teach mankind the names of Rāma, Kṛishṇa and Vasudeva; I clash the wooden clappers, keeping time with the chime of my anklets. I, the Vasudeva, sing of Vasudeva and utter no other name. Knowing the fruits of charity, give me a liberal gift; do not leave my dues unpaid. When once I have told you my message, bear it in mind. Take no load upon you; finish your present duties; do not go to sleep again. Confide in one that deserves charity; truly I assume you, I am your Vasudeva; the merciful saints know me, the men of long experience, who make no distinctions of things. Give heartily a generous gift; forget not the Vasudeva; him all creatures praise, animate and inanimate; I make my bow to him, says Tukā.

## 1361

HE who speaks what is unfit for speech, he is outwardly awake but asleep in his soul. What a cosy corner you have made in your house; you do not know whether it is dark or daylight. I the Vasudeva go on my rounds, I stand outside the door of the house. Bestow some sort of alms on me; if you don't answer, I shall move on. With my cymbals and my dindi in my hand and a song on my lips I raise a loud note; I make no difference between high and low; don't stay asleep to save my alms. I undoubtedly am the Vasudeva; you will find out the truth if you inquire. I am known to the fortunate saints; it is no other that solicits you. Why are you asleep in waking hours? The dog is wide awake at your door. For your advantage Vyāsa wrote; why come you not to meet the Vasudeva? Thus I have roused everyone; I have had an alms from those whose merits led them to bestow one. Tukā says, Some feeble creatures have forgotten the Vasudeva.

## 1362

I SING of Rāma-Kṛishṇa, striking my cymbals and wooden clappers, dancing in time to my song; I have finished my slumbers and go on my rounds. This god pervades city and wilderness; you should seek for him as the aim of your desires, then Vasudeva will turn towards you; you should keep this faith dwelling within you. He loves his own servant dearly; Vasudeva delights in him. Utter his name in assembly; thus acquire Vasudeva for your own. When the end of all things draws near, your efforts will cease whatever your wishes may be. Quit your slumber and awake; bestow some gift on the Vasudeva. Tukā says, Blessed is his life who has relieved the Vasudeva; he need not enter the world or depart any more; he has found a resting-place in Vasudeva.

---

## V.—Dogi

### 1363

EVERYWHERE it is written that the world itself is a beggar! The lord of the world is awake; put some faith in him! Adore, all of you, the only protector of your fields; bring a few leaves and fruit and flowers and water. I wandered long before I reached this city; take no hard task upon yourselves; good deeds and piety are the essential thing. Tukā solicits a gift; O give it with your whole heart.

---

## VI.—Gavagunda

### 1364

I AM the village-wit; the terror of all evil spirits. While I am speaking to one as a friend, another comes along to play its tricks. I challenge everyone, but won't let any one lay a finger on me. Tukā says, I will shut him up; I'll conquer in any wordy warfare.

---

## VII.—Saurya

### 1365

I HAVE lost my old tricks, all my longings have passed away; I am neither a man nor a woman now. The Saurya in her wanderings leaves her own people and consorts with strangers, but ever and anon she is pierced by fond affection for Govinda. They scoff at her as she passes before them, but she takes off her petticoat and throws it round her neck. People are frightened at our dress; we have a quarrelsome way with our tongues. The Lord of Pāṇḍhari stands on the Bhīmā's banks. We are grieved because we are kept aloof; with perfect faith we have laid aside all longings and exchanged our soul for the infinite soul. We will reverence the supreme intellect. In company with drones and fools, we shall dance with faith and devotion. Tukā says, Throw us a copper, and we will dance without shame; we are happy, for in this task we have escaped from worldly cares.

### 1366

"SHE knows neither how to teach others, nor to dance herself, silly creature! She has gone astray and the world laughs at her. Such is not my way; I control my eyes and mind, when I know the tastes and preferences of my audience. I have only the dress of my class. I am unchanged within; I have done well to hide my better self, for thus I earn my living." Tukā says, If you have succeeded in this, do purify your mind; else you will be ruined here and elsewhere.

## 1367

GIVE up money; come away, you slut, why are you caught there? I have asked where we are bound, and that is why I scold you. Now we shall dance, we shall delight ourselves with fond affection for this god; this Govinda has not yet given me what is mine. Why do you go on with that idle prating of yours? Show me all your secrets and tell me where you come from. Tukā says, This is why I have taken the drum in hand, to deliver you from all that clings to you and sets you longing.

## 1368

ONE who is free seeks entanglements; one who is untasked complains that she has neither load nor tie. She is sitting amongst the low-caste Dheds; she has flattered herself of her own will. Listen, O women, these reputable wives shall not make me ashamed. One may live contented in her high station to serve her husband; but another is alarmed, before she is spoken to, and runs away without being beaten. She dislikes her husband and the bed where she sleeps, and so she strays into the harlot's paths. She is blind, though she can see; deaf, though she has ears; dumb, though she can speak. Tukā says, A fall has come to pass in her case; there are some who have lived in this way.

## 1369

"COME with me, blacken your eyes and comb your hair; let us get to the palace gate at Pāṇḍharpura, mount the platform there and dance round and round. Every time we went there, we accepted the kindness of this master; now we need return no more. Now why shall we visit market places, and go round the shops, great and small? We have all been foolish; but now with one impulse let us dance our fill; we feel a deepening bliss; what a joy we have in this one place alone!" Tukā says, Cling to one alone; dismiss anxious fear and fond illusion. We shall show every sign of satisfaction and go back to the spot we belong to.

## 1370

I HAVE been a Saurya, but now I am raised on high; I have left the world; I have taken the drum in my hand. Come, mother Viṭṭhobā, give us our five senses, whole and sound! Do not withdraw yourself, if some of us yield to folly on the sandy shore of the Bhīmā; I have wandered through eighty-four villages to reach your door. For the sake of money alone I have lost the fruit of this migration, but now shame and doubt have vanished; we will dance at your great door. The cloak of error has dropped from our body. What is left? I have taken to quarrelling with the world. I care not for influence or shame. I shall embrace his feet and satisfy the longings of my soul. Tukā says, Let us break with money and the world; how you and I have taken each other's souls in exchange!

## 1371

SAURYA as I am, and vicious woman, I have reverenced all this, and kept in myself an unruffled balance. I have contracted the limit of my wanderings and suffer no one else to enter it. My task is now to sing of Raghu Rāma. I care no more for life, for family or wealth. I have emptied myself of my wickedness; what need is there for concealment now? In whose presence need I feel any shame? What stranger can look upon me now? I have dismissed the world and the company of *sauris;* I have found a joy that is quite different; I have changed my faith and my outward aspect. Soon shame and fear shall disappear, for I have renounced both. I have changed my dress, and I belong to nobody now. Tukā says, I shall draw near to him who gave me this new dress; and all the world shall see it.

## 1372

WE are neither men nor women: we are separated from the world; we have lost shame and desire. Come, Raghu Rāma, take us to your own village; we have no friend but you. We are scorned and censured by the world; the faces of the slanderers are set against us. For your sake we will endure to see our relatives torn from us. Many a time I was sent to you as a messenger; now I can come myself, says Tukā, unashamed of what the world thinks.

## 1373

WITH an upright mien, her person all bedecked, she goes into the bazaar and shows herself off to attract some one's notice. That woman is not truly a *sauri*; she is a dull creature, void of devotion. She parts her hair neatly and dresses herself out. She displays a garland, and a ring and a walk. With a loose gait hoping to earn some money, she visits the houses of the wealthy and dances featly; where there is money to be had, she flings herself about. She looks a fine creature, but she is a Mang at bottom; and not a true *sauri*. She is a dancing slave. Tukā will not associate with her.

## 1374

COME, my Ragho, let a light be kindled on the hill; I have built a house furnished with doors, but no husband inside it. Perish the five children of the neighbour who induced me to sin. I have five children of my own at home stronger than myself; under pressure of the five I swallowed the countless delights of the world. I had built a house and opened a big shop. I was a chosen bride and lustily I romped about. I had opened a big shop, but I had false coin in my purse. You may call me a Hijra, but in truth I am a Yogi, though I have known intercourse sixteen thousand times. Tukā says, However it may be, make haste to cry "Hari!" in this world.

## 1375

I HAVE been born and died, but never offered devotion. Crying "Mine, mine," fast in the toils, I died. Here I paid no heed at all to my teacher's feet. Come, you jade, give up money, give up prating! You will find no path without a teacher; you are wasting labour. People go on eating and dressing and call themselves virtuous, but they turn aside when saints and ascetics visit their houses. They read and recite and grow wise and call themselves saints, but their hearts are flattered when they catch sight of other men's wives. They wear the top knot and the rosary and call themselves ascetics; but there is no compassion in their hearts; be assured they are hypocrites. In this iron age there are many saints about who ramble round a little circuit to fill their stomachs. The saints may say, I am scoffing at them, but I am not scoffing, O brothers. Tukā seeks the feet of the saints with a single hearted devotion.

---

## VIII.—Wagha

### 1376

THE shrine has stood for endless ages; within it reverberates knowledge of the self; about it rages the sudden storm of ecstasy, inspired by this god Mallāri. I wear the shell of pure holiness, the silver ring fastened behind with the button and loop of knowledge. About my neck is fastened a band of renunciation; I will point out the path of this devotion. My alms vessel is my heart; its pulsations are the bells I ring. My turmeric bag contains a treasure of knowledge: it is never empty throughout all ages. I have visited the four houses, passing on the pilgrimage of life. Mallāri has showed favour to me; I have dwelt in the sense of identity. When this god inspires me, I am possessed by a frenzy of love; see! Tukā is set barking and growls in a fit of madness.

---

## IX—Sarvada

### 1377

LISTEN, brothers, to what the Sarvada says— Here the mother of two sons shall be ruined. They shall scorn her, and let all the world know. One is wise without thrashing; but he will never be happy. Listen further to what the Sarvada says—

A truthful man goes down to the lowest pit of hell; when all the world tells you this, you can be sure of it. Speak falsely, men and women; you will escape all sorrow. Hear the Sarvada's words! Some one else will be ruined. One who calls things his own and looks after them—a thief shall break into his house; so call nothing your own and go to sleep comfortably; everything will be looked after well, and you will feel quite secure about thieves. I will tell you another grand tale. A chaste woman shall come to sorrow here; she is born of the five elements, so she ought to feel no security. Let her commit adultery and she shall be made happy. Listen to me once more and obey. When a present is offered, he who does not stop the offer is no honest man. Tukā says, O mother, whatever name you give to this, let the wretch go back to his own place.

---

## X.—An Incident in Preaching

### 1378

AS he looks at the preacher's beard, the goatherd weeps and sobs. Every one imagines it is real love, but the sentiment within him is quite different. He remembers the hoofs and pastern of a goat he has lost; he cannot govern his sorrow; words cannot express it, so he weeps for his loss. When the preacher lifts his fingers in teaching, he thinks of its two horns and four feet; and cries out "Yes!" He recalls his billy goat that is dead. He was truly fond of his goat, so at last he uttered its name. Tukā says, Our secret thoughts come to light.

---

## XXXII

# Abhangs employing the Language of Common Occupations

### 1379

I HAVE got the grain ready to be pounded; my companion in the toil is a pure heart and mind. Therefore remembrance takes hold of me and wakens me in the last hour of the day. O dear companion, your strokes and mine are equal, so long as I enjoy your company ! See how one sifts, another separates, a third purifies it to perfect clearness ! When the pounding is finished, the mind does the cooking, mixing sugar and milk together. Food is prepared for thee, Udbhava and Akrūra; the third is father Nārāyaṇa himself. Tukā says, I love to go to my mother's house, so my mind quickly summons me thither.

### 1380

PRAISES to Nārāyaṇa ! bring the grain together; chaff and corn separate of themselves. Hold the pestle with care above the spot where it is to fall, deliver your blow carefully and steadily. With perfect attention I deal my blows steadily. The bracelets ring with steady music; sweet is the song; let us sing on ! There is no weariness about this pounding, so long as we forget the difference between you and me. Tukā says When his form is truly reflected in the mirror of the mind, the food will be clearly prepared in consequence of that.

## 1381

WE take a handful of clean corn and fill the mouth of the mill; if we fill it with dirt, then we spoil everything. O dear companion, fan your corn and clean it! O wicked one, why have you spoiled what was ready? See that what you have in your fan is clean, or you will spoil everything, you wretch! What you have in the fan you can look after; if you grind rubbish, you will spoil your dinner. While you have it in your fan, attend to it; if you grind it as it is, you will waste everything. As you grind it, the stones rattle—can't you hear it?—where are your eyes and ears? While it is in the fan, you can clean it; but if you do not take the trouble, you will get into difficulties.

## 1382

HOW can I tell the pleasure of grinding corn? It will satisfy you well, my friend. If it is clear, you can turn the mill swiftly, you feel pleasure in every part of your frame. When you eat clean food, body and mind are satisfied; it needs little fire beneath the pot. Clean corn you can cook easily and well; it brings no disgust or waste with it. Tukā says, We all love clean food; it will not turn your husband's heart from you.

## XXXIII

# The Faithful Devotee Described under the Image of a Paik

### 1383

A PAIK by caste recognizes a paik and honours him alone; if any take to arms for their stomach's sake, they are recognized as pressed men. The natural gift is true, but tricks and dodges will come out when they are tested. Tukā says, We will honour men as gods when we see proof that they have attained their end.

### 1384

A PAIK who guards the people becomes the chief of his race; the others seek a livelihood and are commonplace men. When the enemy advances, they run away and perish. They are wounded in the back and bring contempt on themselves, while thieves return whole and are honoured. He who fronts the robbers is a true paik; he will slay them all and strip them. Tukā says, Talk will not make a paik; those only will succeed in it who are trained from their birth.

### 1385

ALL the paiks belong to one master; but their value differs according to their strength; in their master's escort one is placed high, another low One is set near him, another far away. The man of low breeding has a place set apart for himself; high breeding commands high esteem and complete trust. If one is a true paik he is set above all; a good man has rank as well as wages. Tukā says, Death awaits all, but the fear of death would disgrace them; the absence of it would set a value upon them.

## 1386

PAIKS occupy ranks high and low according as they are divided into strong and feeble. Some are intent on their master's service, others are worthless and self-seeking. He who makes a display when there is no need, he bears the high name of a paik in vain. If you reckon all together, there are many high and low, but brave and valiant few among them. Tukā says, Their master knows how to honour them; he treats a paik according to the worth he has seen in him.

## 1387

TO be a paik you must earn your wages; a true paik is one who does true service; a paik knows where his master may be wounded; he himself is beyond fear of wounds. When a paik has lived with two or three masters, he is distinguished as one of the trade. He is well called a paik who fills his office well, and gives victory to his master. Tukā says, A paik can find no home unless he resorts to his master's house.

## 1388

IF a paik is honoured by his master, then all the world dreads him. Paiks generous of their lives are a noble sight; the leaders wear jewelled crowns. In their own right they enjoy their master's grandeur, his splendour and all his happiness. Countless are the tribes of mean wretches; their succession is never broken; they always are coming and going. Tukā says, The paik has filled his office well, if he has served his master, much or little.

## 1389

HE is a paik who protects the tenants with their families and plucks up strangers and rogues by the roots. He alone is a paik, a head among paiks, who is completely devoted to his master's service. He considers his own person no more than grass, he looks on gold as a stone; nothing comes between him and his master. A paik is worth nothing, if he is not trustworthy; nothing if he tells lies. Tukā says, His master will suffer no loss, for the paik will take care of him.

## 1390

THE paiks have cleared the roads and pathways, driving away multitudes of enemies. They win over their enemies and appoint them houses to live in; their own friends they protect. When they hear men chatting at random, they can tell their own friends from strangers. When men quit the path, they chastise them for a lesson to others. Tukā says, They spread confidence throughout the world and so increase men's comforts.

## 1391

HE is a paik who knows the fidelity required of a paik, the tactics of thieves, their resorts and tricks; he can keep himself safe and deceive others; he can win the day completely. He will stop any attack and leave no trace of himself; such a paik the world accounts their lord. Thus a paik makes all the world his paiks, even such as were not respected before. Tukā says, He who has paiks like these, he is a strong master amid the three worlds.

## 1392

A PAIK knows the happiness of his office, therefore he has gladly accepted it in exchange for his own life. He faces volleys of arrows and bullets when they come, though an infinite shower of them be poured forth; when an uproar arises, he steps in front of his master; his bright harness shows well upon him. The paik enjoys boundless happiness, if he is pure and brave within and without. Tukā says, He is wise who sees this to be true; he performs his part and is happy.

## 1393

OF a paik this much is reckoned true, that he is stout and intelligent and obedient from his heart. There is no comfort without a henchman; the citizens cannot get rid of trouble and care. Be then a true paik prodigal of life; such men are furnished with all by their masters. Those who know not the delight of being a paik, fie on them, their lives are wasted. Tukā says, The covenant takes but a moment to make, yet it yields endless comfort.

# XXXIV

# Worldly Comforts described under the Image of a Blanket.

### 1394

THE children of Gokula exchanged their blankets among themselves; each one cried, "I look like Kānhobā;" into such a frenzy he threw his playmates. "I will not contradict them," said Kṛishṇa, for he saw nothing wrong in their saying so. Tukā says, He merely disguised them; he did not take away from them their frailty.

### 1395

WE began to play at hide and seek; I lost my blanket; so I fell on Kānhobā's neck, crying "Come, Gopāla, let me search you! I am stripped naked, I have lost everything." Tukā says, Nevertheless, my intellect was weak; this did not restore me to repose in him.

### 1396

THERE was a heap of blankets and mine was amongst them; show me some trace of mine; you have made this confusion; put an end to it! If mine is spoiled, you will have to give me another. Tukā says, O God, put away the proud idea that you are great and I am small.

## 1397

I WILL not fall on your neck for nothing; don't stir a step, Gopāla! I will tell about your mischief at home and leave you nothing to say. There was a curtain drawn between us; it is lifted now and we are face to face. Tukā says, My last word is this, I have embraced you and I will not leave you.

## 1398

AS long as "You" and "I" are left separate in thought, in the world too we shall be left separate. Give me back my blanket, then we shall be friends together. As long as you are hostile, we shall stay apart; you must not be so treacherous. Tukā says, You know all, O God; you make me rebuke you as though we were quarrelling.

## 1399

YOU were born with these mischievous tricks, and therefore, O Gopāla, you won't give them up. We see it is your practice to take and to give nothing back; my blanket was a big one, but you won't give it me; leave me at least a waist cloth. Tukā says, I have given up all desires, for I have smelt out the hook here.

## 1400

WHEN once he has seized your blanket, he will not give it up, no, not for your life. Hollo! there is a thief in the house! Run and catch him; he is rummaging the four corners. I have caught him, but I cannot tell who he is; I have lit a lamp, I have kindled a wick in my body.

It is no use running, you won't catch him; I stand crying aloud; Tukā is robbed of all his worldly wealth.

## 1401

WHAT, O God, what shall I wear now? What others had given me that too I have lost. This thief does not distinguish between rich men and poor; where he sees a house empty he breaks into it. I have not left even a broken potsherd, not my cloak which I had of the five elements. Tukā says, I have been severed from the world; I have been singled out to lose the one thing I had.

## 1402

I WAS taking care of my own, when a thief from within seized all in my house; he was there before I came, though I did not know it. He took away my blanket and left me bare. Tukā says, When a thief behaves like an honest man, you can expect no justice.

## 1403

MY blanket has been stolen; whom shall I tell about it? Nobody cares for a feeble creature like me. I shall never get it back; I have neither money nor authority. Merchants and traders, some of you, listen; look for my blanket. Tukā says, Cry aloud after my blanket, while the market place is full.

## 1404

I HAVE got my blanket back; I have found where it went to. The thief was an honest man; Pundalika has set him behind his back.

Where is the thief? There is one spot where he dwells, you need not look for him anywhere else. Other people's blankets were stolen before mine, and mine got mixed with theirs. They searched for theirs and found them; I will do the same. Tukā says, I have gained after all; I lost a torn blanket, and I have got a new one.

## XXXV

# Devotion described under the Image of a Woman addressing her Paramour.

### 1405

LET people cast me out as a whorish woman, yet I will not forget him who wears the garland of wild flowers. I have abandoned reputation, I care nothing for it; I neither fear death nor hope for life. I hear not when people speak to me. Tukā says, I am filled with desire for Hari.

### 1406

MY first husband disappointed my passion, so I have turned my hopes to adultery; I need him near me night and day; I have not a moment of pleasure apart from him. Forget me and my affairs and my estate. Tukā says, I have passionately desired the infinite one.

### 1407

THIS is still my practice; I shall not quit it; I have sat down near Govinda. I have forcibly entered my new home and made myself queen; I have chosen for myself dark-blue Brahmā. I have enjoyed intercourse with the mighty one, says Tukā; now I have neither fear nor care.

## 1408

YOU and I are nothing to each other; this was my secret, and now I have made it known. My adultery has been published, I am despised among the people. You need not love me any more, says Tukā, I am grown mad for God.

## 1409

I HAVE forgotten my family and my duties, my husband, my relatives, the comfort of my home. I have forgotten honour and shame, along with fear and apprehension; my soul is enamoured of the infinite one. Tukā says, Now, who will tempt me back? I have become deaf to everything.

## 1410

I NEITHER see nor hear nor speak of anything else; this Hari alone dwells in my soul; I have no more a mother's home or a mother-in-law's, I have made both into one. Tukā says, Long ago I was charged with a contentious spirit; I have proved the charge to be true.

## 1411

WE shall enjoy complete pleasure for ever; we have broken through the snares of illusion. For the sake of this we have abandoned our husbands; we have fallen in love with this stranger. Tukā says, I shall take such a draught that I shall conceive no more.

## 1412

NOW we shall nourish our love by laughter and jest; it is an inward sweetness that never cloys. In happy service we shall sport with one another, Nārāyaṇa and myself. Tukā says, I have ceased to care for the world; I have got my spouse to myself.

## 1413

LET none of you come near me; you women who dwell with your mothers-in-law. You cannot bear the slander of the world; the vile reproaches they fling upon me. Tukā says, We care not for the world; we are free; we have run away with this controller of the senses.

## 1414

THE lessons you taught me I remembered as long as I was a stranger to Hari; at last I lost all sense of the body; who then could regard your instructions? Tukā says, The infinite one dwells in my heart; the eternal one bids me look not at what is momentary.

## 1415

LISTEN to my words; dance not the dance that I dance; as long as you desire what lies behind you, do not give up the world. Tukā says, What is the use of hypocrisy! you will have neither your husband nor Govinda.

## 1416

HITHERTO you and I both were ignorant; we lived and sported fondly with our husbands; now I have become unrestrained in wickedness; I delight in doing what I should not do. Tukā says, I have forgotten both my families, Nārāyaṇa dwells in my mind.

## 1417

AT my mother-in-law's house I hate my husband; at my mother's house I pine for him. I am an adulteress, no one will touch me; now I shall live in the state which my past actions have created for me. Tukā says, I shall have gained a name for improper conduct; why should I be ashamed now?

## 1418

I DIED before the hour of death; since then I have done as I pleased. Now behold my wondrous state; behold, but utter no idle words over it. Tukā says, You are timorous women; how can you associate with me or be compared to me!

## 1419

I AM enjoying happiness with a stranger; let him lift me up and place me by him. One who has set fire to the world with his own hand must not look back at it. Tukā says, We must go straight to our goal, as a moth flies straight at the flame.

## 1420

YOU will find the case other than what you hear, O women. There is no happiness from worldly husbands, though we entangle ourselves in love of them. Tukā says, If you will harden your hearts, leave them and come with me.

## 1421

INSIDE and outside you are useless; I want no such woman for a companion. In the presence of God none need fear nor threaten anyone; all that is needed is to restrain one's own mind. Tukā says, Without some initiation a strayed woman could not practise this.

## 1422

WE shall never agree with a crowd of women; each has a different view of her own. If one waits to weigh them, time is wasted; the idea is deceptive and fruitful in shame. Tukā says, Go on with your logical cavilling, do not tread our path.

## 1423

MY tongue never stops telling its delight; my spirit is immersed at his feet. You, who think fit, listen to me freely; I for my part have followed him. Tukā says, You may wander in many directions, for my part, I am settled here.

## 1424

IF I do not tell you this secret, you will never know it; so I have put away the thought of shame. Now I join my hands and entreat you; do not try me to the uttermost. Tukā says, We are sitting near him; we wait to see what Hari will do.

# NOTES

| Abhanga. | Line. | |
|---|---|---|
| **16** | 3 | To read the Vedas was an ancient privilege of the Brāhmaṇas and Tukā was a Śūdra. |
| **21** | 6 | As a sign of resolution made. |
| **29** | | This Abhanga is by Tukā's brother. A few by this writer have been translated as specimens, but most of them have been omitted. |
| **30** | 1 | A gang of labourers. |
| | 9 | I.e., hell. |
| **34** | 1 | Kunbi, the peasant class of the Deccan. |
| **37** | 1 | The desires, as often, are spoken of under the image of a herd of unruly cows. |
| **38** | 6 | A *Math* is a school where Sanskrit and philosophy are taught. |
| | 13 | There are many ascetics who seek by austerities to bend the unseen powers to their will. Some such devotee is referred to; I do not know the meaning of his cry. |
| | 16 | Agama, a Śāstra (or Scripture) containing magical spells. The reference is specially to the Atharva-Veda. |
| **44** | 2 | "I am not a regular religious mendicant." |
| **55** | 1 | Tukā's illustrations are frequently drawn from the language of trade. |
| | 5 | Recurring to the constant idea that men receive from God something proportioned to what they bring—their faith—and also to what they desire. |
| **61** | 4 | The leaves of the neem-tree are made into plaisters. |
| **62** | 8 | The triple hill is Kailāsa, the hill of heaven. |
| | 14 | The seventeenth principle in the Self (Purusha); this, like much else in Tukā, is a reminiscence of the Sānkhya philosophy. |
| **80** | | Rāghava, Keśava and Bābāji were those reformers who popularized Kṛishna worship in |

| Abhanga. | Line. | |
|---|---|---|
| | | the Deccan in the fifteenth century. Tukā relates that Bābāji met him in a dream. |
| **85** | 1 | The goddess Viṭṭhobā considered as a female. |
| **95** to **96** | | Two of the Krishṇa Abhangas are inserted here as specimens of the poet's delight in Kṛishṇa. |
| **101** | 12 | Possibly, "I resolved to live in it," or "I resolved to repair it." |
| **105** to **111** | | Complaints of Tukā's wife. |
| **105** | 10 | It is usual to smear the floors of Hindu houses with cow-dung, which is warm to the feet, and is esteemed clean. |
| **110** | 1 | People come to feed him out of respect. |
| **111** | 1 | The first words are the wife's ; then follows Tukā's answer. |
| **115** to **118** | | Relating to the incident of Tukā's persecution by Mumbājī. |
| **115** | 1 | Tukā wished to walk round the temple of Viṭṭhobā at Dehu ; Mumbāji had closed the road with thorns, to protect his field ; Tukā removed the thorns and Mumbāji assaulted him with one of the bushes. |
| | 2 | Or "I ought not to have forgotten the old rule, 'Leave the wicked alone'." |
| **120** | | When Tukā was staying at Lohogaon at the invitation of the villagers, the wife of a Teli, who was entertaining him, poured some hot oil over him. |
| **121** to **122** | | A young woman who attended Tukā's services fell in love with him ; these are the verses in which he rebuked her overtures. |
| **123** to **125** | | Written when Lohogaon was attacked by a band of dacoits. |
| **127** | 1 | Even ; i.e., placed close by, side by side. |
| | 4 | The heavens of the Vedic deities do not compare in happiness with the joy of union with Viṭṭhobā. |

Abhanga. Line.

**128** 3 The Tulsi is a small dark herb (*Ocimum Sanctum*), common everywhere in India. It is specially associated with Vishṇu; according to one account Tulsi was a female disciple of Vishṇu, who excited the jealousy of his wife Lakshmī and by her was turned into this herb.

**132** 3 The colour of Kṛishṇa is dark blue.

**133** 6 The disc is one of the emblems of Vishṇu; it is a missile like a quoit for use in war.

**142** 4 A scientific belief!

**143** 10 *Andropogon Muricatum*, whose roots—more familiar than its name—furnish the fragrant "tatties" or screens for Indian doors and windows.

10 The "Betel" nut is the fruit of the Areca palm—familiar in England in the form of tooth paste. Fragments of it are wrapped in the betel leaf, or leaf of the pepper-vine along with lime and spices, and chewed as a stimulant and digestive. All over the East this preparation is highly esteemed and is frequently offered to visitors as a mark of respect. It is to be noted that the name betel really belongs to the leaf and is wrongly though usually applied to the nut.

**147** 10 Refers to the power of Kṛishṇa to create illusions.

**152** 5 Brass heads of Garuḍa, erected along the path of the pilgrims.

**158** 3 Because no one wants liberation.

4 The tulsi plinth is a square structure like an altar, three feet high, with a tulsi plant growing on it. This may frequently be found in the courtyard of a Hindu house.

**159** 2 The Pātil is the headman of a village. Here Viṭṭhobā is meant; the number of his arms is a usual attribute of divinity and the number of his wives is that of Kṛishṇa's.

Abhanga. Line.

160 2 The eighth lunar month of the year, when the sun is in Kārtika or the Pleiades. The eleventh of Kārtika is about the 8th of November, when Vishṇu is supposed to arise from four months' sleep; it is a great festival at Pāṇḍhari.

163 21 It is not certain who Tukā's servant is.

166 1 An inām is an inheritable freehold estate.

172 1 The Vedas—or rather the Vedāntins—assert that the only way in which the absolute can be described is by saying of it—*neti* "not this." Tukā is here arguing against this position.

176 4 The vilanti is the mark above the line that indicates "i" in Sanskrit.

216 12 If an object is reflected in a mirror, then we can give the name of the object to the reflection also, though in actuality it is absent from it. So Hari is seen reflected in us and the world, but is not actually attained except by coming into contact with himself.

221 1 Explains the nature of the creative act and God's interest in the world.

228 1 The Smṛiti represents a girl under two years of age as enjoyed by a Gandharva; under four, by Fire; under six, by the Moon; in the marriage ceremony the bridegroom reminds her of this when he claims her as his wife.

254 2 The banyan.

"The fig-tree, not that kind for fruit renowned,
But such as at this day to Indians known in
Malabar or Deccan,
Branching so broad and long that in the ground
The bended twigs take root and daughters grow
About the mother tree, a pillared shade,
High over arched, and echoing walks between."

It is a sacred tree, but not so sacred as its taller relative, the pipal, *ficus religiosa*.

| Abhanga. | Line. | |
|---|---|---|
| | 7 | The staff is formed of three rods bound together; it symbolises concentration of the mind. |
| | 7 | The Aśoka, *Jonesia asoca.* |
| **262** | 4 | Śiva wears the crescent moon on his head; perhaps as an emblem of Time, as his destructive power is associated with the passage of Time. |
| **271** | 5 | The three syllables are formed by the three letters V-tth-l. |
| **280** | 1 | Refers to Vishṇu abandoning his dinner which had been served by Lakshmī and running to help the elephant Gajendra. |
| | 6 | It is said that Muchakunda, a devotee of Vishṇu, went to Vaikuṇṭha to seek him. Vishṇu lay down and pretended to be asleep, in order to test his patience. The devotee, annoyed by this, gave him a kick in the chest; and Vishṇu still wears the mark of this as an ornament. |
| **290** | 5 | Refers to the Lion-Avatār when Vishṇu emerged from the wooden pillar to confound the atheist. The half male and half female form is a representation of Śiva (Ardh-nāri), in which he appears conjoined with Pārbati, one side of the body being male, one female. |
| **300** | 1 | See the preceding note. |
| **320** | 7 | The wheel is a Persian wheel for raising water. It is a large wheel at the side of a pond, with vessels attached to its circumference. As it revolves, each vessel is filled with water when it dips in the pond, and subsequently empties itself into a channel at the side of the wheel for the purpose of irrigation. |
| **322** | 6 | How can a dying man find these gifts? |
| **324** | 12 | Who art ready to grant even the whole world as a boon. |
| **330** | 13 | See Yoga in Appendix II. |
| **331** | 12 | Man is frequently compared to an ox working an oil-mill. |

| Abhanga. | Line. | |
|---|---|---|
| 337 | 2 | Cf. Appendix III, *the four stages.* Tukā means neither one stage nor another brings satisfaction. |
| 341 | 7 | Protect one side of your field by lighting a fire there, and another side by staying there yourself. |
| 342 | 8 | Floats are made out of the empty skins of pumpkins, to assist beginners to learn to swim. |
| 337 | | A Lalita Abhang. Lalita is a kind of dance performed at the end of certain religious festivities, e.g., those in connexion with the birth of Rāma and Kṛishṇa. |
| 382 | | Written apparently after a visit to the temple when he received no consolation. |
| 406 | 7 | Identifying Viṭṭhobā with Vishṇu. |
| 407 | 5 | Cowries are still used in India as very small change. |
| 411 | 7 | To sit like a creditor:—to sit and starve oneself at a debtor's door, to force him into payment. An old Indian method of exacting payment from debtors of high position, now forbidden by British law. |
| 425 | 1 | Seems to imply a belief that man's soul was originally united with God's. |
| 454 | 4 | The performer at Kirtana sits or stands on a raised platform at the end of the room. |
| 465 | 5 | A tóla, 180 grains Troy. |
| 493 | 1 | The name Brahmācharya is given both to a Brāhmaṇa youth who is still a pupil, and to a sect of Brāhmaṇa ascetics. |
| 507 | 5 | One may often see in the streets a trained bull accompanied by his master, both dressed in a curious garb of gaudy rags. The bull's accomplishments are very limited. |
| | 5, 6 | Kinds of grain. |
| 512 | 1 | Kṛishṇa's companions. |
| | 5 | Bājri, a coarse grain. |

| Abhanga. | Line. | |
|---|---|---|
| **539** | 6 | At Gokula, when the Brāhmanas refused to honour Kṛishṇa, as he was the son of a Vaiśya; Kṛishṇa inspired their wives with devotion to him, and they brought him food. |
| **542** | 6 | A Tamburā is a guitar with four wires. |
| **563** | 1 | Exaggerating the value of the gift. |
| **586** | 7 | Indian babies are usually carried in this way with one arm encircling the body. |
| **604—613** | | Here, under the pretence of abusing Viṭṭhobā, Tukā playfully expresses confidence in him. |
| **604** | | He advises him in his own interest not to quarrel with his worshippers. |
| **609** | 6 | You give us the bliss of devotion instead of worldly interests. You cheat us out of our worldly interests. |
| **613** | 1 | Honour, great or small, is the least of God's gifts. |
| **676** | 4 | The grain can be made into food. |
| **687** | 8 | Devotees of all bands wear garlands. |
| **695** | 6 | In anticipation of the rain, at the end of the hot weather. |
| **704** | 11 | The diamond is not broken; it is driven into the substance of the hammer or anvil. |
| **707** | 5 | Even the obstinate steel shows itself corruptible. |
| **708** | 1 | The root of the pipul (*sterilis mala robora ficus*) will penetrate almost any rock or masonry. |
| **719** | 9 | A strip of land is left waste as a boundary between two fields and no doubt this vexes the careful eyes of the husbandman. |
| **723** | | A Vasudeva is a religious mendicant who makes his round before day break wearing a cap of peacock's feathers and jingling a set of bells. He wakes up the villagers for their work. |
| **723** | 2 | The two wives are the good and bad impulses. The children are designs of all kinds. "This country" is Viṭṭhobā's shrine. |

| Abhanga. | Line. | |
|---|---|---|
| | 8 | The four companions are devotion, knowledge, renunciation and duty. |
| | 10 | The thorns are infidelity and sensuality. |
| 724 | | The Kāvada carries by a yoke on his shoulders two vessels of Ganges water and takes it to bathe the linga at some shrine. |
| | 6 | i.e., join my profession ; let your water drip on the road like mine. |
| 726 | 16 | Every Hindu family has an ancestral god or goddess who is occasionally visited even from a distance. |
| 780 | 6 | From the first step of creation the principle was declared that there is no difference between the first and last step. |
| 763 | 5 | Prosperity and accomplishment are the names of the two servants of Gaṇesha. They are terms of general application. |
| | 10 | A reference to the valour of Kṛishṇa. |
| 774 | 4 | Forming plans and also entertaining doubts about them. |
| 825 | 8 | The body. |
| 828 | 6 | Ashes rubbed by the devotee on his person. |
| 859 | 10 | The further bank of the sea of the world. |
| 867 | 5 | *Upādhi*, an object of sense viewed as a metamorphosis of the spirit or an external limit unnaturally placed upon it. |
| 875 | 6 | The spirit bears the same relation to the material world as butter does to the sour butter milk which is left after churning. |
| 891 | 5 | The sectarian mark worn on the forehead by Vaishnavas resembles (accidentally) the letter V. |
| 907 | 10 | A platform is made for an image (simhāsana); and certain stones found near the Narbadā are worshipped as emblems of Śiva. |
| 921 | 5 | Parisa, the stone that turns iron into gold; Moharā is a jewel that will not allow a thread wound round it to be burned. |

| Abhanga. | Line. | |
|---|---|---|
| 946 | 2 | The Châmbhārs are a low caste of leather workers. |
| 978 | 5 | Personal knowledge of God. |
| 993 | 3 | Dôm-dom, a Mahommedan cry; perhaps a corruption of Din-din ("faith"). |
| 1003 | 2 | By rolling on the earth. |
| 1012 | 1 | In offerings to the gods. |
| 1041 | 2 | By seeking truth through debate and discussion. |
| 1055 | 5 | The gods are often honoured by lighting lamps before their images. |
| 1062 | 5 | The dog in a village is a general scavenger. |
| 1065 | | This depicts the selfish prudence of a worldly-minded man going on pilgrimage. The corn referred to is the private store in his house. |
| 1088 | 4 | Bracelets are a symbol of marriage, as a ring is among European nations. A widow wears no bracelets. |
| 1093 | 5 | The death of very young babies is ascribed to a mischievous goddess named Satvāi, who kills them on the fifth day. |
| 1098 | | Denounces the crime of selling a daughter in marriage. The "twice-born" are the Brāhmaṇas, who are born a second time when they are invested with the sacred thread. A Bania is a general dealer, especially in grocery. |
| 1111 | 4 | Refers to the building of the bridge to Ceylon, which was done by the aid of the monkey Nala, who was able to make stones swim in water. |
| 1129 | | Danka, a drum, used to proclaim the festivity. A band of singers (Gondhaḷa) come and place an image of the goddess Bhavâni on a platform and honour it with song. |
| 1130 | 1 | The "house of god" here means "my thoughts about the deity." Or possibly it means "my shrine at Paṇḍhari." |

| Abhanga. | Line. | |
|---|---|---|
| 1135 | 5 | This is of course the language the Gondhala would use about Bhavāni. Tukā uses it of Viṭṭhala. |
| 1155 | | Refers to impostors of magical pretensions. |
| 1156 | 8 | Satvāi is a mischievous female demon. |
| 1158 | 3 | Demon powers that insist on sacrifices to propitiate them. |
| 1159 | | The Śāktas are a sect that worship the female energy, with impure orgiastic rites. |
| 1162 | 9 | The female power that he worships. |
| 1164 | | Possibly against the use of spells. |
| 1167 | | Against dramatising episodes in the life of Kṛishṇa as a public amusement. |
| 1168 | 5 | Spirits, " (madhya)," honey, " (madhu)." |
| 1169 | 1 | These village gods (Bhairobā, Maisoba) are represented by stones smeared with red oxide of mercury. |
| 1170 | 1 | The "Jeshtadevi" are the deities who preside over the confinement of women. The term, which means "exalted deities," is a euphemism. |
| 1177 | | "Rasa" is the kernel and "Bhosa" the chaff, they have changed places. |
| 1190 | 6 | He is not successful either in this world or the next. |
| 1191 | | Apparently describes an impostor who pretends to supernatural powers. |
| | 8 | He shows some stone of pretended magical powers and worships the female organ. |
| 1193 | 4 | The darbha grass *Poa cynosureides* ; he puts it in his hair. He takes hold of the tip of his nose and pretends to practise prāṇāyāma, i.e., regular breathing according to the rules of the Yogis. |
| 1196 | 6 | The ascetic's gourd ; the rind of the gourd used for carrying water. |

Abhanga. Line.

1200 This impostor carries about the stones which are used as emblematic of the gods and pretends he cannot afford to make a proper receptacle for them. Accordingly he asks for alms for that purpose. The stones in question are black ammonite fossils found in Northern India.

1205 1 Gósāi is a corruption of Go-svāmi, controller of the senses, and is a title applied to many religious mendicants.

3 How can a wicked man make others better than himself?

1212 4 The words of Kṛishṇa's mother.

1227 3 The mountain is Govardana, which Kṛishṇa lifted up to shield the cowherds from the rain.

1228 The mystic meaning is that Kṛishṇa relieves mankind from the burden of following the Vedic precepts.

1230 1 A jungle fire.

1233 6 Who gives up sacrificial rites.

1235 1 *Nauclea Cadamba*, a small tree.

1238 1 Allegorically Kali represents self-will.

1239 1 Allegorically the cows are the senses.

1251 1 The pot is suspended in a sling and as Kṛishṇa dips his arms in it the curds trickle down them, the cowherds open their mouths to receive the stream. The butter stolen by Kṛishṇa represents allegorically divine knowledge.

1258 1 The eternal Brahma, Parabrahma, the original unmodified spirit.

1263 1 The words of the cowherds to each other.

1265 3 The jungle of the world.

1267 1 Allegorically the cows represent the senses. Karma follows the self continually.

6 Khodā, a log of wood fastened to the neck of the cow and hanging down between the front legs, to prevent it from straying. Here the log fettering the cow is the world as perceived by the senses.

Abhanga. Line.

9 Pādi, the leader of the herd; here, the intellect, viewed as the head of the senses. "Obstinate as this chief cow is, how can she run quite ahead of you?"

9 Until you reach salvation (lit: "till the cow reaches its stable.")

1269 1 "The cow whose udders are filled" is devotion as contrasted with ceremonial religion.

1270 6 "Home," i.e., back to the world again; if by devotion we can avoid re-birth.

1272 1 Represents the protestations made against religion by those who feel it will compel them to resign the pleasures of the world. The more violent this language is, the better pleased God is to see that men recognize the nature of religion.

1280 2 Kṛishna is speaking to the boys.

Allegorically, let my worshippers merge in me (as the advaita school desire).

4 I.e., let the timid cling to the world.

1308 The allegorical meaning is that we should have no secrets from God.

1313 5 Śiva taught this spell to Bhavāni and it enabled her to escape re-birth.

7 Reading नित्य; or, reading नीच, "the old is pleasant, the new is undesirable;" the old name of Rāma is sweeter than the new terms of the philosophers.

1318 1 It is related that Rāma's mother, while pregnant with him, remained in a state of ecstacy.

5 Rāma took all the people of Ayodhya to heaven with him.

1334 Sututu is a game in which the players on one side have to run between two goals, while those on the other side try to catch them. It is a condition that each player as he runs must continue crying "Sututu" without stopping. Allegorically the game represents life; the oppos-

Abhanga. Line.

ing players are the forces of the world, between which the soul has to make its way. This is not quite the same antithesis as that between Śiva, the universal, and Jiva, the individual soul. To illustrate this we must identify the player who runs with the universal soul striving to assert itself against the manifold forces which make up the Jiva or individual life. But Tukā in the last line seems to view the whole struggle as something which may be avoided by recourse to simple devotion. So possibly the game represents the struggle to attain salvation by works. Aham and Soham ("I and mine" "I am he") are two compendious phrases to indicate (i) self-will and separation from the divine, (ii) unity with it.

1335 Tipari is a circular dance in which each player carries a short stick which he strikes rythmically against his neighbours sticks turning first to the right and then to the left. It is not a contentious game, and therefore represents allegorically the unity of love between Viṭṭhobā and the saints.

1337 1 The twelve, i.e., the eleven senses and the vital air or breath; or, counting another way, the sixteen, i.e., the eleven senses and five vital airs. We may make up seventeen by adding the controlling self.

1340 Chenduphali is a game resembling cricket on a small scale. Like Sututu, being played between two sides, it represents in some way the struggle of life. "Catching the ball" represents dealing with the world in a right spirit; possibly observing the prescribed forms of ceremonial religion. Tukā means to deprecate this and recommends faith.

1341 5 It is an incident of the game that the defeated players have to carry the others.

1342 Atyapātya is the most popular of these games. It is played on a field marked out as in

Abhanga. Line.

the accompanying diagram. The players of one side stand at A and have to run to B without being touched; the players of the opposite side stand one on each of the cross lines and try to touch them as they pass. They may each move up and down his own cross line; the captain of the side may also move up and down the longitudinal line from A to B. The interpretation is the same as in the preceding Abhanga. The captain is the individual; the players on his side are the senses; opposed to them are the temptations of the world.

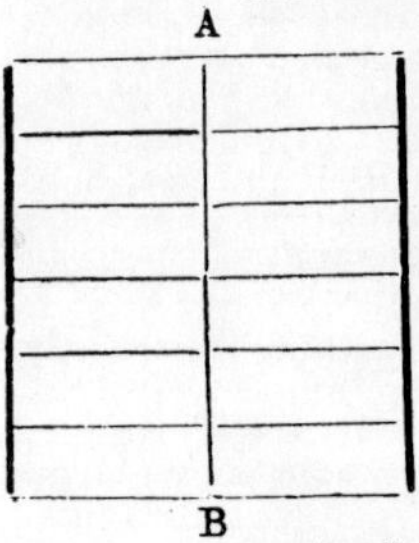


7 *Nava* either (i) need or (ii) nine referring to the nine organs of sense.

1343 Witudăndu, a sort of miniature cricket; the witi is the bat. The game seems to represent in general language the turmoil of life.

1344 Phugdi, a game of girls, in which two girls seize each other's hands and spin round and round. It represents mystically the union of God and the worshipper.

6 Mulbad (i) the part of the head where the hair is fastened, (ii) the head of the spinal cord, where the power of concentration resides.

1345 In this Abhang the same game of Phugdi seems to represent the turmoil of life.

1346 Humbari; in this game the players see which can keep up a humming noise longest. Allegorically this contest represents the effort of man to comprehend or praise the nature of God.

7 Refers to the story of Pūtanā.

11 Uncle Kansa.

1347 Hamāmā, a game resembling Sututu.

1348 16 Sūrya's son is Yama.

Abhanga. Line.

**1349** Riddles, resembling English riddles, e.g., "My first is in Heaven; my second in the company of musicians; my third in the Vania's shop." (Hara tāla).

**1351** Johāra is a salutation employed by members of the low castes. The Mahārs are such a caste employed as messengers in collecting the revenue. The language used by the collector of the revenue is here employed to remind the listener how he will have to pay off the debts incurred by his actions in the past.

**1352** 1 The gate-keeper of the village is usually a Mahār.

**1353** The application of these lines remains quite obscure.

**1354** Lakhótā; a messenger carrying a sealed packet. Most of the poems have no reference to the occupation of this personage; the point of contact is "be like a trusty messenger."

**1355** Góndhalas are religious mendicants who recite songs in honour of deities, male or female. These verses are in honour of Viṭṭhóbā considered as female.

12 Sarangdhara.

**1356** The apparatus of worship usually employed by the Gondhalas is replaced imaginatively by tudes and feelings of the mind.

**1357** Viṭṭhobā described as feminine.

**1358** Vasudevas are religious mendicants who appear in the very early morning just before daylight and waken the village with their songs. The name is that of the father of Kṛishṇa and the verses often play on the double sense of the word.

**1359** 6 Chipalya, or large wooden castanets, are employed to keep time in singing.

**1363** Jógi, a corruption of Yógi, a general term for naked ascetics.

Abhanga. Line.

1364 A Gāvagunda is a fellow who has made himself conspicuous for coarse wit and has perhaps some claims to be considered a magician.

1365 A Saurya is a woman leading an irregular life, nominally devoted to some god, but practically a prostitute. Such women are brought into existence by the custom of dedicating girls to certain gods, which prevents them from marrying. Khandóbā at Jejuri near Poonā is one of these gods; the girls devoted to him are called Muralis. They are still fairly numerous in Poonā, though the custom of dedicating them has been declared illegal by the British Government. Tukā seems to have in view a Saurya who has turned to Viṭṭhōbā for consolation; but it is not clear whether he supposes her to have given up her trade or not. The purpose of the abhangs is not clear; but they may be intended to show that devotion is accessible to anyone. Possibly Tukā intended these poems to become known to this class of women and to elevate them; but this is uncertain.

1368 Possibly the Saurya here rebukes those reputable women who proudly think themselves superior to her.

1370 7 The eighty-four lakhs of re-incarnations.

1373 Apparently a rebuke from a regenerate to an unregenerate Saurya.

1374 Of the same type as the above.

1376 A Vāghā is a male companion of a Saurya. He speaks in language praising Khandobā, but so constructed that it would apply to Kṛishṇa.

1377 The Sarvada is a magician, who pretends to foretell the future. The language applies (i) to some supposed responses of her to a client, which are purposely mysterious, (ii) to the process of the soul's emancipation. This seems to take the form of an attack on Dvaitism; "the mother of two souls" is Brahma, on the

Abhanga. Line.

supposition that the individual and the universal self are distinct.

1879 Rice is pounded to get rid of the husks; it is placed in a hollow in the ground and struck with two long pestles, wielded like paviour's rammers by two women standing opposite each other. The process requires them to keep good time together, hence it is taken allegorically to represent unity between God and his worshipper.

6 After the rice is pounded it is sifted in a fan to separate the husks and the refuse.

1880 6 The bracelets on the arms of the women.

1881 Grinding is performed at a hand-mill, by two women sitting opposite each other. This is a tedious employment, like pounding. Possibly Tukā thought these songs of his would be found agreeable to lighten the toil and at the same time interest the people in religion.

1383 A paik is a man-at-arms paid to accompany and defend a rich man. Nothing in English represents its meaning, which hovers between "henchman" and private detective. Here the paik represents the true devotee of religion.

1394-1404 These really belong to the Kṛishṇa abhangs The blanket is the comfort of the worldly pleasures which religion takes from a man. But in the end religion compensates him by giving him a higher pleasure.

1405-1424 The intention is to indicate that as a woman renounces the world for her paramour, so men should renounce it for religion.

1406 1 My first husband, the world.

1415 Do not pretend to give up the world or talk about doing so till you are truly ready for the step.

# APPENDIX I

## Proper Names

AHALYĀ.—The first woman created by Brahmā, wife of Gautama. She was seduced by Indra; and being cursed by Gautama became a stone. Rāma afterwards delivered her.

AJAMELA.—A degenerate Brāhmaṇa, who was saved by reciting Nārāyaṇa's name.

AKRŪRA.—Kṛishṇā's uncle, who was sent by Kansa to fetch Kṛishṇa from Gokula that he might be slain. Akrūra went unwillingly, and Kṛishṇa disclosed to him his own true nature.

AMBARĪSHA.—A solar king of Barsi, who observed strictly the Ekādaśī fast and broke it according to rule before the end of the day. On one occasion a Durvāsa Rishi came to him as a guest, and was asked to bathe before dinner. He took so long in bathing that Ambarīsha drank a sip of water to keep his rule. Durvāsa offended invoked the female demon Kṛityā to destroy him; but Ambarīsha sought protection from Vishṇu, who destroyed the demon with his disc.

AMRĀVATI.—The heaven of Indra.

ANJANI.—The mother of Hanumana by Vāyu, Hanumana went on the expedition to Lankā, under Sugrīva, the monkey-king, and on his return so great a flood of milk was poured from his mother's breast that it broke through the hills between Nāsik and Saptaśṛinga.

BABHRU.—The son of Arjuna by Chitrāngī, who fought against his father in the war of the Mahābhārata. He severed Arjuna's head with an arrow, but it was reunited by the aid of a magic stone. Tukā says it was by the dispensation of Providence that so great a warrior was slain by so young a one.

BALI.—King of Mahābalipura, descended from Pralhāda and Hiraṇyakaśipu. Though a virtuous monarch he became arrogant and neglected the gods. To punish this Vishṇu assumed the form of a dwarf Brāhmaṇa beggar, and asked as a boon the gift of as much land as he could cover in three steps. This having been granted, the dwarf suddenly expanded and covered in two steps heaven and earth. Bali fell before him in adoration, and was granted the empire of the nether world, Pātāla. Vishṇu condescended to become a door-keeper of the entrance of his kingdom there.

BALLĀLA.—"Mighty one"; a name of Gaṇapati.

BHĀNUDĀSA.—A Brāhmaṇa saint who lived at Pāṇḍhari.

BHARATA.—Son of Daśaratha and Kaikeyī; elder brother of Rāma. His mother procured the exile of Rāma in order to place Bharata on the throne, but it was agreed that Rāma should finally return after fourteen years.

BHAVĀNI.—The wife of Śiva. She unites many attributes, frequently appearing as a warrior goddess.

BHILLI.—Literally "Bhil woman." A woman of the forest tribe of Bhils, who presented Rāma with some fruit which she had bitten to see if it was sweet. Rāma accepted the offering on account of the spirit in which it was made.

BHIMAKI.—Daughter of Bhīma.

BIBHISHANA.—Brother of Rāvaṇa, who deserted to the side of Rāma and assisted him.

CHAITANYA.—A Brāhmaṇa by birth (A.D. 1485), who initiated a reform movement in Upper India. He attacked the licentious orgies of the worshippers of the female energy; and following Kabīr refused to recognize caste. He exalted Kṛishṇa into the position of supreme Deity accessible by devotion—Bhakti. The chief scene of his work was Jaganātha, though he travelled much throughout Northern India. The circumstances of his death (A.D. 1527) are unknown. Among his followers in the Deccan were Bābā Chaitanya, Keśava Chaitanya and Rāghava Chaitanya, to whose inspiration Tukā owed a good deal.

CHĀMUNDĀ.—A name of Bhavānī.

CHANDRABHĀGA.—A digit of the moon.

CHĀNGADEVA.—A yogi of Vateshwar in Khāndesh, who was converted by Dnyāndeva to the school of devotion (Bhaktimārga).

DASAVANTI.—A corruption of Jāśoda or Yeśodā.

DHRUVA.—The grandson of Manu. Though a boy, he performed such austerities that he was raised to heaven as the Polar Star.

DNYANESHWARA.—A Marātha saint of the fourteenth century, who wrote a commentary on Bhagavadgītā.

DRAUPADĪ.—The daughter of Drupada, a solar prince, who married the five Pāṇḍava brothers. She was lost in gambling by one of them, Yudhisthira, and became the property of the Kauravas. The war of the Mahābhārata followed till Draupadī was finally rescued.

DVARKA.—A town in Kathiāwār containing a famous shrine of Kṛishṇa, still a place of pilgrimage.

EKANATHA.—A Marātha saint of the sixteenth century who lived at Paithan, in the Nizam's territory. He composed a metrical translation of Śrimat Bhāgavat, which was probably known to Tukā.

GAJENDRA.—An elephant whose foot was seized by an alligator. In his distress he cried to Vishṇu, who came to the rescue and destroyed the alligator.

GANIKA.—A courtesan who renounced her profession and was saved by reciting the name of Hari.

GARUDA.—A creature with the head and wings of a bird and the body of a man. The vehicle of Vishṇu.

GAURI.—"Fair in complexion"; an epithet of Bhavānī, Śiva's wife.

GAYA.—A town in Bengal containing the pipal tree under which Buddha meditated for five years. Still a place of pilgrimage.

GODAVARI.—A sacred river.

GOVINDA.—A name of Kṛishṇa meaning both "Keeper of cows" and "Controller of the senses."

HANUMANTA.—The son of Anjanī, a monkey queen, and Vāyu, the wind. The chief general of the monkeys, who assisted Rāma in his campaign against Rāvaṇa.

HARA.—A name of Śiva.

HARI.—"One who removes" the sins of men; a name of Vishṇu.

INDRAVANI.—A small river on the bank of which is situated Dehu, the birth place of Tukā.

JANAKA.—Father-in-law of Rāma; father of Sītā.

JANAKI.—Daughter of Jānaka; Sītā.

JANARDANA.—"Destroyer of re-birth"; a name of Vishṇu.

KABIR.—A Hindu reformer of Northern India (? A.D. 1338-1449). He was a follower of Rāmānanda; probably a Muhammadan by birth, who adopted a reformed Hinduism. His doctrines are contained in the Sukh Nidan and resemble those of Vaishṇavas generally. He opposed idolatry.

KALI, or Kaliya, the serpent which lived in the Yamunā and poisoned its water. Kṛishṇa, pretending he was going to look for a chendu or ball that was lost, jumped into the stream and after a famous contest drove Kali away.

KAMADHENU.—A cow produced at the churning of the Milk Sea, and afterwards owned by Vaśishṭha, which had the power of granting wishes.

KARNA.—Son of Kuntī by the sun; he fought against his half brothers the Pāṇḍavas, and was killed in a battle by Arjuna. He is famous for his generosity and is said to have given away his own teeth to Kṛishṇa disguised as a Brāhmaṇa.

KĀNHOBĀ.—A name of Kṛishṇa.

KAUSALYĀ.—The wife of Daśaratha and mother of Rāma.

KAUSTUMBHA.—A jewel produced at the churning of the ocean, and worn by Vishṇu on his neck.

KESAVA.—A name of Vishṇu: (origin uncertain).

KESIRĀJA.—"Controller of Keśi." Keśi was a horse-headed demon killed by the infant Kṛishṇa.

KUMBHAPĀKĀ.—A region in hell where sinners are immersed in boiling oil.

KUBJA.—A deformed menial servant of Kansa, who was straightened by Kṛishṇa.

LAKSHMĪ.—The wife of Vishṇu, and goddess of wealth and prosperity.

MADANA.—A name of Kāma, the God of love.

MALLAR.—A name of Khandobā, as victor over Malla, a local king of the Deccan. The name may also be applied to Kṛishṇa, as victor over the gymnasts of Kansa, called "Mallas."

MERU.—A mythical mountain, the centre of the world, with three peaks, one of which is Kailāsa, or the heaven of Śiva, another Svarga, the heaven of Indra.

MUKTĀBĀĪ.—The sister of the Marāthā poet Dnyāndeva, who herself composed religious poetry.

MURĀRI.—A name of Kṛishṇa, in consequence of his killing the demon Mura.

NALA.—A king of the solar race, who lived at the close of the Vedic period. He became the husband of Damayantī, who chose him herself according to a romantic tale preserved in the Mahābhārata. Afterwards he lost all his wealth in gambling and deserted her; but she recovered him by proclaiming that she would choose another husband. The king of Oudh came to ask for her hand, and Nala accompanied him as his charioteer; he was recognized by Damayantī and they were reunited.

NĀMDEVA.—A Marātha saint of the fourteenth century.

NĀRADA.—One of the Rishis who appears among the attendants of Vishṇu as a musician accompanied by Tumbaru.

NĀRĀYANA.—"Whose abode is in the crater," a name of Vishṇu.

NARMADĀ, also Narbadā, a sacred river of Central India; inferior in sanctity only to the Ganges. Indeed according to the Reva Purāṇa the sanctity of the Ganges disappears in Samvat year 1951 (A.D. 1895), while that of Narmadā continues for ever.

PĀNDURANGA.—"The joy of the Pāṇḍava," a name of Viṭṭhobā.

PĀNDAVA.—The lunar princes of Hastināpura, whose quarrel with their cousins, the Kauravas, brought on the war of the Mahābhārata.

PRALHĀDA.—The pious son of Hiraṇyakaśipu, who rebuked his father's atheism. At the rebuke the lion-avatār, Narsinh, issued from the pillar and rent Hiraṇyakaśipu.

Putanā.—A demoness sent by Kansa to destroy Kṛishṇa by suckling him with her poisonous milk. However, Kṛishṇa was too strong for her and sucked all the blood out of her body and killed her.

Rādha.—The wife of Ayana-Gosha, the favourite mistress of Kṛishṇa.

Rāghava.—"Descendant of Raghu." A name of Rāma.

Raghunath.—See above.

Rakhumai.—A name of Bhīmakī.

Rāvana.—The king of Lankā or Ceylon, who carried off Sītā, the wife of Rāma. The war by which she was recovered forms the subject of the Rāmāyaṇa.

Rudra.—A name of Śiva, one of the trinity of gods.

Rudra.—A Vedic god of storms, identified in later times with Śiva.

Sadāsiva.—"Always prosperous." A name of Śiva.

Sanaka.—One of the four great Rishis with Sanandana, Sanātana, and Sujāta. Sanaka was the preceptor of Nārada, and author of the doctrine of Bhakti or devotion.

Satrajita.—King of the country near Dwārka.

Satwai.—A corruption of Shashthibai, a mischievous female goddess who exercises her powers on the sixth night after the birth of a child, and often kills it.

SATYABHĀMĀ.—Sister of Satrājita, and wife of Kṛishṇa At the instigation of Nārada, Hanumāna, when he came to Dwārka, tried to see if Kṛishṇa was as truly an incarnation of Vishṇu as his own Rāma was, Kṛishṇa accordingly changed his durbar into that of Rāma, and sent Garuḍa to bring Hanumāna to see it. He asked Satyabhāmā to represent Sītā; but she failed to do so and incurred ridicule. Accordingly Rukhmiṇī, his other wife, became Sītā. This is one victory of Rukhmiṇī over Satyabhāmā; the other was on the occasion when Satyabhāmā gave away Kṛishṇa in charity to Nārada, under the mistaken idea that she would thus secure him as a husband for ever. To recover him at all, she was told to give to Brāhmaṇas his weight in gold. No gold however was enough to weigh down Kṛishṇa; and Rukhmiṇī had to come to the rescue. She put a single leaf of tulsi in the scales, and this, as the symbol of unselfish devotion, was sufficient to make up the weight.

ŚAMBHU.—"The origin of blessings," a name of Śiva.

ŚANKARA.—A name of Śiva.

ŚIBI.—A Solar king famous for his generosity. One day a dove flew into his court pursued by a hawk, and Śibi to save the dove offered the hawk a piece of his own flesh. When this was cut off both the hawk and the dove manifested their own true forms and conferred on him many boons.

ŚRINGA.—A Rishi who wears a horn on his forehead; invoked in seasons of drought.

Śriyala.—A king of the Solar race, who consented to give his son to supply a meal for Śiva, when he came to him disguised as a Brāhmaṇa. Tukā confounds Śiva here with Kṛishṇa, either accidentally or perhaps from a view that they are ultimately the same.

Śankhasura.—A demon in the form of a conch shell who concealed the Vedas within himself and took them down into the sea. Vishnu assumed his fish incarnation, destroyed the demon, and rescued the scriptures.

Śuka.—A saint who preached Śrímat Bhāgvata to king Parīkshit.

Sopana.—The brother of the Marātha poet Dnyāndeva.

Sudama.—A playmate of Kṛishṇa's childhood. When Kṛishṇa revealed his true form to him, being very poor, he could only offer him three handfuls of rice which Kṛishṇa accepted.

Suta.—A charioteer whose preaching of the Purāṇas was attended by 88,000 Rishis in Nimishāraṇya, a forest near the Ganges.

Svarga.—The paradise of Indra.

Tāmradhvaja.—A lunar king famous for his generosity. Kṛishṇa and Arjuna came disguised as Brāhmaṇa beggars to his court and he consented to give them the right half of his body. While his body was being sawn in two by his wife and son, a tear dropped from his left eye. Kṛishṇa then declared that the offering was contaminated by this but Tāmradhvaja explained that the tear was one of devotion, on which the gods relented, made him whole and blessed him.

TRIJATA.—A giantess in the service of Rāvaṇa, who was appointed to guard Sītā. She was moved with compassion for Sītā and condoled with her.

TUMBARU.—A musician who appears as a companion of Nārada.

UDDHAVA.—A descendant of the Yādava or Lunar race, to whom Kṛishṇa delivered Ch. XI of Śrīmat Bhagavat.

UPAMANYA.—The son of poor Brāhmaṇa parents. Once when he asked his mother for milk, she replied that she had none and he must pray to God for milk. This he accordingly did, going to the forest and praying to Vishṇu, who took him to the sea of milk.

VAIKUNTHA.—The paradise of Vishṇu.

VALHA.—A corruption of Vālmīki, the reputed author of the Rāmāyaṇa. He is said to have belonged to a tribe of robbers, and to have attained divine knowledge under the guidance of Nārada. He received from him the direction to invert the letters of Rāma and to recite the name as Marā, "Die thou;" and he continued reciting this name till he was surrounded by an anthill.

VALHAKHILLYA.—Sixty thousand dwarf Rishis sprung from the hair of Brahmā.

VASISHTA.—One of the seven Rishis represented by the seven stars of the Great Bear. He was a family priest of the Solar race to which Rāma belonged, and is the reputed author of several hymns in the Rig Veda.

VASUDEVA.—The father of Kṛishṇa, a prince of the Lunar Yādava race.

VASUKI.—The serpent used by the gods and demons as a churning rope at the churning of the ocean. Sometimes identified—though wrongly —with Śesha, the primeval serpent on which Vishṇu lay before the creation.

VĀYU.—The wind-god, the father of Hanumāna.

VEMUNADA.—" The sound of the flute," *Venu* being a bamboo flute. A spot near the Chandrabhāga where Kṛishṇa used to play his flute, and a temple now stands in honour of Punḍalika.

VETALA.—The king of goblins; he haunts burial grounds.

VIDURA.—The son of Vyāsa by a slave girl; a faithful friend of the Pāṇḍavas.

VIMALARJUNA.—The name of two white *Arjuna* trees that stood in Nanda's courtyard. They were two nymphs—Gandharvas—Nala and Kubara, who had been changed into trees by Nārada as a punishment for their sensualities. Kṛishṇa rooted them up as he passed between them and at the touch of the god they attained their original form.

VISVĀMITRA.—A Kshatriya prince of the Lunar race, who became a great Rishi. He appears in constant conflict with the Brāhmaṇa Vaśishṭa; and like him is represented by one of the stars in the Great Bear. He protected Rāma and assisted him in arranging his marriage with Sītā.

VRINDAVANA.—" Forest of *Vṛinda*," a tree into which the wife of the demon Jalandhara was transformed, as a punishment for her passion for Vishṇu. The name of a forest near Mathurā, where Kṛishṇa spent his childhood with cowherds and the damsels. Also in modern usage frequently the name of the small altar in the courtyard of a Hindu house where the tulsi plant is grown.

VYANKOBA.—"Crawling"; a name of the infant Kṛishṇa.

VYĀSA.—Lit. the distributor, a title applied in general to the authors of the Vedas and Purāṇas, of whom 28 are mentioned. The most celebrated was the son of Parāśara and Satyavatī, from whom the Pāṇḍava and Kaurava brothers were both descended. He is said to have compiled the Vedas and the Mahābhārata.

YADAVA.—A race of invaders of India, to whom Kṛishṇa belonged.

YAMADHARMA.—A name of Yama, viewed as the upholder of righteous conduct. The ruler of the nether world.

YESODA.—The wife of the herdsman Nanda, to whom Kṛishṇa was entrusted.

---

## APPENDIX II

# Ceremonies and Beliefs referred to by Tukārāma

*The neem-fruit ceremony* (निंबलोण). —Leaves of the neem tree, with salt, etc., are waved round the head of a person and thrown away, to carry off an evil influence.

*The eighty-four lakhs* of re-births (8,400,000). This is usually given as the number that are necessary.

*The primal form* (स्वरूप) —The native essence of God not contracted or disfigured by the world.

*The eleventh day* of each half of the month is observed by the Hindus generally and especially by Vaishṇavas as a solemn fast.

*Yoga.*—A method of liberating the spirit from the material world. To follow it, certain postures of the body must first be practised; these will assist the concentration and ultimately the liberation of the spirit.

*The wishing cow.*—See Kāmdhenu.

*My mother's house.*—A little Hindu girl after her marriage—or rather betrothal—goes to live in the house of her husband, where her mother-in-law drills her into the ways of the new family. She has often reason to regret the indulgence of her "mother's house"; and the mother-in-law's house is appropriately employed by Tukā as an image of the uncomfortable world.

*Chintāmani.*—A gem of Svarga supposed to yield its possessor every wish.

*Waving a Lamp.*—A lamp is waved round a person as a sign of blessing, to remove evil influences from him.

*Sāligrām.*—A whirl-shaped fossil shell resembling the conch of Vishṇu, and accepted as a symbol of him. It is found in the bed of the Gaṇḍakī, a tributary of the Ganges.

*The Sea of the World.*—Perhaps more properly, "the river of the world," a large flood which the traveller has to cross.

*The Sea of Milk.*—Conceived as surrounding Vaikuṇṭha, the paradise of Vishṇu.

*The ascetic's staff.*—A triple rod, formed of three staves fastened together, and often carried by ascetics. These indicate mystically the three stages of life they have passed through, pupilage, wordly life, and renunciation.

---

# APPENDIX III

## Certain Classifications which are mentioned by Tukārāma

*The three Worlds.*—Heaven, Earth, Hell.

*The three aspects of merit* (and demerit.)-(i) संचित (Sanchita) merit stored up, (ii) प्रारब्ध (Prārabdha) merit in action, (iii) क्रियमाण (Kriamāṇa) merit which has yet to operate.

*The three qualities* of created beings.—(i) सत्व Truth or goodness, (ii) रास् Passion or foulness, (iii) तमस् Darkness.

*The triad of knowledge.*—(i) Knower, (ii) Known, (iii) Process of knowing.

*The three fevers.*—(i) आधिभौतिक (Adhibhautika)

tāpa), fever caused by the five elements, (ii) आधिदैविक (Adhidaivika) fever caused by demons, (iii) आध्यात्मिक (Adhyātmika tāpa), fever caused by diseases of the mind.

*The four Vedas.*—Rig Veda, Yajur Veda, Sāma Veda, Atharva Veda.

*The four stages of life.*—ब्रह्मचर्य (Bramacharya), the unmarried life of a student; गृहस्थ (Gṛihastha), the householder's life; वानप्रस्थ (Vānaprastha), living in the forest; सन्यास (Sanyāsa), abandonment of the world.

*The four stages of speech.*—(i) परा (Parā), the first stirring of breath; (ii) पश्यंती (Paśyantī), the whisper of the breast; (iii) मध्यमा (Madhyamā), the middle stage; (iv) वैखरी (Vaíkharī), articulate utterance.

*The four kinds of liberation.*—(i) सलोकता (Salokatā), or dwelling in the same heaven with God; (ii) समीपता (Samīpatā), being near him; (iii) सरूपता (Sarūpatā), possessing similarity of form with him; (iv) सायुज्यता (Sāyujyatā), complete absorption in him.

*The four means of attaining union.*—(i) शमदमादि (Śamadamādi), or restraining the senses; (ii) वैराग्य (Vairāgya), or restraining the mind; (iii) विवेक (Viveka), discriminating matter and mind; (iv) मुमुक्षा (Mumukshā), or desire for liberation.

*The five vital breaths.*—उदान (Udāna), the breath rising from the chest; प्राण (Prāṇa), the breath passing through the nose; अपान (Apāna), the abdominal breath, below the navel; समान (Samāna), the navel breath; व्यान (Vyāna), the breath in the limbs.

*The five fires used at sacrifices.*—(i) आहावनीय (Ahāvanīya), (ii) गार्हपत्य (Gārhapatya), (iii) दक्षिणाग्नि (Dakshiṇāgni), (iv) सभ्य (Sabhya), (v) आवसथ्य (Avasathya). Their shapes are various—square, circular, semi-circular, hexagonal, octagonal.

*The five elements.*—Earth, air, fire, water, and ether.

*The six tasks.*—Study, teaching, sacrificing, causing sacrifices to be made, giving and receiving gifts.

*The six enemies.*—(i) काम (Kāma), desire (ii) क्रोध (Krodha), anger; (iii) लोभ (Lobha), covetous.

ness; (iv) माह (Moha), infatuated love; (v) मत्सर (Matsara), evny; (vi) मद (Mada), pride.

*The six stages of life.*—(i) Existence, (ii) birth, (iii) growth, (iv) maturity, (v) decay, (vi) death.

*The six Śastras.*—Six learned works,—three of which relate to grammar, one to ceremonies, one to mathematics, one to explanation of obscure words in the Vedas.

*The six enchantments.*—(i) जारण (Jārana) causing another's body to waste, (ii) मारण (Māraṇa) causing the death of another, (iii) उच्चाटन (Uchchāṭana), causing another to remove from his habitation, (iv) स्तंभन (Stambhana) stopping another's motion, (v) मोहन (Mohana) casting an illusion over another, (vi) वशीकरण (Vaśīkaraṇa) reducing another to subjection.

*The seven regions of hell.*—(1) Atala, (2) Vitala, (3) Sutala, (4) Rasatala, (5) Talātala, (6) Mahātala, (7) Pātāla.

*The eight limbs*, or the eight parts of the body which touch the ground when a prostration is made, the forehead, nose, the two shoulders, the two knees, and the toes

*The eight mystic powers.*—(i) to make oneself exceedingly small, (ii) to make oneself exceedingly large, (iii) to become light, (iv) to become heavy, (v) to touch the sun and moon, (vi) to make predictions, (vii) to subdue, (viii) to create.

*The nine forms of worship.*—(i) श्रवण (śravaṇa) hearing, (ii) कीर्तन (kīrtana) celebrating praise, (iii) स्मरण (smaraṇa) meditation, (iv) पादसेवन (pādasevana) worshipping the feet, (v) अर्चन (archana) worshipping an image, (vi) वंदन (vandana) salutation, (vii) दास्य (dāsya) attendance, (viii) सख्य (sakhya) friendship, (ix) आत्मनिवेदन (ātmanivedana) communion.

*The ten gifts presented after death.*—(1) sesamum seed, (2) cotton, (3) iron, (4) salt, (5) udīda, a black grain, (6) oil, (7) rice, (8) wheat, (9) a pair of shoes, (10) an umbrella.

*The ten avatars or incarnations of Vishnu.*—Fish, tortoise, boar, lion, the dwarf, Paraśurāma, Rāma Krishṇa, Buddha, Kalki.

*The eleven senses.*—The five senses of perception, (eye, ear, nose, tongue, touch); the five of action, (hands, feet, speech, excretory organ, generative organ), and the mind controlling them.

*The fourteen worlds.*—Bhu (earth), bhuvah (space), svah (heaven), mahah, janah, tapah, satya. Also the seven lower regions, atala, vitala, utala, mahātala, rasatala, talātala, pātāla.

*The sixteen presents* offered to an image or to a great man.—(1) sandal wood, (2) flowers, (3) rice, (4) betelnuts, (5) camphor, (6) incense, (7) a lamp, (8) some sweet food, (9) water for the feet, (10) water to drink, (11) cloth, (12) an ornament, (13) money, (14) a seat, (15) leaves, (16) fruit.

*The eighteen Purāṇas*, collections of doctrines and mythology.